The Incarnate Word

The Mercersburg Theology Study Series
Volume 4

The Mercersburg Theology Study Series is an attempt to make available for the first time, in attractive, readable, and scholarly modern editions, the key writings of the 19th-century movement known as the Mercersburg Theology. We believe this will be an important contribution to the scholarly community and to the broader reading public, who can at last be properly introduced to this unique blend of American and European, Reformed and catholic theology.

PLANNED VOLUMES IN THE SERIES
(TITLES SUBJECT TO CHANGE):

The Church in History: Selected Writings of Philip Schaff
Edited by David Bains and Theodore L. Trost

"One, Holy, Catholic, and Apostolic": Nevin's Writings on Ecclesiology
Edited by Sam Hamstra

The Sacraments and Christian Formation
Edited by David Layman

Essays in Church History
Edited by Nick Needham

The Early Creeds
Edited by Charles Yrigoyen

The Heidelberg Catechism
Edited by Lee Barrett

The Mercersburg Liturgy
Edited by Michael Farley

Schaff's America and Related Writings
Edited by Stephen Graham

Philosophy and the Contemporary World
Edited by Adam S. Borneman

Mercersburg and Its Critics
Edited by Darryl G. Hart

See www.mercersburgtheology.org for more about the series, as well as a treasury of resources for Mercersburg research.

The Incarnate Word
Selected Writings on Christology

By
JOHN WILLIAMSON NEVIN
PHILIP SCHAFF and DANIEL GANS

Edited by
WILLIAM B. EVANS

General Editor:
W. BRADFORD LITTLEJOHN

Foreword by
OLIVER CRISP

WIPF & STOCK · Eugene, Oregon

THE INCARNATE WORD
Selected Writings on Christology

The Mercersburg Theology Study Series 4

Copyright © 2014 William B. Evans and W. Bradford Littlejohn. All rights reserved. Except for brief quotations in critical publications or reviews, no part of this book may be reproduced in any manner without prior written permission from the publisher. Write: Permissions. Wipf and Stock Publishers, 199 W. 8th Ave., Suite 3, Eugene, OR 97401.

Wipf & Stock
An Imprint of Wipf and Stock Publishers
199 W. 8th Ave., Suite 3
Eugene, OR 97401

www.wipfandstock.com

ISBN 13: 978-1-62564-523-4

Manufactured in the U.S.A.   10/24/2014

Contents

Foreword by Oliver Crisp   vii
*Editorial Approach and Acknowledgments
   by Bradford Littlejohn and William B. Evans*   xi
General Introduction by William B. Evans   xv

ARTICLE 1
"Sartorius on the Person and Work of Christ"   1
(by John W. Nevin)

ARTICLE 2
"The New Creation in Christ"   29
(by John W. Nevin)

ARTICLE 3
"Wilberforce on the Incarnation"   46
(by John W. Nevin)

ARTICLE 4
"Liebner's Christology"   87
(by John W. Nevin)

ARTICLE 5
"Cur Deus Homo?"   113
(by John W. Nevin)

ARTICLE 6
"Jesus and the Resurrection"   136
(by John W. Nevin)

Article 7
"The Moral Character of Jesus Christ"   159
(by Philip Schaff)

Article 8
"The Person of Christ"   210
(by Daniel Gans)

Bibliography   239
Subject and Author Index   247

Foreword

by Oliver Crisp

Though seldom reported in ecclesiastical histories, the most important representatives of the three major trajectories in nineteenth century American Reformed theology each had a particular relationship to one seat of higher education, namely, Princeton. It was here that Jonathan Edwards ended of his life as the College of New Jersey's third President. It was here that the theology of the Hodges, especially Charles Hodge and his disciple Benjamin Warfield, was established as the touchstone of orthodox Reformed thought in nineteenth century America at the Seminary adjacent to the college, founded at the beginning of that century in 1812. It was here too that John Williamson Nevin had his theological training with Hodge as his teacher. He even filled in for Hodge, teaching his classes whilst his mentor was abroad in German-speaking Europe, learning about liberal theology from some of its greatest exponents. Yet the only version of "Princeton" theology that is remembered in popular accounts today is that strain associated with Hodge, which he famously characterized as an orthodoxy that had not changed one iota during his tenure there.

The facts are rather different. Hodge was schooled in the common sense philosophy that swept away Edwardsian idealism in the spring cleaning of the College that John Witherspoon instigated upon arriving from Scotland. Hodge's "orthodoxy" represented a particular way of understanding Reformed theology, one that was consonant with the Scotch Philosophy (as it was called) culled from the likes of Thomas Reid and Dugald Stewart. This influence can be seen in the sort of approach Hodge countenanced: sensible, reasonable, empirical, appealing to the plain sense of Scripture, and the subordinate standard of the Westminster Confession. But with this came a suspicion of things numinous, sacramental, and idealist. This included a rather complex relationship to the legacy of Edwards, whose views Hodge regarded as incipient pantheism. It also led to the opening up of theological distance between himself and Nevin, his erstwhile student. Upon his return from Europe to the security of his position in New Jersey, Hodge spent the rest of his academic life resisting the encroachment of the liberalism he had encountered overseas. By contrast, Nevin stayed at home, learnt German to read the authors Hodge encountered in person, and became enamored of the idealism that infused the Mediating Theology even though he resisted some of the doctrine in which it was expressed. His gradual disillusionment with Hodge's approach is mirrored in his move from Princeton, eventually settling in Mercersburg where he was joined by a native German-speaker, Philip Schaff. Together they forged a different path to the one being hammered out in Princeton. Instead of Reformed theology in the mode of Scottish common sense realism, they developed a European-influenced theology indebted to the German idealism Hodge had shrugged off.

The results speak for themselves. Whereas Hodge conceived of the Incarnation as the necessary pre-requisite to Atonement, the work of Christ as a penal satisfaction, and the sacraments as little more than Zwinglian memorials, Nevin came to think of the whole of theology as being imbued with sacramental resonance. The Incarnation was not merely a condition for soteriology. It was the means by which humanity would be transformed, being united into one organism with Christ as its head. Borrowing language from Calvin dipped in the idealism of Schelling and Hegel, Nevin expatiated on the mystical body of Christ, on the real sacramental presence of Christ in the Eucharist, and on the fundamental importance of the Church as the visible manifestation of His presence in the world in a number of different essays, articles and reviews, and in his great work, *The Mystical Presence*. This was Reformed theology of a very different stripe to that championed by Hodge and his epigone. Thoroughly Catholic, it took Christology, understood sacramentally, as its touchstone.

It is one of the great gifts of the Mercersberg Study Series, the fourth volume of which you now hold in your hands, that this legacy is now being recovered. In time, we may hope that Nevin and Schaff will take their rightful place in the pantheon of Reformed theologians, as thinkers whose work developed and extended the christological and sacramental insights of the Magisterial Reformation in Geneva, Strasbourg, and Canterbury in particular, which the *Princetonian* theology of the Hodges has all but eclipsed.

Like several prominent nineteenth century American Protestant institutions of theological education, the small Seminary of the German Reformed Church in Mercersburg had its own organ, *The Mercersburg Review*. Like others of his contemporaries, including Hodge and Edwards Amasa Park, Nevin was an inveterate essayist and reviewer, writing about the latest ideas to emerge from European presses in the *Review*, and taking on Hodge in particular in several battles (including the dispute about Calvin's sacramental legacy, in which Hodge was clearly on the back foot). He was also a churchman. His concern for the denomination he served, and for the wider Christian Church, is evident in his published works as well as in his homiletics. For these reasons, this collection offers an invaluable window into the inner workings of Nevin, of Schaff, and of one of the products of Mercersburg theology, Daniel Gans, regarding what is arguably the central motif of their thought: the person and work of Christ. These papers, essays, reviews, and a sermon, demonstrate the vitality and importance of this small but determined group of Reformed thinkers whose work is a sort of herald of the ecumenical retrieval theology that characterizes much constructive dogmatics today, whether or not it is Reformed in nature. For those desirous of a richly sacramental, and incarnational approach to this particular theological tradition the pieces collected together here offer rich and nourishing fare.

Editorial Approach and Acknowledgments

by Bradford Littlejohn and William B. Evans

The purpose of this series is to reprint the key writings of the Mercersburg theologians in a way that is both fully faithful to the original and yet easily accessible to non-specialist modern readers. These twin goals, often in conflict, have determined our editorial approach throughout. We have sought to do justice to both by being very hesitant to make any alterations to the original, but being very free with additions to the original in the form of annotations.

We have decided to leave spelling, capitalization, and emphasis exactly as in the original, except in cases of clear typographical errors, which have been silently corrected. We have, however, taken a few liberties in altering punctuation—primarily comma usage, which is occasionally quite idiosyncratic and awkward in the original texts, but also other punctuation conventions which are nonstandard and potentially confusing today. We have also adopted standard modern conventions such as the italicization of book titles and foreign-language words. The entirety of the text has been re-typeset and re-formatted to render it as clear and accessible as possible; pagination, of course, has accordingly been changed. In the absence of original section headings, we have supplied our own in brackets.

Original footnotes are retained, though for ease of typesetting, they have been subsumed within the series of numbered footnotes which includes the annotations we have added to this edition. Our own annotations and additions, which comprise the majority of the footnotes, are wholly enclosed in brackets, whether that be within a footnote that was original, or around an entire footnote when it is one that we have added.

Source citations in the original have been retained in their original form (with the exception of Schaff's scripture references in article 7, which were given in a confusing and obsolete form), but where necessary, we have provided expanded citation information in brackets or numerated footnotes, and have sought to direct the reader toward modern editions of these works, where they exist. Where citations are lacking in the original, we have tried as much as possible to provide them in our footnotes.

In the annotations we have added (generally in the footnotes, though very occasionally in the body text—all marked with brackets), we have attempted to be comprehensive without becoming cumbersome. In addition to offering citations for works referenced in the original, these additions fall under three further headings:

1) Translation

2) Unfamiliar terms and historical figures

3) Additional source material

4) Commentary

We have attempted to be comprehensive in providing translations of any untranslated foreign-language quotations in these works, and have wherever possible made use of existing translations in standard modern editions, to which the reader is referred.

Additional annotations serve to elucidate any unfamiliar words, concepts, or (especially) historical figures to which the authors refer, and where applicable, to provide references to sources where the reader may pursue further information (for these additional sources, only abbreviated citations are provided in the footnotes; for full bibliographical information, see the bibliography).

We have also sought to shed light on the issues under discussion. Although most commentary on the texts has been reserved for the General Introduction and the Editor's Introductions to each article, further brief commentary on specific points of importance has occasionally been provided in footnotes to facilitate understanding of the significance of the arguments,

We hope that our practice throughout will help bring these remarkable texts to life again for a new century, while also allowing the authors to be heard in their own authentic voices.

ACKNOWLEDGMENTS

As the general editor, I would like to thank Bill Evans for his remarkable work on this volume over the past couple years. This volume posed special challenges in the form of the extensive use of nineteenth-century German texts, which Bill diligently tracked down whenever possible. His editorial thoroughness and precision left very little work for me to do as the general editor, a great boon at a very busy time in my life. The main credit I can take is merely my success in recruiting someone who was clearly the right man for the job. The texts in this volume wrestle with some of the most profound and complex theological problems that we find handled anywhere in the Mercersburg writings; indeed, these are problems that have exercised the greatest minds throughout the Christian theological tradition. To do justice to these texts, synthesizing them and introducing them for the modern reader, required not merely editorial or historical expertise, but a theologian well-versed in the conceptual problems and the history of the tradition. Bill was more than up to the task, drawing upon his own extensive reflections on Christology in the Reformed tradition in order to bring these texts to life and highlight their importance for the modern reader.

Finally, I would again like to thank Christian Amondson at Wipf and Stock and Deborah Clemens of the Mercersburg Society for their ongoing enthusiastic support of this project, and the whole Mercersburg Society for lending it generous financial support. I would also like to thank Todd Billings, Kang Yup-Na, Martha Moore-Keish, and Dawn DeVries for making possible a special session at the American Academy of Religion annual meeting on our Mercersburg series; among other things, this gave Bill an opportunity to develop many of the important reflections which you will find expanded upon here in his Volume Introduction.

* * *

As volume editor, I must offer hearty thanks to series editor Bradford Littlejohn and to the other members of the editorial team. In addition to spearheading this worthy project, Bradford in particular has been a source of encouragement and wise counsel at each juncture. It is quite safe to say that this series, and this volume in particular, would not have appeared without his capable and creative leadership. When the story of the current revival of scholarly and popular interest in the Mercersburg Theology is finally told, his name will be prominent in the narrative. Concrete evidence of this ongoing revival of interest was on display at a joint session of the Nineteenth-Century Theology Group and the Reformed Theology and History Group at the 2013 annual meeting of the American Academy of Religion—a session that offered a wonderful opportunity to explore some of the themes presented in this volume. Thanks are also due to the special-collections librarians at the McCain Library of Erskine College and the James H. Thomason Library of Presbyterian College, who graciously made rare volumes in their collections available to the editor. In addition, Mrs. Ilse Engler of Due West, South Carolina helped to track down some elusive German quotations. Finally, I must thank my wife Fay for her patience and good cheer throughout the project.

General Introduction

by William B. Evans

The Mercersburg Theology that we associate especially with John W. Nevin and Philip Schaff was, in retrospect, remarkably comprehensive in scope. That is, it had something distinctive to say about many of the traditional loci of theology and important aspects of Christian ministry. Key figures of the movement reflected with depth and subtlety on any number of issues having to do with theological method and the relationship of faith and reason, biblical interpretation, applied soteriology, ecclesiology, catechesis and Christian nurture, worship and liturgics, and the role of tradition and historical inquiry in the life of the church. But if any one topic in theology has claim to centrality for Mercersburg it is Christology.[1] And for this reason, Christology touches on nearly everything else—theology proper, theological anthropology, soteriology, hermeneutics, and ecclesiology.

As we examine the Mercersburg materials in any depth we see that, for Nevin, Schaff, and their students, the Incarnation is the central event of history, the ontological ground of all created reality, and the epistemological key to all truth. In short, Christ is central to both the orders of creation and redemption. As Nevin put it, "The Incarnation is the deepest and most comprehensive fact, in the economy of the world. Jesus Christ authenticates himself, and all truth and reality besides; or rather all truth and reality are such, only by the relation in which they stand to him, as their great centre and last ground."[2]

---

1. On this aspect of the Mercersburg Theology, see, e.g., Muller, "Gerhart on the 'Christ Idea.'"
2. Nevin, "The Apostles' Creed," 315.

Thus we might say that the Mercersburg movement was "Christ intoxicated," and for this reason materials dealing significantly with Christology are found in many of the Mercersburg writings beyond the limited scope of this particular collection. While the primary purpose of this "Editor's Introduction" is to provide context for the reading of the materials in this volume, of necessity we must cast our net more broadly.

This centrality of Christology is evident in a number of ways. We must always keep in mind Mercersburg's close association of Christ's person and work. The Incarnation is no mere *conditio sine qua non* for Christ's work; it is itself an essential part of that work. Moreover, these writers were concerned, for example, to see the transformation of Christ's humanity by the Holy Spirit in the resurrection as essential to his objective work of salvation and to the subjective appropriation of salvation by the Christian.

Related to this, there is also the role of Christ's person in the application of salvation to the Christian through union with Christ. Indeed, these writers are insistent that salvation takes place through participation in the very person of Christ, and not merely on the basis of what Christ has done in some external sense. Thus, to utilize Roger Newell's useful distinction between "appropriationist" and "participationist" soteriologies,[3] Mercersburg is resoundingly participationist.

Yet another distinctive of the Mercersburg Christology, particularly in its American context, is the extraordinary attention paid to the incarnate humanity of Christ. Again, far from being a mere condition of possibility for Christ's redemptive work, the humanity of Christ is itself salvific in that it is the locus of redemption. And, building on insights of Schleiermacher and the German Mediating theologians, Mercersburg also views the humanity of Christ as essential to our knowledge of the divine presence in Christ. Thus, in keeping with larger nineteenth-century trends, there is a sort of "Christology from below" at work here.[4]

In this Introduction we will explore the larger background and historical context of the Mercersburg Christology. Then we will examine some distinctive features of the Mercersburg approach to the doctrine of Christ and the salvation accomplished in him. Finally, we will explore some interpretive questions and problems that emerge.

3. See Newell, "Participation and Atonement."
4. See, e.g., Philip Schaff, "The Moral Character of Jesus Christ" in this volume.

I. HISTORICAL BACKGROUND

The Mercersburg Theology in general, and its Christology in particular, were not formulated in a vacuum. That is to say, while some of the conceptual apparatus and conclusions may seem foreign or alien today, they made considerable sense in the broader context of discussion in the mid-nineteenth century. For our purposes we see at least four significant contextually driven developments in the Mercersburg Theology—a reaction against older Anglo-American empiricist influences and an embracing of Germanic idealist and organic ways of thinking, a new appreciation for the centrality of Christology in theology, a repudiation of the abstractions common to prevailing forms of American Reformed theology, and a reaction against the subjectivity of American evangelical revivalism in favor of churchly objectivity.[5]

A. German Idealism and Organicism

The late eighteenth and early nineteenth century saw the ascendancy in America of the philosophical system known as Scottish Common Sense realism. Framed in opposition to the skepticism of Scottish philosopher David Hume (1711–76), whose radical empiricism and view of the mind as but a series of isolated perceptions undercut metaphysical claims, the Scottish Realism of Thomas Reid as it was transmitted to America by John Witherspoon held that ideas are not mental objects but rather mental acts of direct perception, and utilized a "common sense" empiricism confident in the mind's epistemic capacity to organize empirical data rightly.[6] This way of thinking was, as is often noted, reflexively dualistic—carefully distinguishing mind and matter, subject and object, body and soul, flesh and spirit, God and world, the natural and the supernatural, and so forth—in opposition to the monisms of the day (idealism and materialism). Sydney Ahlstrom notes,

> The Scottish Philosophy was an apologetical philosophy, par excellence. And the secret of its success, I think, lay in its dualism,

---

5. The material in this section draws extensively on the more extended account of these issues in my *Imputation and Impartation*.

6. On Reid and the Scottish Common Sense philosophy, see Grave, *The Scottish Philosophy of Common Sense*. For treatments of the influence of Scottish Realism in America, see Ahlstrom, "The Scottish Philosophy"; May, *The Enlightenment in America*; Bozeman, *Age of Science*; Holifield, *Gentlemen Theologians*, 110–26; Noll, "Common Sense Traditions."

> epistemological, ontological, and cosmological. Its other advantages were auxiliary. Reid's theory affirmed a clean subject-object distinction. The world which men perceived was in no sense constituted by consciousness. On the mind-matter problem dualism facilitated an all-out attack on both materialism and idealism, as well as the pantheism that either type of monistic analysis could lead to. Furthermore, by a firm separation of the Creator and His creation, the Scottish thinkers preserved the orthodox notion of God's transcendence, and made revelation necessary.... The Scottish philosophy, in short, was a winning combination.[7]

And with this disjunctive impulse naturally came a heavy focus on static particularity and a preference for induction over deduction. As T. D. Bozeman has shown, rather than deducing truth from first principles, Reid and his followers stressed the observation of discrete phenomena and the generalizations that flowed from them, and "Baconian" method became the watchword of the day.[8]

But by the middle of the nineteenth century the limitations of Scottish Common Sense were becoming evident to many, and, in a shift ably and extensively chronicled by Bruce Kuklick, some American thinkers turned to a variety of idealist currents of thought coming out of Germany, especially the metaphysical idealism of Hegel and Schelling.[9] The Mercersburg Theology, of course, was an instance of this.

Like the Scottish Common Sense thinkers, Immanuel Kant sought to deal with Hume's skepticism by appealing to the activity of the mind, but his more radical proposals precipitated an epistemological and theological crisis that still impacts Western thought.[10] Calling attention to the mind's contributions, Kant argued that relational categories of time, space, modality, and so forth are imposed by the mind on sensory data, and this recognition of the active role of the knowing subject undercut the clean subject-object distinction of earlier thought. Coupled with this, the empirical basis of Kant's epistemology implied that we can only have knowledge of phenomena, or things as they appear to

---

7. Ahlstrom, "Scottish Philosophy," 267–68. See also Riley, *American Thought*, 123; Loetscher, *Facing the Enlightenment*, 33; Kuklick, *Churchmen and Philosophers*, 78.

8. Bozeman, *Age of Science*, 23–30, 44–70.

9. See Kucklick, *Churchmen and Philosophers*, 117–229.

10. Helpful treatments of Kant's significance for theology include Fackenheim, "Immanuel Kant"; Frei, "Niebuhr's Theological Background," 9–64, esp. 16–21, 32–40.

us. Noumenal reality, such as God, human freedom, and things as they really are in themselves, is not accessible to reason.

Hegel and Schelling responded to the pessimism of Kant's epistemological and metaphysical dualisms with idealist ontologies that focused on the ultimate unity of all reality, a unity framed in terms of Absolute mind as the source and ground of all finite particularity.[11] Such idealist ontologies transcended many traditional epistemological and metaphysical dualisms—subject and object, finite and infinite, matter and spirit, natural and supernatural, *a priori* and *a posteriori*.

The implications of such idealism were substantial. As Christology was recast in idealist terms, the focus shifted from the union of two dissimilar natures to the explicit realization of the idea of divine-human unity in history.[12] But this shift in turn posed another problem. Was this realization fulfilled in a single individual (as Hegel himself maintained), or was this realization better understood as occurring in the human race as a whole (as some of Hegel's more radical followers such as D. F. Strauss argued)?[13] Another issue here had to do with the question of whether the Incarnation would have occurred even apart from sin, as the idealist framework of thinking seemed to suggest. Not surprisingly, both of these questions are engaged at length in the materials collected in this volume, and Christology serves as a sort of test case for the role of philosophical idealism in the Mercersburg Theology.

This idealism also resulted in more organic and dynamic approaches to history. If history itself is, as Hegel argued, the unfolding of Absolute Spirit in finite consciousness, then history is naturally viewed in developmental and organic terms. Such thinking stood in stark contrast with the static and disjunctive categories of the earlier Common Sense historiography, particularly as it insistently raised questions of organic continuity with the Catholic pre-Reformation past. Thus it should not surprise that the Mercersburg theologians were persistently accused of Catholicizing tendencies, and that some either dallied with conversion to Rome (as in the case of John Nevin) or actually converted (Daniel Gans). It was also this idealist cast of thinking, with its deep concern for history, continuity, and unity, that that placed the Mercersburg Theology at odds with the mainstream of American

---

11. On these developments, see Copleston, *Fichte to Nietzsche*, 1–31.
12. See Hodgson, "Hegel."
13. On this question, see McCormack, "Person of Christ," 163.

Protestantism, with its democratic populism and nominalism, and that prompted persistent accusations of "transcendentalism."[14]

B. Christocentric Approaches to Theology

While much earlier Enlightenment theology had viewed Christ in ethical rather than redemptive terms, that is, as little more than a (perhaps dispensable) teacher and example of moral truth, with Friedrich D. E. Schleiermacher (1768–1834) a new epoch in theology began in which Christ was seen as both central and essential. Schleiermacher had responded to the epistemological challenges of Kant by seeking to ground religion and theology in something deeper and more fundamental than reason or morality. He found this in a particular sort of human experience, a "feeling [*Gefühl*] of utter dependence upon the Whence," in which God is immediately present to human consciousness.[15] He then presented Jesus Christ as the archetypal ideal of humanity that has been fully realized in history. What distinguishes Jesus from other human beings, whose God-consciousness is fragmentary rather than constant, is "the constant potency of his God-consciousness" and his "unclouded blessedness" (i.e., sinlessness), which "was a veritable existence of God in him."[16]

As the instantiation of this new level of God-consciousness in history, Jesus Christ is the culmination of human destiny, and here Schleiermacher draws on the Pauline conception of Christ as the "Second Adam," the one in whom humanity is redeemed and raised to a new level of existence. Christians are incorporated into this new reality through their union and solidarity with Christ, as they are assumed "into the power of His God-consciousness" and "into the fellowship of His unclouded blessedness."[17] Thus "Christianity is," as Schleiermacher famously declared, "a monotheistic faith belonging to the teleological type of religion, and is essentially distinguished from other such faiths

---

14. See, e.g., Nevin, "New Creation in Christ" in this volume. The extent to which Mercersburg was swimming against the stream of popular religiosity in nineteenth-century America is evident from a careful reading of Hatch, *Democratization of American Christianity*.

15. See Schleiermacher, *The Christian Faith*, 5–26.

16. Ibid., 385.

17. On Schleiermacher's view of Jesus as the archetypal ideal, see Niebuhr, *Schleiermacher on Christ*, 219.

by the fact that in it everything is related to the redemption accomplished by Jesus of Nazareth."[18]

Schleiermacher's impact on subsequent theology was profound. While many found his location of religion in the realm of "feeling" to be too subjective, his christocentrism inaugurated a period in which Christology was seen as central to the theological enterprise, and in which it often became the organizing principle of dogmatics.[19] Another result was a striking emphasis upon the humanity of Christ. For Schleiermacher, solidarity with the archetypal humanity of Christ is the means whereby the blessings of salvation are received. Furthermore, as we have seen, Schleiermacher viewed the divine reality in Christ as a function of his humanity, and while many of his successors found this formulation inadequate, they nevertheless generally utilized a "Christology from below" that reasoned from the sublimity of his humanity to his deity.

This christocentrism is especially evident in the so-called "Mediating Theologians"—those, particularly in Germany, who sought to mediate between Schleiermacher and Hegel on the one hand, and orthodoxy on the other. Here we think particularly of J. A. G. Neander (1789-1850), I. A. Dorner (1809-84), Richard Rothe (1799-1867), and Carl Ullmann (1796-1865), who assumed the idealism and christocentrism of the period, but who moved in the direction of orthodoxy.[20] For example, they were suspicious of what they took to be the pantheistic tendencies in Hegel, and of Schleiermacher's lack of attention to the doctrine of the Trinity. In addition, Hegel was criticized for making sin a necessary moment in the dialectical unfolding of the Absolute rather than the contingent moral disaster that the Christian Scriptures present. Finally, in their Christology they moved back in the direction of Chalcedonian orthodoxy.[21] As we will see, the Christology of Mercersburg is scarcely imaginable apart from these developments.

18. Schleiermacher, *Christian Faith*, 52.

19. For an extended account of this development, see TeSelle, *Christ in Context*.

20. On this German mediating theology (*Vermittlungstheologie*), see Pfleiderer, *Theology in Germany*, 131–153; Holte, *Die Vermittlungstheologie*; Welch, *Protestant Thought*, I: 269–291. For an excellent treatment of the influence of the mediating theologians on American theology (including Mercersburg) see Aubert, *German Roots*.

21. Because Schleiermacher viewed the divine reality in Christ as a function of his humanity, the humanity of Christ was required to carry considerably more theological freight than is necessary with the earlier two-natures doctrine. This results,

C. The Nineteenth-Century American Reformed Theological Context

Another important context for the Mercersburg Theology was the larger environment of American Reformed theology, which was anything but monolithic during this period. The debates were sometimes fierce, and it is not without reason that Mark Noll observes that this was a time when "Calvinists got down to the serious business of beating up on each other."[22] In fact, the Mercersburg theologians were engaged in a contentious three-way conversation regarding Christology and applied soteriology—with the New England Calvinists to the north and with the champions of Reformed federal orthodoxy at Princeton to the east. But in order to understand these debates more fully we must have some broader context.

Here we will recall that for Calvin, with his strongly Christocentric trinitarianism, the person of Christ was central to both the accomplishment of redemption and the application of redemption to the Christian. What the Father sent the Son to accomplish is applied to the Christian by the Holy Spirit. Crucial to this application of redemption for Calvin was the believer's union by faith and the Holy Spirit with the person of Christ, and in particular with the incarnate humanity, through which the *duplex gratia* (double grace) of forensic justification and the transforming power of God is received.[23] Thus, for Calvin all of salvation is a matter of "participation in Christ." It is "in Christ" and not simply on the basis of what Christ has done in some outward sense, and the rich sacramental theology of Calvin (especially his view of the Lord's Supper) must be understood in light of this participationist soteriology.

But as Reformed theology developed in the period after Calvin there was a perceived need to establish stable school-text positions over against Roman Catholic, Lutheran, and other alternatives. In particular, they were concerned to distinguish forensic justification from sanctification in order that there was no possibility of confusing the two, and they also wanted more fully to explain the relation of nature and grace.

---

as several generations of Schleiermacher interpreters have noted, in a certain docetic tinge. See H. R. Mackintosh, *Person of Jesus Christ*, 255; TeSelle, *Christ in Context*, 82–83; Gunton, *Yesterday and Today*, 98–100.

22. Noll, *America's God*, 262.

23. See, e.g., Calvin, *Theological Treatises*, 308; *Commentary* on John 6:51; *Commentary* on Ephesians 5:30; Institutes III.11.9. See also Wallace, *Calvin's Doctrine of Word and Sacrament*, 146–149; Evans, *Imputation and Impartation*, 7–41; Garcia, *Life in Christ*.

Thus the tendency in mature federal theology from the late seventeenth century onward was to speak of two forms of solidarity with Christ—an extrinsic legal union whereby the forensic benefits of salvation are conveyed and a vital or spiritual union whereby the Christian experiences the transforming power of God. Accompanying this was an *ordo salutis* framework in which the elements of soteriology were logically and temporally schematized such that the forensic precedes the transformatory. With regard to the relationship of nature (or human capacities) and grace, many Reformed orthodox began to speak, in Aristotelian fashion, of the infusion of gracious habits as the foundation for faith and obedience, and amidst all this scholastic apparatus the older Reformed emphasis on union with the humanity of Christ began to recede.

In short, the Christian's solidarity with Christ came to be framed in more extrinsic terms. All this was intended to safeguard the gratuity of justification from works righteousness, and the assumption for many came to be that justification cannot be associated in any sense with what God does in us. But this came at the expense of making the forensic, and salvation itself, rather abstract. Justification was abstracted from the ongoing life of faith and obedience, and salvation itself was abstracted from the person of Christ. Thus notions of "virtual communion," or the reception of the benefits of salvation, often replaced Calvin's more concrete notion of union with the very person of Christ, and the reception of salvation was framed in "appropriationist" rather than "participationist" terms.

This extrinsic impulse was most fully developed in the American context by the Old Princeton theologian Charles Hodge, who insisted that justification precedes sanctification in temporal as well as logical priority, and that justification entails only an extrinsic, legal relationship with Christ. Calvin's emphasis on realistic union with the incarnate humanity of Christ was dismissed by Hodge as irrational mysticism that threatened the forensic nature of justification.[24] Thus, in the later federal theology, the importance of the Incarnation recedes and the incarnate humanity of Christ becomes little more than a prerequisite for the atonement.

This extrinsic appropriationist trend accelerates in the New England Calvinist trajectory from the Edwardseans to Nathaniel

---

24. See the exchanges between Nevin and Hodge in DeBie, ed., *Coena Mystica*, volume 2 of this series.

William Taylor. Convinced that traditional federal theology did not comport with the emerging revivalism (because the notion of a definite substitutionary atonement seemed to undercut gospel proclamation in that one cannot say that Christ died for all) and that it was implicitly antinomian (because *ordo salutis* conceptions of a punctiliar, once-for-all forensic decree of justification upon the exercise of faith were thought to undercut the need for ongoing obedience and holiness of life), the New England Calvinists adopted the Grotian or Governmental view of the atonement (which understood the death of Christ as a demonstration by the divine moral governor that sin will be punished, rather than as a vicarious death in place of sinners), jettisoned all notions of imputation (in both hamartiology and soteriology), and spoke only of a "moral union" of shared sentiment between Christ and the believer.[25] One result of all this was that the theme of union with Christ largely dropped out of New England Calvinist discourse by the mid-nineteenth century, which prompted Charles Hodge to quip, "[T]he Christian feels disposed to say with Mary, They have taken away my Lord, and I know not where they have laid him."[26]

The Mercersburg Theology was in critical dialogue with both of these "appropriationist" options. Responding to the federal theology bifurcation of union, Nevin contended that both the legal and the spiritual unions are ultimately extrinsic and abstracted from the person of Christ.[27] Likewise, Nevin also opposed the New England Calvinist notion of a moral union as extrinsic, as issuing in a flat moralism, and as ultimately sub-Christian.[28] Against these "appropriationist" options,

---

25. See Evans, "Imputation and Impartation," 228–67. The continuity of the Edwardsean trajectory from Jonathan Edwards to N. W. Taylor is ably explored by Sweeney, *Nathaniel Taylor*.

26. Hodge, "Beman on the Atonement," 115.

27. Nevin wrote in the *Mystical Presence*, 46–47: "The relation of believers to Christ, then, is more again than that of a simply *legal* union. His is indeed the representative of his people, and what he has done and suffered on their behalf is counted to their benefit, as though it had been done by themselves. They have an interest in his merits, a title to all the advantages secured by his life and death. But this external imputation rests at last on an inward, real unity of life, without which it could have no reason or force.... Of course, once more, the communion in question is not simply with Christ in his *divine nature* separately taken, or with the *Holy Ghost* as the representative of his presence in the world. It does not hold in the influences of the Spirit merely, enlightening the soul and moving it to holy affections and purposes.

28. Nevin, *Mystical Presence*, 44, writes: "In this view, the relation is more again

Nevin and the robustly participationist Mercersburg Theology insisted that salvation is to be found in Christ, not simply on the basis of what Christ has done. As Nevin himself put it, "It is a new creation *in Jesus Christ*, not by him in the way of mere outward power."[29]

D. From Abstract Predestinarianism and Subjective Revivalism to a Concretely Objective Ecclesiology

The Mercersburg Christology was also closely connected with ecclesiology or the doctrine of the church. They sensed that ecclesiology was determined by even more fundamental christological commitments. "We come," Nevin said, "to the true conception of the Church through a true and sound Christology (as in the Creed), and in no other way."[30] In short, Nevin and the Mercersburg theologians sensed that much more was at stake in the ecclesiological discussions of the day.

J. H. Nichols observed that the "Mercersburg view of Christ and the church was defined in constant polemic contrast with the speculative predestinarianism of Princeton."[31] He was half right. Once again the two foils mentioned in the section above—New England Calvinism and Old Princeton—served as dialogue partners. On the one hand, Nevin, of course, reacted strongly against the "New-Measures" revivalism of the day and the theological codification of it by New England theologians such as Nathaniel William Taylor.[32] Such subjective and individualistic thinking, according to Nevin, had no place for the church understood as the organic body of Christ and for the sacraments as genuine means of grace. On the other hand, the Mercersburg thinkers were also convinced that the predestinarian Calvinism of Princeton

---

than a simply *moral* union. Such a union we have, where two or more persons are bound together by inward agreement, sympathy, and correspondence. Every common friendship is of this sort. It is the relation of the disciple to the master, whom he loves and reveres. It is the relation of the devout Jew to Moses, his venerated lawgiver and prophet. It holds also undoubtedly between the believer and Christ. . . . But Christianity includes more than such a moral union, separately considered. This union itself is only the result here of a relation more inward and deep." See also Nevin, "New Creation in Christ."

29. Nevin, *Mystical Presence*, 198.

30. Nevin, "Wilberforce on the Incarnation," 86. For an incisive examination of the Mercersburg ecclesiology, see Littlejohn, *Mercersburg Theology*.

31. Nichols, *Romanticism*, 141.

32. See Nevin, *The Anxious Bench*.

rendered the corporate life of the church (especially the sacraments as real means of grace) a meaningless abstraction.[33]

The Mercersburg theologians were quick to describe what they saw as defective soteriologies and ecclesiologies in terms of christological heresies (it is also interesting to note how quickly Nevin and Hodge in their controversy over the Lord's Supper sought to identify christological problems in the other's position). On the one hand, they persistently distanced themselves from the position that salvation was simply a matter of the immortal soul, as if Christ had not really entered this world as a complete human being in order to redeem human beings in their entirety. This they associated with the christological heresy of Gnostic Docetism. On the other hand, they opposed conceptions of salvation and the church that viewed salvation as merely the perfecting of this worldly existence, which they associated with the Ebionite heresy of the early church period. As Nevin put it,

> The idea of the Christian redemption is never that of a salvation which consists in the mere perfecting of the order of man's present life (Ebionitic humanitarianism); nor yet that of a salvation which has to do with his soul only, magically transferred to some other state (Gnostic spiritualism); it looks always to a deliverance that shall make him as a part of the present world superior to its constitutional curse, carrying him victoriously through it, and crowning him at last with immortality in his whole person, body as well as soul.[34]

Rather, the church is an organic unity, the body of Christ. Because of the mystical union between Christ and the church, the church is the very presence of Christ on earth, and thus it is, in a carefully circumscribed sense, a continuation of the Incarnation. Nevin writes, "In a deep sense, then, Christ himself is made perfect in the Church, as the head in our natural organization requires the body in order to its completion. There can be no Church without Christ, but we may reverse the proposition also and say, no Church, no Christ."[35] Thus, in the church a new and higher supernatural and christologically conditioned principle

33. See Nevin, "Hodge on the Ephesians."

34. Nevin, "Jesus and the Resurrection," p. 154–55.

35. Nevin, "The Church," 66. Nevin is also careful to note that this relationship of mystical union between Christ and the church does not imply that the church is somehow a continuation of the hypostatic union. See Nevin, "Wilberforce on the Incarnation," 71.

of existence has been introduced into human existence, and this New Creation is communicated to human beings through the sacramental mediation of the church.

II. DISTINCTIVE FEATURES OF THE MERCERSBURG CHRISTOLOGY

In the section above we noted that the Mercersburg Theology was highly contextual—it was responsive to the issues and concerns of its age. Here we must recognize, however, that the focus of the Mercersburg Theology is more on what might be termed "applied Christology," that is, Christology in service to soteriology and ecclesiology. Thus we find rather little discussion of christological technicalities for their own sake. In addition, the focus of discussion is especially on the incarnate humanity of Christ as the particular means whereby salvation is both accomplished and mediated to Christians. With this in mind, there are certain distinctive characteristics that require further elaboration here.

A. Christ as the Irenaean Second Adam

The Mercersburg Theology followed Schleiermacher and the Mediating Theologians in viewing Christ as the "Second Adam," that is, as the goal and fulfillment of the human race as created and as the one in whom humanity is restored and brought into union with God. Thus the human race is determined by two relational realities—being "in Adam" and being "in Christ," and the framework of thinking here, as the Mercersburg Theologians deploy it, is fundamentally Irenaean.[36] For our purposes, three themes in the church father Irenaeus are particularly important for understanding Mercersburg. First, there is the parallel between the first Adam and the Second Adam, Jesus Christ. Christ lives the full course of human life in obedience to God, an obedience that Adam failed to achieve. Second, there is the solidarity of human beings in these two figures. Humanity participates in Adam by natural generation, and Christians participate in Christ through spiritual and sacramental incorporation into the mystical body of Christ, the church. The line of thinking here is corporate rather than individualistic, and

---

36. This Irenaean aspect is noted by Nichols, *Romanticism*, 144–45. See especially Irenaeus, *Against Heresies*, I: 440–458. For a provocative reading of Irenaeus in dialogue with Calvin, see Canlis, *Calvin's Ladder*.

Nevin, for example, never tires of saying that the church is not a "sand heap," or simply the aggregate of its individual members. Third, there is the elevation of humanity into union with God by the Incarnation and work of Christ, as humanity is sanctified in Christ. All this is abundantly evident in Mercersburg, and at times Nevin and others reference Irenaeus by name or allude to his theory of recapitulation.[37]

As James Hastings Nichols notes, this basically Irenaean perspective is accompanied by a view of the atonement that emphasizes Christ's death and resurrection as a mighty victory over sin, death, and the devil.[38] In this, of course, we see important similarities with the Eastern Christian tradition.[39] At the same time, the substitutionary dimension of Christ's work that is more characteristic of Latin Christianity is not ignored. Nor does he deny the imputation of the righteousness of Christ to the Christian. Rather, both are placed within a broader context of incorporation and participation—it is only as the human being is united with Christ that his substitutionary work and righteousness avail. Behind this lies the nineteenth-century conviction that merit and demerit inhere in persons, and cannot be abstracted from them. Thus, to be in Adam is to participate in his condemnation, and to be joined with Christ is to participate in his forensic righteousness.[40]

B. The "Fallen Humanity" of Christ

But what sort of humanity did the Logos assume in the Incarnation and elevate into union with God? The Mercersburg theologians persistently, and somewhat provocatively, described it as a "fallen humanity" that is

---

37. See, e.g., Nevin, "Noel on Baptism," 248, where he writes, "Humanity is not merely our mature human life, but all the stages also through which this is reached. It includes infancy and childhood as a necessary part of its constitution. . . . Does the nature of the Second Adam take in one half of the necessary life of the race only, while it hopelessly excludes the other? Such a thought goes at once to undermine the whole fact of the Incarnation. Christ must be of the same length and breadth in all respects with humanity as a whole, in order to be at all a real and true Mediator. He must be commensurate with the universal process of humanity from infancy to old age, as well as with its mere numerical extent. . . . He sanctified infancy and childhood, says Irenaeus, by making them stages of his own life. This expresses a just and sound feeling."

38. Nichols, *Romanticism*, 145–46. See, e.g., Nevin, *Mystical Presence*, 148.

39. These connections to Eastern theology are explored at length in Littlejohn, *Mercersburg*, 124–46.

40. On this, see Evans, *Imputation and Impartation*, 170–71.

then sanctified and elevated. Representative is this statement by Nevin in *The Mystical Presence*:

> In taking our nature upon him, he was made in all respects like as we are, only without sin (Heb. iv. 15. v. 2, 7). He appeared "in the likeness of sinful flesh" (Rom. viii.3); "made of a woman, made under the law" (Gal. iv.4). The humanity which he assumed was fallen, subject to infirmity, and liable to death. In the end, "he was crucified through weakness" (2 Cor. xiii.4). Under all this low estate however, the power of a divine life was always actively present, wrestling as it were with the law of death it was called to conquer, and sure of its proper victory at last. This victory was displayed in the resurrection.[41]

Here Nevin is by no means denying the sinlessness of Christ. Rather, he emphasizes both the solidarity of Christ with those he came to save and the way in which fallen human life is redeemed and elevated in Christ. Broken and weakened humanity was assumed by Christ, and that brokenness has been healed in Christ.

Nevin asserts this position regarding the sinful humanity of Christ in numerous places, but without naming his influences. He would have been aware of the Church of Scotland minister Edward Irving (1792–1834), who seems to have popularized the idea initially and was subsequently deposed from the ministry in 1831, and Nevin the embattled controversialist had obvious reason not to mention one who had been officially designated a heretic by the Scottish Kirk. The "sinful humanity" of Christ was affirmed in the twentieth century by Karl Barth, and especially by Thomas F. Torrance, who regarded the denial of it as the "Latin heresy" leading to an extrinsic view of the relationship between Christ and the Christian, and to an exaggerated preoccupation with the forensic at the expense of realistic solidarity.[42] Torrance's reasoning here is likely a good summary of Nevin's concerns on the issue.

---

41. Nevin, *Mystical Presence*, 194.

42. See Irving, *Orthodox and Catholic Doctrine*; Barth, *Church Dogmatics*, I/2: 151–59; Torrance, *Incarnation*, 61–65; "Karl Barth and the Latin Heresy." More recently, Oliver Crisp has argued that the notion of the "sinful humanity" of Christ is incoherent in light of the doctrine of original sin. See his "Did Christ have a Fallen Human Nature?"

C. The Generic Humanity of Christ

In explaining how this incarnate humanity of Christ serves as the medium of the New Creation, Nevin and the Mercersburg theologians utilized a crucial distinction between individual and generic humanity, between what Nevin termed "the simple man and the universal man." Both the first Adam and the Second Adam serve as the generic heads of their respective communities. The first Adam has to do with humanity as originally created and fallen, the Second Adam with humanity as redeemed, recreated, and elevated through the person and work of Christ.[43]

This generic identity is understood in terms of organic law, a life principle antecedent to any subsequent division into body and soul that determines the identity and character of those in solidarity with the head. The organic law binding Adam and his posterity together is natural, while with the Second Adam a new and higher principle has been introduced into human existence. While supernatural, it nevertheless becomes integral with human existence. Nevin writes,

> Christ's life as a *whole* is borne over into the person of the believer as a like *whole*. The communication is central, and central only; from the last ground of Christ's life to the last ground of ours; by the action of a single, invisible, self-identical spiritual law. The power of Christ's life lodged in the soul begins to work there immediately as the principle of a new creation. In doing so, it works organically according to the law which it includes in its own constitution. That is, it works as a *human* life; and as such becomes a law of regeneration in the body as truly as in the soul.[44]

The distinction between individual and generic humanity enabled Nevin and the Mercersburg thinkers to affirm a real and organic union without effacing the personal distinction between Christ and the Christian, and to avoid a pantheistic mysticism. Nevin wrote,

> We distinguish between the simple man and the universal man, here joined in the same person. The possibility of such a distinction is clear in the case of Adam. His universality is not indeed of the same order with that of Christ, But still the case has full force, for the point now in hand. Adam was at once an

---

43. See Nevin, "Catholic Unity," 40; *Mystical Presence*, 154.
44. Nevin, *Mystical Presence*, 153.

individual and a whole race. All his posterity partake of his life, and grow forth from him as their root. and still his individual person has not been lost on this account. Why then should the life of Christ in the Church, be supposed to conflict with the idea of his separate, distinct personality, under a true human form? Why must we dream of a fusion of persons in the one case, more than in the other? Here is more, it is true, than our relation to Adam. We not only spring from Christ, so far as our new life is concerned, but stand in him perpetually also as our ever living and ever present root. His Person is always thus the actual bearer of our persons. And yet there is no mixture, or flowing of one into the other, as individually viewed. Is not God the last ground of all personality? But does this imply any pantheistic dissipation of his nature, into the general consciousness of the intelligent universe?[45]

The coherence of these notions of the corporate or generic significance of the humanities of Adam and Christ depends upon philosophical presuppositions that may be broadly designated as Platonic in tendency. For Nevin and Mercersburg, this impulse was mediated by and filtered through the organic idealism of Schelling and the German mediating theologians such as Neander and Ullmann. In a description of T. F. Torrance's Christology that applies equally well to that of Nevin, George Hunsinger notes that the sanctified humanity of Christ has "the status of a 'concrete universal.'"[46]

D. Christ and the Spirit

The Mercersburg Theology is also notable for its emphasis on the work of the Holy Spirit in connection with Christology, and it is here that the relationship of pneumatology, Christology, and soteriology becomes especially apparent. In his discussions of the Christian's union and solidarity with Christ, Nevin insists that the Holy Spirit is not a surrogate for the Christ himself, as if the Spirit simply represents an otherwise absent Christ. Rather, the believer is united with the divine-human Christ

---

45. Nevin, *Mystical Presence*, 154.

46. Hunsinger, "Dimension of Depth," 162. The affinity of Nevin for Plato and the Christian Platonist tradition is explored in DiPuccio, "Nevin's Idealistic Philosophy." On the remarkable similarities between Nevin and Thomas F. Torrance with respect to theological method and content, see Evans, "Twin Sons of Different Mothers."

in heaven by the power of the Holy Spirit.[47] And because Christians are united with Christ through his incarnate humanity, it is necessary that this humanity be made spiritually accessible. Thus to this end Nevin and the Mercersburg theologians argue that Christ's humanity has been taken up into the realm of Spirit. Nevin wrote,

> All is spiritual, glorious, heavenly. His whole humanity has been taken up into the sphere of the Spirit, and appears transfigured into the same life. And why then should it not extend itself, in the way of strict organic continuity, as a whole humanity also, by the active presence of Christ's Spirit, over into the persons of his people?[48]

This transformation of Christ's incarnate humanity reaches its climax with the resurrection and ascension of Christ, which constitutes the "final triumph of the Spirit in the glorified humanity of Christ."[49] But the Mercersburg theologians are far from holding that Christ's humanity is somehow dissolved by or into the Holy Spirit. Rather, the point is that the New Creation as it has been inaugurated by the transformation of Christ's humanity is an eschatological form of existence pervaded by the power of the Holy Spirit.[50] An implication of this is, of course, that the work of the Holy Spirit assumes a decisively new character with the resurrection and ascension of Christ. In other words, the Christ-event is decisive for the work of the Holy Spirit. Nevin wrote,

> John goes so far as to say there was no Holy Spirit . . . till Jesus was glorified (John vii.39). This does not mean of course that he did not exist; but it limits the proper effusion of the Spirit, as known under the New Testament, to the Christian dispensation as such. It teaches besides, that the person of Jesus, as the Word made flesh, forms the only channel or medium, by which it was possible for this effusion to take place. The Holy Ghost accordingly, as the Spirit of Christ, is, in the first place, active simply in the Saviour himself. In this view, however, he

---

47. See Nevin, *Mystical Presence*, 47, 170–71, 195–96. See also Evans, *Imputation and Impartation*, 159.

48. Nevin, *Mystical Presence*, 156.

49. Nevin, *Mystical Presence*, 194.

50. Here Nevin and the Mercersburg theologians anticipate themes later to be developed by twentieth-century New Testament scholarship. See, e.g., Vos, *Pauline Eschatology*; "Eschatological Aspect"; Hamilton, *Holy Spirit and Eschatology*, 12–15; Harris, *Raised Immortal*, 53–57, 94–97.

cannot be separated from the person of Christ. He constitutes rather the form, in which the higher nature of Christ reveals its force, In the end, the whole person of the Son of Man is exalted into the same order of existence. Humanity itself in this way, as joined with the everlasting Word, is made to triumph over the law of infirmity and mortality, to which it was previously subject in its own nature, and takes henceforth the character of *spirit*, in distinction from mere flesh.[51]

III. INTERPRETIVE QUESTIONS

Despite the general clarity of the Mercersburg Christology, a number of interpretive questions present themselves. The first has to do with the place of the Incarnation within the broader system of thought. Is it the case, as some contemporaries argued, that the Incarnation has displaced the atonement as the central saving event? To be sure, Nevin did insist that the Incarnation has a certain priority over the atonement, but his concern in these contexts was to underscore the inseparable relationship between Christ's person and his work and that the benefits of Christ cannot be abstracted from his person. As Nevin put it, "Not by the atonement then, as something made over to us separately from Christ's person, are we placed in the possession of salvation and life; but only by the atonement as comprehended in his person itself, and received through faith in this form."[52] Thus, far from slighting the importance of the work of Christ, Mercersburg actually emphasized that work by foregrounding its connection with Christ's person, and in so doing it was able to do highlight the importance of the resurrection and ascension in ways unavailable to their contemporaries who focused primarily on the atonement.

Another question has to do with the divine agent of the elevation of Christ's incarnate fallen humanity. Was it due to the incarnational union with the Logos or to the work of the Holy Spirit? The answer here, in the final analysis, seems to be both, for the divine Word and the Holy Spirit are implicated in this sanctification of the incarnate humanity (sometimes in the same context). For example, Nevin argues that "Humanity itself in this way, as joined with the everlasting Word, is made to triumph over the law of infirmity and mortality, to which

51. Nevin, *Mystical Presence*, 193. See also Nevin, "Apostles' Creed," 330.
52. Nevin, *Mystical Presence*, 208. See also "Apostles' Creed," 343–45.

it was previously subject in its own nature, and takes henceforth the character of *spirit*, in distinction from mere flesh."[53] On balance, however, the emphasis seems to fall more on the work of the Holy Spirit, for it was by the power of the Holy Spirit that the Incarnation initially occurred; it was by the Holy Spirit that Christ was raised from the dead and becomes the agent and source of the New Creation, and it is by the power of the Holy Spirit that believers are united with Christ's incarnate humanity.

Nevin, for one, was aware that such language could be misunderstood—in fact, he was accused of Sabellianism by Charles Hodge because of it.[54] In this context he affirms the personal distinction but also appeals to the perichoresis of the divine Persons: "The persons of the adorable Trinity are indeed distinct. But we must beware of sundering them into abstract subsistences, one without the other. They subsist in the way of the most perfect mutual inbeing and intercommunion."[55]

A third question has to do with whether the Incarnation would have occurred apart from sin. This is a significant matter for this volume in that two of the essays by Nevin deal explicitly with this issue. As we noted earlier, Nevin insists that the Incarnation is much more than a mere precondition for the atonement: "The true order is, the mystery of the Incarnation first, and then the atonement, as growing forth from this."[56] Such statements could be taken to imply, though they probably do not necessitate, that the Incarnation would have occurred even apart from sin. Further complicating the issue is the fact that Nevin and the Mercersburg theologians were the heirs of German organic idealism as it came to them through the mediating theologians. According to this way of thinking, the Incarnation is the telos of creation in which the idea of divine-human unity is finally realized. Consistent with this, Nevin can argue, "The nature of the Messianic idea has its necessity in the constitution of humanity,"[57] and here an ontological necessity of the Incarnation even apart from sin becomes more clear.

The two reviews of German works—by Liebner and Müller—included in this volume do not finally settle the issue for us, at least with

---

53. See Nevin, *Mystical Presence*, 193.
54. See DeBie, ed., *Coena Mystica*, 162–64.
55. Nevin, *Mystical Presence*, 196.
56. Nevin, "Apostles' Creed," 343. See also *Mystical Presence*, 147.
57. Erb, *Nevin's Theology*, 236.

respect to Nevin. In the first, Nevin ably and with some obvious enthusiasm recounts the arguments of Karl Theodor Albert Liebner for the necessity of the Incarnation apart from sin. In the second, Nevin no less ably, though with a bit less enthusiasm, summarizes the case made by Julius Müller for the hamartiological rationale. Müller's case was formidable in its marshaling of biblical evidence. Even more impressive was his presentation of what he took to be the implications of Liebner's view—a confusion of the moral and the metaphysical, a subversion of the freedom of God, and tendencies toward pantheism and universalism. It seems rather clear that Nevin was taken aback by this.[58]

That being said, however, the heart of Nevin's positive argument for the Incarnation—that the Logos had been united with fallen human nature, had sanctified it, and thus had raised humanity to a new level of existence—was, in fact, compatible with either rationale for the Incarnation. And this, in turn, raises a further set of questions that cut to the heart of our understanding of Nevin as a theologian, and of the broader Mercersburg movement. Is Nevin to be understood primarily as an idealist theologian in the tradition of the German mediating theologians? Or is he better seen as a biblical theologian with deep patristic and Reformation roots, who found the apparatus of German idealism quite useful in providing an idiom for articulating certain concerns but who was not slavishly devoted to that apparatus when there were reasons to diverge from it? On balance, the latter interpretation seems better to fit the facts. A careful survey of the biblical citations in the Mercersburg theology materials provides obvious testimony to just how *scriptural* they were, and Nevin's failure to defend an obvious implication of the idealist Christology against Müller's learned onslaught at least suggests a significant measure of independence.[59]

---

58. Nevin's indecision has fascinated historians. Nichols, *Romanticism*, 149–50, wonders, "Did he hang on dead center, unready to decide? Was he already feeling the paralysis of will which was shortly to cripple his speculative interest? This whole aspect of the Mercersburg Christology ran into a question mark and remained unresolved." D. G. Hart, *John Williamson Nevin*, 147, shares Nichols' perplexity and attributes Nevin's indecision to his "plunging into the depths of despair."

59. Hart, *John Williamson Nevin*, 147, suggests that the 1851 review of Müller "was virtually the last time that Nevin would address the significance and nature of Christology in a sustained way." But while it is fair to say that Nevin soon entered a period of inactivity and later turned his attention to other matters, it is not the case that this was his last substantive word on Christology. Witness his 1861 piece "Jesus and the Resurrection" (included in this volume), which is a compelling presentation

The recognition above—that the Mercersburg theology is best understood as Protestant Christian theology based on Scripture and deeply informed by patristic and Reformational insights (and often expressed in an idealist idiom)—is significant for the continuing legacy of the Mercersburg movement. After all, any theology completely tied to nineteenth-century idealism would today be little more than a period piece. But the issues that Mercersburg addressed with such vigor are still with us. American Christianity by and large continues to be profoundly individualistic and "ecclesially challenged." Many American Protestants continue to see the Incarnation as little more than a prelude to and precondition for the atonement, and the incarnate humanity of Christ continues to be largely ignored as a theological factor. Not surprisingly, the importance of the person of Christ for the application of salvation to the Christian, as opposed to the accomplishment of salvation, continues to be overlooked, with the result that the sacraments as mediators of that divine-human person are eclipsed. For all this and more, the Mercersburg theologians still have something of importance to say.

---

of the Mercersburg Christology and distinctive for its presentation in a more biblical rather than philosophical idiom.

ARTICLE 1

"Sartorius on the Person and Work of Christ"

(by John W. Nevin)

EDITOR'S INTRODUCTION

This review essay appeared in the *Mercersburg Review* during the first year of its publication (1849). Given Nevin's interests and the prominence of Christology in his writings to this point, the fact that an American translation of a significant work of this sort by the German Lutheran theologian Ernst Wilhelm Christian Sartorius (1797–1859) attracted Nevin's attention should not surprise. Nevin's review, however, is more a sustained criticism of the translation and the way that, in Nevin's view, the translator had imposed his own baptistic theology on the robustly Lutheran text of Sartorius.

The translator in question was Oakman S. Stearns (1817–1893), a prominent figure among New England Baptists who spent the latter part of his career teaching at the Newton Theological Institution (which in the twentieth century merged with Andover Seminary to form Andover Newton Theological School). Nevin spends the first portion of the review taking issue with the quality of the English translation itself, which he found to be lacking in both accuracy and style, and later he excoriates Stearns for omitting a significant portion of the volume dealing with the sacraments, an act Nevin regarded as a "mutilation" of Sartorius' original text.

But Nevin's deeper objection is to Stearns' "theory of religion" and "Baptistic theology," which views the Incarnation as little more than a means to the end of the atonement. The problem here, according to Nevin, is that Stearns views Christ as an "outward instrument" rather than the one in whom salvation is concretely accomplished and mediated to Christians. In this, Stearns fails to do proper justice to the hypostatic union and to the role and importance of Christ's incarnate humanity. By contrast, for Sartorius Christianity "is a new order of life that has its ground in the Christological fact itself." In Christ's person as the God-man he "reconciles heaven and earth" and effects the union of the divine and human. This organic union of God and man, according to Sartorius, takes place "through the medium of common consciousness" and involves a real communication of attributes from the deity to the humanity and from humanity to deity.

Nevin then turns to the question of how this new order of life is communicated to Christians in the means of grace, especially the sacraments, and here he summarizes the section from the Sartorius original on the sacraments that Stearns had chosen to omit from his translation. Once more, Nevin finds the difference between author and translator to be one of irreconcilably different theological systems rooted in different Christologies. For Stearns and those who hold to his system, Nevin argues, the work of Christ and the benefits of salvation can be separated from the person of Christ: "The work which was required to take away sin, needed indeed a conjunction of divinity and humanity in Christ, to qualify him for its execution; but once executed, it carries with it an independent and separate value in the divine mind, and may be set to the account of men as a mere abstraction in this way, apart from Christ's life altogether." By contrast, for Sartorius the sacraments are real means of grace that, along with the preaching of the Word, convey the divine-human life of Christ. Baptism is the rite of Christian initiation, which then comes to completion in confirmation, and the Christian life that has its inception in baptism is then nurtured and strengthened by the holy supper.

Nevin goes on to argue that such renunciation of sacramental efficacy is characteristic, not only of Stearns' own Baptist tradition, but of "the American churches in general," which he describes as of "Puritan and Methodistic tendency." Here he implicates even the American Lutheran party of Benjamin Kurtz (who edited the *Lutheran Observer*). Such churches may have a deep affection for Martin Luther, especially as they claim to champion the Reformer's doctrine of justification by faith, but the sacramental Luther is not so easily dispensed with. According to Nevin, "The sacramental doctrine of Luther . . . was no outward fungus upon his system. . . . To part with it is to give up the cause of the Reformation itself . . . and to turn his whole theology into a new and different shape."

This charge of declension from the Reformation, of course, was strong language on Nevin's part! In support of it he takes pains to emphasize the commonality of the classic Lutheran and Reformed traditions. While conceding that there were creedal differences, Nevin argues that both of these magisterial Protestant traditions "intended to hold fast to the substance of the ancient sacramental doctrine, as it had stood in the catholic Church from the beginning." In addition, he suggests that this common stance "grew too out of a corresponding Christology."

Here many will sense that, in his desire to make common cause with the Lutheran tradition over against the low-church, anti-sacramental "Puritans" of his day, Nevin overstated his case. Certainly there are important Christological and sacramental differences between the classic Lutheran and Reformed traditions. But Nevin also had a point, in that the sacramental theology of the Reformed confessions was much too high even for many American Presbyterians, as his earlier controversy with Charles Hodge had amply demonstrated.

"Sartorius on the Person and Work of Christ"[1]

1. *Die Lehre von Christi Person und Werk in populairen Vorlesungen vorgetragen von Ernst Sartorius, Doctor der Theologie. Fuenfte Auflage. Hamburg, 1845.*[2]
2. *The Person and Work of Christ.* By Ernest Sartorius, D. D., General Superintendent and Consistorial Director at Koenigsberg, Prussia. Translated by Rev. Oakman S. Stearns, A. M., Boston, 1848.

[AN UNFORTUNATE TRANSLATION]

The second work here named offers itself to the world as a translation of the first. If by a translation, however, we are to understand a true transfer of the sense and spirit of a book out of one language into another, it is wholly a misnomer to apply the term to this case. The original work of Sartorius[3] is one which comes up in full, both in sentiment and style,

---

1. [Originally printed in the *Mercersburg Review* 1:1 (March 1849): 146–69.]

2. [The first edition was published in Hamburg in 1831, followed quickly by second (1834), third (1837), and fourth editions (1841). As noted above, the final and fifth edition was published in 1845. These lectures were initially presented to a popular audience at the University of Dorpat.]

3. [Ernst Wilhelm Christian Sartorius (1797–1859), a German-Lutheran theologian educated at Göttingen who taught successively at the Universities of Göttingen (1818–21), Marburg (1821–24), and Dorpat (1824–35). In 1835 he was called as the General Superintendent of the Union Church (which had united Lutherans and Reformed in a single church body) in the province of East Prussia, and he also served as chaplain of the royal castle church at Königsburg. A staunch defender of the Lutheran Augsburg Confession against the rationalism of the day, Sartorius nevertheless did not support the Old Lutherans who separated from the Prussian Union Church in order to maintain Lutheran distinctives, hence Nevin's comment in this review that the "Lutheranism of Dr. Sartorius, as presented in this work, is by no means of the rigid extreme sort."]

to the wide reputation which has carried it in Germany through five editions, and made it a favorite with all who take an interest in practical piety under a manly and substantial form. No one can read it understandingly without admiration and respect; and the heart must be dull indeed that is not made to kindle, under its simple though profound devotional eloquence, into some corresponding glow of Christian edification. But of all this, it would be hard to form any conception from Mr. Stearns' translation. This is neither elegant, nor intelligent, nor edifying. A most lame, clumsy performance throughout, it presents no single attraction either in thought or expression, no redeeming quality whatever, save in the broken fragments of truth and beauty that still look forth here and there upon the beholder, in spite of the general desolation with which the work has been overwhelmed as a whole. It is indeed Sartorius *in ruins*; a spectacle, whose remains of greatness serve only to render more affectingly sad the chaotic dreariness in which its exhibition mainly consists. Murderous translations are by no means uncommon; but we have seldom met with one which could be said more effectually to kill the life of the author it pretends to honor in this way.

In the first place, Mr. Stearns[4] evidently has had no sufficient knowledge of the German language, and no proper mastery of the English either, to do justice to any undertaking of this sort. His own English, as we have it in his short preface, is anything but easy and smooth. Were his knowledge of the German ever so complete, he lacks altogether the freedom and pliancy of style that are required to make a good translator. But he has brought with him no such advantage to his task. It is only a smattering acquaintance with German, he can be said to possess at best. His knowledge of the language shows itself to be throughout mechanical, superficial, and in a great measure merely external. He has never entered at all into its true genius and life; its idiomatic soul remains, to a great extent, foreign from the view of his understanding. Still less can he be said to be at home in the peculiarities of German thought. There is not a page of his translation accordingly, we might say indeed hardly a sentence in its connections, which does not betray some want of insight, more or less, into the true living sense

4. [Oakman Sprague Stearns (1817–1893). A Baptist minister, author, and educator, Stearns was educated at Waterville College and the Newton Theological Institution, and later served as Professor of Biblical Interpretation at Newton. See Charles Rufus Brown, "American Old Testament Scholars: Oakman Sprague Stearns," in *The Old and New Testament Student* 10 (1890): 7–13.]

of the original work. Take as a specimen, the following extract, which is made to pass for the preface of Sartorius to the last German edition:

> Several years have passed away since the first appearance of this little volume, and now the Fifth Edition is deemed necessary by the continual demand for it. It is absolutely necessary that the doctrine of the incarnation, by the union of divinity and humanity in it, and the re-union of both by it, which was rejected by many theologians out of the historical churches, and had become foreign to and far from the educated and uneducated in general, should be transferred in this artless, familiar manner, from the department of learned theology, to the more common orbit of faith and life, and should be brought to the Christian conscience of readers of every grade, as the basis of all Christianity and of all salvation. Great storms have been raised during this time respecting the proper field of the church, and they have been particularly directed against this fundamental doctrine. They have endeavored to turn away the testimony of the church and its judgement, thereby expecting to tear it asunder and destroy it. Some have spoken of the incarnate Jesus as the Lord of humanity, in the loose generalities of the multitude, and thereby robbed him of the excellence by which he was to increase to a confederate head, and by which he should become the reconciler of everything which sin had separated, even the fountain of life and love from which every favor and power of renovation should flow. He has a very narrow conception of the thing who expects to remove from Christ the concentration of the fulness of the Godhead. He most assuredly misunderstands himself, because if in him all fulness dwells, every favor, even grace for grace must come from him, and by means of him we become partakers of the divine nature.
>
> These storms, however, have to a great degree blown over or turned out to be mere wind. Indeed, the church has strengthened itself, established itself, and made itself fast during the roar of the storm, clinging the more tenaciously to the reconciliation of heaven and earth by faith in Jesus Christ, the mighty God eternally generated from the Father, and the mighty man generated from the virgin Mary. This union of time and eternity cannot be removed. The denial of the divinity of Christ humbles him to an idol or a demi-god, and leads to a heathenish idolatry, or it degrades him to a mere man, and thereby sinks his religion behind Judaism. Very evidently everything spiritual and human becomes him who is the king of the heavenly kingdom, who was exalted from the cross to the right hand of the majesty, not

to conquer, but to receive the name which the Father has given, by virtue of which he shall obtain the homage of both angels and men.

In spite of the stormy movements of the time, therefore, while the world renews the evidence of the Scriptures and the church respecting the Son of God, and the Son of man the mediator between God and man, Jesus Christ our Lord, who though in the image of God, humbled himself, and took upon himself the form of a servant, was obedient to the death of the cross, and from his humiliation is now exalted for us over all the world to his praise and for our salvation, this discussion will remain immovable by the side of that which is old and unchangeable. Neither the contents nor the form of this little book ought to suffer any material change. The circumstances of the time seem to demand the very same things. Indeed, they present themselves as another proper occasion for giving the book both in Germany and in other lands, by means of translations, a larger circle of readers. Its design is to meet not so much the wants of a theological public as those of a Christian public. Accordingly, the Fifth edition appears with every essential correspondence to the earlier ones. As I would not, however, omit any amount of care manifest in the other editions, I have inserted when and where it was proper, individual additions and emendations, and thereby increased the pages somewhat.

May this work receive the blessing of him concerning whom it treats. May it receive the sanction of the Lord who renovated the condition of the world by reconciling it to himself. May it aid in establishing the Christian reader upon the precious cornerstone, without which every church organization founded upon some other basis than the rock of confession, which was first testified to by the apostles before the Lord gave to them the shutting up of the heavenly kingdom, is founded only upon the sand. This is the first and chief thing to be done by the church, that worshipping in the name of Jesus, every knee may bow, and every tongue confess that he is the Lord to the glory of God the Father.[5]

To be properly estimated, this should be compared with the original German text. As however a large part of our readers must be supposed unable to try it in that way, we subjoin the true sense of the

---

5. [Ernest Sartorius, *The Person and Work of Christ*, trans. Oakman S. Stearns (Boston: Gould, Kendall & Lincoln, 1848), xi–xiv.]

original in a different version. It will be easy to see, by the comparison, first that the "translation" just quoted has in part no clear sense whatever; and secondly, that such sense as it has is materially different from that intended by Sartorius:

> Fourteen years have elapsed since the first appearance of these lectures, of which the continued demand now calls for a *fifth* edition. The doctrine of the *God-man*, of the union of divinity and humanity in him, and the reconciliation of both through him (a doctrine by many theologians long since thrust out of the church into mere history, and that had grown strange to the Christian community, cultivated as well as uncultivated) by these unpretending lectures came forth again from the sphere of scientific theology into more general contact with faith and life, and was anew brought nigh to the Christian consciousness of readers of every standing as the foundation on which Christianity with its whole salvation rests. Great storms have swept since that time over the field of the Church, and have directed their strength in particular against this foundation, bearing witness thus to its true character in this view, while seeking to unsettle it, and so to overthrow the church built upon it. It has been pretended to dissolve the God-man Jesus, the Lord of humanity, into the loose generality of the human race; robbing this thus of the head, from which the whole should grow up into a well compacted body (Eph. iv. 15f.) of the mediator through whom is to be reconciled all that has been separated by *sin* (Col. i. 20) and of the fountain of life and love from which all should draw grace and power of renovation. The concentration of the fulness of the Godhead in the One Christ (Col. ii. 9) it was affected to set aside as something poor and narrow; while in truth such judgment was itself too narrow to see, how all fulness dwells in *him* for this reason precisely, that all may receive thence grace for grace, and become through *him* partakers of the divine nature (John i. 16; 2 Pet. i. 4).
>
> Those storms have to a great extent blown over, or are sunk at least into common winds; in the midst of their raging, however, the Church visibly gained strength, planting herself with new and more firm resolution on the rock of her all-reconciling faith in Jesus Christ, 'true God begotten of the Father in eternity and also true man born of the Virgin Mary.' She cannot recede from this ground which binds eternity and time into one; since the denial of Christ's divinity either sinks him to the character of an idol or demi-god, leading in this way to heathenish idolatry, or

else reduces him to a mere man, and so falls back into Judaism. Assuredly all the spiritual and fleshly powers of the world will be found unable to prevail over the king Messiah who has been exalted from the cross to the right hand of majesty, or to take from him the name which is given him of the Father, so high and glorious as to compel the homage of angels and men.

In the face accordingly of all the stormy agitations of the time, these lectures have stood immovably fast to the firmly seated, ancient (though never old, but rather always world-renewing) testimony of the Bible and the Church, concerning the Son of God and of Man, the Mediator between God and man, our Lord Jesus Christ; who being in divine form equal with God, nevertheless emptied himself and took upon him the form of a servant, and became obedient even to the death of the cross, and now is exalted from such humiliation over all the world for his own glory and our salvation (Phil. ii. 5ff.). No material change therefore has been made in the contents of this little volume, as it has passed through different editions, nor even in its form; for this, as it had from outward popular occasion adapted itself to a wide Christian rather than theological public, was just what procured for the work its extensive circulation, and this indeed not in Germany only, but by translations also in foreign lands. So this fifth edition also appears in substantial agreement with those which have gone before; only I wished to show my continued interest in the earlier work, and for this reason have introduced single additions and improvements, as it seemed worth while, which have increased somewhat also the number of pages.

Under his blessing now of whom it treats, under the blessing of the Lord, who has brought into the world not so much a constitution as an atonement, may this little book still farther contribute to build Christian readers on that precious foundation and corner-stone, without which all church organization, the great concern of the present time, will be built upon the sand, and not on the rock of that confession (Matt. xvi. 16ff.) which the Apostles were required first to make, before the keys of the kingdom of heaven were given to them by the Lord. This it is which the Church needs first and above all, that at the name of Jesus every knee should bow in worship, and every tongue *confess* harmoniously with his people, that he is Lord to the glory of God the Father.

Koenigsberg, Passion week, 1845.

This will be sufficient, for all readers, to justify in full the sweeping censure we have allowed ourselves to pronounce on Mr. Stearns' translation. Harsh and exaggerated as the judgment might seem on first view, it will easily be perceived that it falls not a whit short of the sober truth. The translation is no translation whatever, but a miserable travesty and caricature rather of the respectable work in whose name it appears. It is such a wrong indeed upon the character and reputation of Sartorius, that under any proper system of international literary law, he would be authorized to sue for heavy damages, as a grossly misrepresented and slandered man. "The translation," we are told in the preface, "is designedly free, and as expressive of the views of the author as the time and means of the translator would allow." A good translation must be in any case *free*; that is not bound slavishly to the letter at the expense of the spirit and sense. But in the case before us, the freedom is such as flows from weakness and not from strength. It is helplessly, wilfully, and for this reason slavishly independent. Its liberty stands only in the power it has to go wrong, without understanding the fact. A strange freedom truly, that turns words and sentences continually from their proper sense, misled by its own mechanical dictionary-guided ignorance, and turns an author on every page into a shape which can hardly be said to reflect a single feature of his native face. If the "time and means" of Mr. Stearns allowed no more than this, it had been better, we think, to turn his resources to some other work. It is no apology for such a wrong as this, that the doer of the work could do it no better. Why should he, in such case, feel bound to try it at all? The world would not have suffered any irreparable loss—Sartorius himself might well have borne the disappointment—if the little book in question had been left to go untranslated; at least till some more competent hand, with proper "time and means," had offered itself for the purpose. The thanks of the translator are tendered, in conclusion, to the Rev. Dr. Sears, President of the Newton Theological Institution, for suggesting the translation, "and for any aid he has generously afforded him during the progress of it." No doubt Dr. Sears recommended the work as worthy of being translated, as any one would who was able to appreciate its value; but it is not to be imagined for a moment that he is responsible in any way for the character of the translation. He is known to be one of the most accomplished German scholars in the country; and to involve him even indirectly in the endorsement of such a production must be taken as a wrong to his reputation, only less flagrant than the wholesale slaughter of poor Dr. Sartorius himself. How such a work could pass muster with the common religious press might seem strange; for it abounds in sentences and entire passages that have no sense whatever, and as a whole is made exceedingly tasteless and dull; but newspaper notices, we all know, are not generally in such cases the fruit of much consideration or care. They go by presumption, far more than by insight. This has been well illustrated, in the present case.[6]

[THEOLOGICAL DEFECTS]

Our interest, however, in this translation is something deeper than its merely literary character. As a bungling attempt to turn a good German author into English, its merits fall so low that it might seem scarcely worth while to make it the subject of criticism; although even in this view there is such a wrong involved in it as ought not to go unnoticed and unrebuked. But along with the literary defect of this translation must be taken into consideration also a general theological defect, which goes, of course, so far as it prevails, to aggravate the other evil. Some illustration of this may be found in the two phases of the preface already presented; which indeed have been given in full, for the purpose partly of bringing into view what is now stated.

The truth is, the religious theory of Mr. Stearns differs very materially from that of the author whose work he has here undertaken to translate. Of this he is himself aware, to some extent. Sartorius, he tells us, is a Lutheran, with certain peculiarities, which he, of course, as a New England Baptist is not prepared to endorse or accept. It is plain enough, however, at the same time, that his sense of such difference between himself and his author remains always in the end very partial and narrow. The peculiarities in question are taken to be in part verbal only, technical forms of different schools, and, in other cases, mere outward and accidental excrescences (traditional *crotchets*) rather than living and necessary elements in the inward constitution of the system to which they belong. It is quietly taken for granted accordingly, that this system is, in all substantial respects, one and the same with that of

---

6. Even the scholarly editor of the *Methodist Quarterly Review* (Dr. M'Clintock) is so far misled, on the faith probably of the respectable publishing firm, Gould, Kendall & Lincoln, Boston, as to say: "The translation appears to be faithful, and is in general well expressed." [*Methodist Quarterly Review* (January 1849): 154.]

the translator himself. Mr. Stearns has been honestly persuaded, in his own mind, that his general scheme of evangelical religion is identical with the scheme of Sartorius, and the *evangelical* German school generally, to which he belongs—barring only a few old-fashioned European prejudices, now fast going into disuse; and he has set himself to translate this work, and carried through the undertaking as he best could, without the least imagination probably that he was bending the inward habit of the work throughout to a form of thinking altogether strange and foreign from its own. And yet it is so in fact. Without the least *consciousness* of any such wrong, and much less with any malicious intent to bring it to pass, he has, nevertheless, contrived to surround Sartorius with a theological nimbus, or *cloud*, which, so far as it can be seen through at all, makes it very difficult, if not indeed absolutely impossible, for any merely English reader to catch even a dim outline of his true German person.

The great object of the work, as is shown by the preface to the fifth edition already quoted, is to assert the glorious mystery of the incarnation, with its necessary consequences, as the one only sure and immovable foundation of religion, over against the rationalistic and pantheistic errors with which it has been opposed, particularly in modern Germany. This mystery is of course accepted by all evangelical bodies in this country also, from the most churchly away out to the most unchurchly, as the foundation of the gospel, in opposition to all sorts of Unitarianism. Mr. Stearns accordingly finds no difficulty in making common cause with Sartorius on this ground. A tract on the Person and Work of Christ falls in easily with his theory of religion, as based on the conception of a supernatural redemption wrought out by his death; and no hesitation is felt about taking it in the sense of this theory, leaving all awkward *inconcinnities*[7] to fetch themselves right as they best can. Here, however, is a grand mistake. The mystery of the incarnation, in its relation to Christianity, is something very different to Sartorius, from all it is made to be, or felt to be, in the Baptistic theology of Mr. Stearns. There is a stress laid upon the fact, a deep sense, a world of significance and force, made to go along with it, in the one case, which come not into view to any similar extent in the other. It is after all a different *christology*, that comes before us in the two cases.

---

7. [I.e., incongruities.]

[The Incarnation No Mere Outward Contrivance]

With Sartorius, Christianity is a new order of life that has its ground in the christological fact itself. The incarnation is viewed not simply as an outward contrivance, to open the way for the work of redemption, but as the real foundation in which the entire mystery not only starts, but continues also to hold from beginning to end. It is the union of divinity and humanity in Christ, which not simply qualifies him for the work he was appointed to perform, but of itself involves in his person that reconciliation between heaven and earth, God and man, which the idea of redemption requires, and for which there could be no room in any other form. He is in his very constitution our peace, in whom first the sundered worlds just mentioned are made one, for the very purpose of bringing them together afterwards in the way of a general salvation. It is in virtue only of what he is in this view, as the head of our human life, that it becomes possible for the race beyond him, through union with his mystical body and by conjunction with him as its centre and head, to partake also of the divine nature. Thus it is that "this ground binds eternity and time into one," reconciles heaven and earth, not circuitously and instrumentally only, but immediately and at once, in Jesus Christ. This is very distinctly stated by Sartorius in the preface to the first edition of his work, which it may be well to give here also in full:[8]

8. Travestied in Mr. Stearns' translation as follows: "The subject herein discussed was originally presented to a mixed assembly in the form of lectures. Lectures on another subject had already been given by Prof. Struve, by whose very kind assistance and instigation the poor were accommodated during Passion-week in the great lecture-room of our university. I now give them to the public, partly because others desire it, and partly because I myself wish by these unassuming discourses to establish a fixed and determined knowledge of the peculiar evangelical doctrine of salvation, in a larger circle than that in which it is now found, even among such laymen as err concerning true Christianity rather in knowledge than in good will. Of these there are at the present time more than is generally supposed. I have, therefore, discussed the doctrine of the incarnation of the Son of God, the more extensively, because I wished to show intelligibly, that the work of redemption, as connected with the divine benevolence, depends upon a personal union in Christ of divinity and humanity. Moreover, this great doctrine is peculiarly practical and requisite in an age when an unchristian rationalism is striving to destroy it by a foolish indifference, and is making bold efforts to deny the revealed truth of the Bible. This discussion, besides furnishing a correct knowledge to the laity, will, it is hoped, contribute to the purity, importance and completeness of the doctrine as believed by the church, maintaining as it does the only true and self-evident medium between two antagonistic errors. Finally, if the publishing these Lectures shall remove any unavoidable mistake in a single passage during their delivery, or shall give any proof in this time of jealousy with respect to

After the example set by Professor Struve,[9] at the beginning of the year before, the following lectures were delivered during Passion week of the present year, in aid of the poor supported by the Benevolent Society of this place, in the large lecture room of our university, before a mixed audience, which gave them encouraging attention to the close. They are now printed, partly to satisfy the wish of others, and partly from my own desire that their unpretending form may serve to promote, in more remote circles also, a definite and practical acquaintance with the peculiar saving truths of the gospel among those of the laity, who are often wanting in right knowledge far more than in good will towards true Christianity: and of whom there are more at the present time than is generally supposed. I have accordingly dwelt at large on the doctrine of the incarnation of the Son of God, as I wished to show, for common apprehension, how his work of redemption, together with all his benefits, rests for us throughout upon the union of divinity with humanity in his person; and of what practical moment and how necessary to salvation therefore this great doctrine is, which an unchristian rationalism, with stupid indifference and in plain contradiction to the Bible, is endeavoring to bring out of credit. The work may contribute besides to bring the purity, consistency and completeness of the church doctrine, which ever maintains the alone true and sure medium between opposite errors, into proper acknowledgment also with the laity. Finally, the publication of the lectures will remove any misunderstanding of single passages, such as is unavoidable with mere oral delivery, and furnish clear proof at the same time to such as share the reigning prejudice against evangelical Christianity, that no new-fashioned mysticism has been presented here, but only the old, well authenticated bible Christianity of our fathers, which alone can claim, as long as the Augsburg Confession stands, a legitimate authority in our Church. However many may have fallen from it, the truth itself is not for this reason fallen, but shall continue to stand when heaven and earth even pass away.

Dorpat, May, 1831.

---

evangelical Christianity, that there is in this doctrine no new-fangled mysticism, but only the firmly-settled Bible-Christianity of our fathers; which is to stand as long as the Augsburg Confession shall have a lawful existence in our church, then my object will be accomplished. Though the times may degenerate, and many may fall away, truth itself never changes, but will continue when the heavens and earth have passed away." [Sartorius, *Person and Work of Christ* (Stearns trans.), ix–x.]

9. [Friedrich Georg Wilhelm von Struve (1793–1864) was Professor of Astronomy and director of the famed observatory at the University of Dorpat.]

In carrying out his design, Sartorius dwells at length, in the first place, on the nature of the great mystery of godliness, "God manifest in the flesh," the way and manner of the union of divinity with humanity in Jesus Christ as the basis on which rests the whole superstructure of the Christian salvation. In the next place, the value and power of the fact for the purposes of redemption are shown. Finally, the process is explained by which all is made to pass over to the actual benefit of the human race.

The mystery of the incarnation is presented to us as "the assumption of the human nature by the Son of God into the unity of his person." It throws us back at once on the eternal sonship of Christ, and the doctrine of the divine trinity. This, however, is not absolutely peculiar to revelation. Some trace of it at least is to be found in philosophy and heathen mythology. The God of the mere deist is a lifeless abstraction. "There is hardly any ancient system of religion, in the East or West, which reveals not some glimmering of the doctrine of the trinity; the traces of it are to be met at the opposite poles, in India and Scandinavia." Peculiar to revelation rather, as its foundation truth, is the announcement that the eternal Word has become flesh, under a personal historical form, in Jesus of Nazareth, the Son of the Virgin Mary.

> The latest enemies of Christianity (Dr. Strauss and his followers[10]) have assailed it by asserting a general incarnation of God in humanity as a whole, in such way as to deny it under an individual separate form in Jesus Christ, nay, to repudiate the idea of this as narrow particularism. This is a gross error, which sees not in the first place, how estranged from God the human race has become by sin, so as to be wholly incapacitated within itself for a re-union with divinity without a mediator; and in the second place, does not consider that, in the perfect Mediator all the fullness of the Godhead dwells, just for this reason, that out of his fullness all may receive grace for grace, John i. 16, and not by any means that it may remain selfishly shut up in his person. So in the body of the sun, light is not concentrated,

---

10. [David Friedrich Strauss (1808–74), a German New Testament scholar, is best known for his *The Life of Jesus Critically Examined* (German: *Das Leben Jesu, kritisch bearbeitet* [Tübingen: Osiander, 1835–36]). Strauss agreed with G. W. F. Hegel on the central importance of the idea of divine-human unity, but, concluding that the gospel materials were permeated with myth, found the concrete expression of this idea of divine-human unity in the human race as a whole. See Strauss, *Life of Jesus*; Frei, "David Friedrich Strauss"; Barth, *Protestant Theology*, 541–68.]

to remain there fixed, but rather that all the world may be enlightened by it; whereas when many stars twinkle in place of the one orb of day, we have at best but the dusk of night. Into such night dusk would those lead us, who rob the planets of their sun, while in room of the one God-man, who is the Saviour of all and the Light of the world, they affect to proclaim *all* men, and especially, the heroes of the race, an incarnation of deity. They deny both, the personal oneness and glory of Christ, as well as his true universality; for the last consists just in this, that as the *one* divine head of his Church, he comprehends under himself *all* its members (Eph. iv. 15, 16) and communicates to them his truth, grace and righteousness, forming them thus into one body. Where on the contrary the royal head is made to fail, the members fall asunder in helpless broken disorder, and there is no room to speak farther of a kingdom of Christ or a Church of God, or of any redemption and salvation of the human race. Here, then, if anywhere, it behooves us to abide by the Scriptures, which in most direct contradiction to this modern wisdom or folly expressly assure us, Col. i. 19: "It pleased the Father that in him (in Jesus Christ) should all fulness dwell; and ii. 9: In him dwelleth all the fullness of the Godhead bodily."[11]

The incarnation under this personal, historical character, is shown to be an act of *free* condescension on the side of God. It implies no essential *change* in the divine nature. At the same time, the human nature assumed by the Son of God, must be allowed to be in all respects real and complete. It was no phantom or show only, but a true body joined with a reasonable soul. Lastly, the union of the two natures, while it leaves them distinct, must be regarded as organic, involving a strict personal unity in the form of a common undivided consciousness.

> Without such a personal union of divinity and humanity, no redemption could be accomplished; for the very nature of it stands just in this, that grace brings together what by nature and sin are sundered, namely, God and man; a mere man could of himself as little redeem the world as he could create it; and God of himself, though able to create, uphold and govern the world, cannot either make reconciliation for it, since this requires a union of the sundered parts, and such a free satisfaction for sin as he only

---

11. This fine passage, so intimately related to the deep significance of the christological mystery as held by Sartorius, his translator entirely omits; connecting what goes before and what follows, in a continuous paragraph, with a violence that fairly kills the original, to make out, what is, after all, only an *apparition* of sense.

can render, who stands at once over the law and under the law. The error before us is accordingly at war with the whole Bible. Throughout, in the entire life of our Lord, we are confronted with only one personality, one *I*, one undivided, though in its contents, most manifold self-consciousness.

Sartorius next considers how the two natures, in this personal union, condition and affect each other. There must be, through the medium of the common consciousness in which they meet, a mutual communication, to some extent, of states and properties. Only so can the divine and human be regarded as coming fully together, in such way as the idea of a true and proper redemption and reconciliation requires. Hence the most opposite predicates can be affirmed of the common person. Secondly, the properties of the divine nature attach, through the central consciousness, to the human. Thirdly, the properties of the human nature attach, in the same way, to the divine.[12] With such constitution, the mystery of the Saviour's person, in order that it may be still more fully understood, must be followed through the successive stages of his humiliation and exaltation, till all becomes complete finally in the glory of his second coming.

The way is opened thus, at length, for contemplating the *work* of Christ, the end in which the mystery of his person reveals its meaning and power. This occupies the sixth, seventh and eighth lectures. All is made to grow out of the fact of the incarnation.

> So closely is the whole joined with this as its root, that to describe the wonderful constitution of Christ's person is itself to set forth in some measure its object. If we cast a retrospective glance over the entire portrait of the God-man, as presented to us in both his natures, in their union and in his different states of humiliation and exaltation, so as to bring all as much as possible to one grand impression, we must at once feel that the end and purpose of it is to effect the inmost union and fellowship of divinity and humanity, and in this way to glorify the love of God as well as secure the happiness and salvation of men.

12. Mr. Stearns, with amusing awkwardness, makes Sartorius say here just the same thing in his second and third conclusions; in the first case, "by means of the communicated union of consciousness, the attributes of the divine nature belong to the human," while in the second, "by means of the reciprocal consciousness, the human nature receives also the attributes of the divine nature." [See Sartorius, *Person and Work of Christ* (Stearns trans.), 56, 60.]

Man is formed for religion, as the perfection of his being. This holds only in union with God, whose love is the ground of all good. Sin sunders us all naturally from his presence. Our salvation requires that it should be taken out of the way. This is accomplished only through the satisfaction of Christ, which, in virtue of his inward living relation to the race, and the theanthropic mystery of his person, carries with it a true reconciling and saving force for all mankind.

[The Sacraments Real Means of Grace]

The next inquiry regards the application of this grace to particular men, the transition of what is accomplished primarily in Christ over to his people. This leads to the consideration of the *means of grace*, namely, the word and sacraments, as they have been divinely lodged in the keeping of the Church for this purpose. Next follows a view of the several stages in the process of salvation; after which the whole discussion concludes with a brief survey, in the last lecture, of the prophetical, priestly and kingly offices, as executed by Christ in the character of Mediator.

Throughout, thus, the person of the Saviour is represented as lying, inwardly and truly, at the foundation of the whole Christian salvation. "Christ is himself the living substance of Christianity"; which accordingly, from first to last, serves but to unfold or bring out the deep contents of his life. His work holds always and only in the mystery of his person, and is of force for others in no other way than as they are brought to have part in this as its constant support and ground. "In him dwells all fullness; all the predictions of the prophets, all the ideals of sacred poetry, all the deepest thoughts of true philosophy, are fulfilled and actualized in him, in whom God became manifest in the flesh (I Tim. iii. 16) that we might behold his glory, as that of the only begotten Son of the Father, and receive from his fullness grace for grace, John i. 14–18." *In him*, not *by* him simply, all things which are in heaven and which are on earth, are reconciled, united and comprehended under one head (Eph. i. 10, Col. i. 20).

All this, rightly apprehended, is something materially different, we say, from the christology of Mr. Stearns. Without being aware of the fact, he has in his mind throughout quite another conception of the theanthropic mystery, and quite another scheme accordingly of the Christian salvation. Sartorius is a Lutheran, honestly and earnestly true to the substance of Luther's faith, though now in the bosom of the United German Church. Mr. Stearns is a Baptist, immersed all over in the unmystical element of his own creed. These two systems are by no means the same; and the difference is not simply accidental. It falls back, in the end, to the idea of Christ's person, and in this way necessarily conditions the theory and life of religion throughout. The Baptistic Christ is not in full the Lutheran Christ. He may be acknowledged in the same terms to a certain extent; but his constitution is not the same, and he stands in a different relation to the work of redemption. The Baptistic christology is not itself the new world of grace, in which the whole gospel stands revealed as a living fact, but forms rather the outward machinery which heaven has contrived for saving men. The *work* which was required to take away sin, needed indeed a conjunction of divinity with humanity in Christ, to qualify him for its execution; but once executed, it carries with it an independent and separate value in the divine mind, and may be set to the account of men as a mere abstraction in this way, apart from Christ's life altogether. The person of the Saviour is not viewed as the principle and root strictly of the whole Christian salvation, but only as its outward occasion or instrument, brought in gloriously to make way for the action of grace under another form; just as the electric telegraph is employed as a medium for bringing a word to pass a thousand miles off, which could not be made to take effect in any other way, although it is in no sense itself the very form and substance of the word so spoken. So regarded, the hypostatical union itself assumes a more or less shadowy and unreal character, leaning at one time towards Gnosticism, or at another saving itself again only in the form of Nestorian dualism.[13] The sense of an inward, *organic* union is, in a great measure, wanting. The true *universalness* of Christ's humanity comes not into view. The *reconciliation* of heaven and earth, which lies in the

13. [Gnosticism and Nestorianism were early-church heresies. The Christology of Gnosticism (from the Greek word *gnosis*, meaning "knowledge") held that Jesus was a messenger from the eternal realm bringing saving knowledge. Many Gnostics held to a docetic (from the Greek word meaning "to seem") Christology, maintaining that Jesus only "seemed" to be human. Nestorianism was the fifth-century movement associated with Nestorius, bishop of Constantinople from AD 428–31. Seeking to preserve the integrity of Christ's humanity, Nestorius objected to the use of the term *Theotokos* ("God-bearer") for the Virgin Mary on the grounds that God has no mother, and he spoke of the union of deity and humanity in Christ as a "conjunction" rather than a "union." All this was seen as threatening the unity of the person of the God-Man, and Nestorius was condemned at the Council of Ephesus in 431.]

mystery of the incarnation itself, and involves potentially and necessarily all the atonement and redemption that follow, is not perceived. The deep, rich, overwhelming sense of the living *fact*, is not understood or felt. In place of it, we have only an orthodox abstraction. Then the redemption which follows is, of course, apprehended under a corresponding character. Christ executes all his offices in a comparatively outward way, parallel thus in kind with the Old Testament prophets, priests and kings, only rising above them in degree, "*primus inter pares*" ["first among equals"]. He reveals truth, buys righteousness, and exerts power, all in an external instrumental manner; instead of being in fact, as he always claims to be, in the very constitution of his own person, *the* way, *the* truth, *the* resurrection and *the* life, all in the most real and absolute sense, in whom, as well as by whom only, it is possible for any of the children of men to be saved. An abstract conception of the work of redemption again brings with it necessarily also a like abstract idea of the way in which men are made partakers of its grace. The process is lifted into the sphere of pure thought. All turns on supernatural acts of God on one side, and the exercises of individual experience on the other, that come after all to no steady union in the way of spiritual life. The mystical, sacramental interest in religion is practically undervalued, or we may say, rather to a great extent subverted altogether, in order to make room more effectually for what are conceived to be the far higher claims of piety under a different form.

It is easy enough to feel this want of congruity between Sartorius and his translator throughout; but it comes to its most glaring exposure where the subject of the sacraments is brought forward. In the nature of the case, this could not be left out of sight in the original work. No christology, no scheme of Christianity, can be *Lutheran* which leads not to the idea of sacramental grace, the *mystery* of Christ's presence in the sacraments, as an essential, inseparable element of the gospel. Sartorius accordingly devotes a whole lecture mainly to this subject—a rich, instructive and edifying discourse, for any one whose mind is prepared at all to sympathize with the ancient faith of the Church. But what now becomes of this most unbaptistic chapter of the work, in the hands of Mr. Stearns? The whole of it is quietly suppressed, with only the following explanation, in the way of a short note, at the beginning of the next lecture: "The previous chapter discusses the Lutheran view of baptism and the Lord's Supper, but is omitted in the translation as inapplicable to the ideas upon that subject held by Christians generally on this side of the water."[14]

Let us now look for a moment to the lecture in question, that we may understand how much is involved in the summary renunciation, thus made in behalf, not only of the Baptist body, but of the American churches in general.

The means of grace, according to Sartorius, have their force only in the Church, constituted by the Holy Ghost, to hold them in charge and administer them as organs for men's salvation. They are, first, the *word*, in the two-fold form of law and gospel; then the two holy sacraments, *baptism* and the *Lord's supper*. These are not properly *our* works, but acts of grace performed towards us by Christ, through the Church, which we are required to accept believingly in this character. Baptism is the seal of our ingrafting into Christ. We are born under the curse of original sin; but grace interposes, through Christ, to bring us out of that state, extending to us, even in infancy, the visible pledge of such deliverence in this holy mystery.

> Hence it is called the laver of *regeneration*, Tit. iii. 5; because by it the child, though at first still unconscious, passes out of the kingdom of the world and its spirit into the kingdom of God and his Spirit, and from a child of the flesh becomes a child of grace, on whom is impressed anew the seal of his original destination to the image of God and the inheritance of eternal life, while in the Church of Christ, of which he is a member, all means and helps are furnished for reaching this end.

The objective value of it is not affected, in the case of infants, by the consideration that they cannot at once appropriate it by faith. It remains always at hand, as a divine fact, notwithstanding, for their use and appropriation through the whole of their lives. Does a man become truly and properly the child of his natural parents, only when he wakes first to the clear sense of what is comprised in such relation? Baptism, in this case, comes to its completion of right in *confirmation*. Again, as the Christian life begins in this first sacrament, so it is fed and supported by the second, the holy supper. Here Christ imparts to us his flesh and blood, that is, the power of his own divine-human life; for he is, in truth, the living bread, of which all must partake or perish. There is, indeed, no change of the bread and wine into the substance

14. [Sartorius, *Person and Work of Christ* (Stearns trans.), 128.]

of Christ, as the Roman Church teaches; but still there is a real union between them, above sense, according to his own word. "We will not envy those," says Sartorius,

> who see in this meal only an outward figurative memorial of an absent Christ, which makes nothing more of him to be present, than what they may think along with it out of their own minds. Such, verily, would do better to contemplate a crucifix, or an *ecce homo*, or some other image of Jesus, than to eat a piece of bread and drink a sip of wine, destroying thus the recollection sign in the very act of its reception.

All this, of course, is at full variance with the system of Mr. Stearns. He allows no such efficacy to baptism, and dreams of no such mystery in the Lord's Supper.[15] It is easy thus to see and understand why he should be disposed to set aside the whole chapter as out of date. What, however, must we think of the *honesty* of such conduct? Be the merits of the suppressed lecture what they may, it is certain that, for Sartorius himself, it has been of indispensable account in the discussion of his general subject. It goes necessarily, with him, to make out the completeness and integrity of the book; he would not be willing at all, as a good Lutheran, to stand charged before the world with a christological theory from which, by any possibility, the idea of sacramental grace could be divorced in such wholesale style. The probability is that he would prefer decidedly the suppression of the whole work to any mutilation so terrible as this must appear to be in his eyes. What right then, we may well ask, has any translator, standing in a wholly different system of religious thought, to mutilate the book in this way and still publish it *in Sartorius' name*? It may be proper, in certain cases, to abridge another man's work for more general popular use; though, even then, to be at all honest, the

---

15. [Baptist theology has historically viewed the sacraments as signs of divine grace already received rather than instrumental means of grace, and thus it prefers to speak of "ordinances" commanded by Christ rather than "sacraments." According to the Baptist Second London and Philadelphia Confessions, "Baptism and the Lord's Supper are ordinances of positive and sovereign institution, appointed by the Lord Jesus, the only Lawgiver, to be continued in his Church to the end of the world" (Schaff, ed., *Creeds of Christendom*, III: 741). Compare Westminster Confession of Faith 27.1-2: "Sacraments are holy signs and seals of the covenant of grace, immediately instituted by God, to represent Christ and his benefits, and to confirm our interest in him; . . . There is in every sacrament a spiritual relation, or sacramental union, between the sign and the thing signified; whence it comes to pass, that the names and effects of the one are attributed to the other."]

abridgement must be published *as such*, and is bound besides to be true to the sum and substance of the full work. It is, however, quite another thing to change or expunge a single passage or even a single word, by which the true sense and spirit of the original is expressed at any point, in such a way as to bring in another sense quite foreign from the author's mind. This is spiritual forgery, which deserves to be abhorred of all good men. No small noise was made a few years since, about certain liberties of this sort, taken with D'Aubigne's *History of the Reformation*, by the American Tract Society.[16] But that wrong, generally condemned, we believe, was small indeed as compared with the highhanded violence here perpetrated on Sartorius; and it must be regarded as a sign of the general obtuseness of the American Church to the claims of the high interest here concerned, that so glaring a wrong should be able to proclaim itself with so little danger of shocking the common sense of Christian propriety. Let the case be put into a new shape. Suppose a Baptist tract, gutted of its baptistic peculiarities, or some good Puritan work *catholicized* for the use of the Roman Church by the careful obliteration of a whole section on justification by faith, and we should not soon hear the last of the stealthy-footed, cowl-mantled stratagem. Can it be less *jesuitic*[17] to play the same game under a Protestant evangelical guise? We think not.

But this is not all. The case reveals a radically wrong conception of the entire theological system represented by Sartorius, and of its

---

16. [For an account of this controversy by the author, see "Preface to the Oliver & Boyds Edition Revised by the Author," in D'Aubigné, *History of the Reformation*, I: 3–8. D'Aubigné writes on pp. 3–4: "At the end of the year 1844, I received several letters from the United States, informing me that, besides 75,000 copies of my History put in circulation by different American booksellers, The American Tract Society had printed and edition of 24,000 copies, which they sold through the instrumentality of more than a hundred hawkers (*colporteurs*), principally in the New Settlements, which no bookseller can reach, but whither the pope ceases not from sending active emissaries; they added, that the committee of this society, composed of different denominations, and among others of Episcopalians and Baptists, were rendered uneasy by certain passages in my history, and had thought proper, with the best intentions, either to modify or retrench them; they informed me, lastly, that two Presbyterian synods, astonished at these changes, had publicly accused the Society of mutilating the work, and that there had arisen (wrote one of the most respectable men in the United States, himself a Presbyterian, and not a member of the Society) so violent a discussion, that "the Committee will inevitably be ruined unless you interfere to rescue it."]

17. [Members of the Roman Catholic Society of Jesus (Jesuits) were known for their casuistry.]

relation to the theory of religion in whose service he is here enlisted. It is quite common, we know, for all evangelical sects as the Church now stands, not excepting Baptists of every hue and name, to claim inward affinity with *Luther* as the father of the Reformation, and to glory in his doctrine as only carried out to its purest form in their own faith and practice. His prejudices about the sacraments, and some other things, they, of course, have consigned to the tomb of the Capulets[18] (with due indulgence to the dormitancies of so great a Homer), but only to stick the faster to the true life and marrow of his divinity, as found in the doctrine of justification by faith. But only see the contradiction which all this carries upon its very face. "Saul among the prophets!" was not, surely, a greater incongruity than the idea of Luther quietly seated among these various sects ("*die himmlische Propheten*")[19] and consenting to be taught "the way of God more perfectly" at their feet. What a compliment, moreover, to the cause of the Reformation to conceive of its great leaders generally, and most of all the very Moses of its glorious exodus, as having no power to discriminate between the essential and the accidental in so clear a case as this of the sacraments is now taken to be; but actually filling all Europe with their noise about it, as though it belonged in some way to the very core of Christianity, when any child may now see that they were driving at a shadow from first to last. The whole conception is absurd. The sacramental doctrine of Luther, so far as the substance of it is concerned, was no outward fungus upon his system. It lies imbedded in its inmost life. To part with it is to give up the cause of the Reformation itself, as it stood in his mind, and to turn his whole theology into a new and different shape. To think of the Baptistic theory of religion as one and the same with the evangelical Lutheran, *only* divested of his sacramental doctrine—as though this were an old cocked hat to be kept on or laid off at pleasure—can only show the shallow character of the whole theology for which any such thought is possible. So in the case before us, to drop the chapter on the sacraments and yet pretend to be satisfied with the rest of the book as sound

18. [An allusion to the death scene in Shakespeare's "Romeo and Juliet," Act IV, Scene 3.]

19. [Nevin's reference to *die himmlische Propheten* ("the heavenly prophets") alludes to Martin Luther's 1525 work *Wider die himmlischen Propheten, von den Bildern und Sakrament*, written against Andreas Karlstadt and other *Schwärmer* (religious enthusiasts claiming immediate divine inspiration as the basis for their views). See Luther, *Against the Heavenly Prophets*.]

and good, must be taken as a gross inconsistency. Any christology that can admit the idea of a Church with no divine powers, no grace in its sacraments, no room in its bosom for infants, no mystical presence of Christ's life in the Lord's supper—be its claims to respect in any other view what they may—must be counted utterly foreign from the entire mind of Sartorius, and cannot possibly be the same that is presented to us in this little book. However it may be with others, *his* view of Christ's person (like that of Luther) necessarily involves such a conception of the Christian salvation as brings along with it in the end all that the sacramental interest includes. His scheme of religion thus, in the nature of the case, is materially different throughout from that into whose service he is here forcibly *translated* by Mr. Stearns.

Still farther. The Lutheranism of Dr. Sartorius, as presented in this work, is by no means of the rigid extreme sort; so that in the case before us it might seem to be set aside in favor simply of the old Reformed or Calvinistic doctrine of the sacraments, as this stood in the sixteenth century. Even in that case, the wrong would, of course, still merit sharp rebuke. But the opposition here is not between the two forms of the original Protestant doctrine. There are a few sentences, perhaps, in Sartorius to which a true follower of Calvin might demur; but the body of his doctrine, beyond all doubt, is the same that is most distinctly taught in the writings of Calvin, and embodied in all the classic confessions of the Reformed Church. There was a difference between the two creeds, of course; but such as it was, it lies away beyond the Baptistic horizon with which we are here concerned. Both sides of the old Protestantism intended to hold fast to the substance of the ancient sacramental doctrine, as it had stood in the catholic Church from the beginning. Both held the sacraments to be *mysteries*, regarded them as *organs* of grace, looked through them by faith to the *presence* of Christ's life, as objectively and truly comprehended in their solemn transaction. All this grew too out of a corresponding christology, by which room was made for the idea of a concrete Church, with divine resources and capabilities, commensurate, in all respects, with the entire extent of our human fall, and fitted in this way to cover the case of infants no less than that of adults. All this, however, and nothing more than this, is just the conception which Mr. Stearns, true to his Baptist feeling, undertakes to expunge from the doctrine of Christ's Person and Work, "as inapplicable to the ideas upon that subject held by Christians generally, on this side of the water." This deserves to be well considered and borne in mind.

But now finally, what are we to think of the declaration here made of Christians generally on this side of the Atlantic? The reference is, of course, not simply to the Baptist body, but to the so-called evangelical denominations in general. It is taken for granted that they have collectively fallen away from the old doctrine of the sacraments, as here represented; that their system of religion excludes it; that it has come to be, in short, on all sides, obsolete and out of date.[20] Is this representation correct? We fear that there is but too much reason for it, in the actual state of the Church. It is sometimes resented indeed, as harsh and unkind, to speak of any falling away from the original Protestant ground in the posture of our modern churches. But the evidence of the fact, so far as the general Puritan and Methodistic tendency is concerned, is too clear in the case of the sacraments to bear any controversy; and it can only be by making no account of the interest in consideration that the reality and momentous significance of the fact are so generally thrust out of sight. This, however, is itself one of the strongest evidences of the very change, which it is affected in this way to overlook or despise. It is the want of the old faith in the sacraments, precisely, which makes the question of the sacraments, and along with this the whole subject of the Church, to be for so many of so little interest and meaning. With all this agrees, but too well, the low style in which these divine mysteries are spoken of in every direction, and the determined resistance which is made to the idea of everything like sacramental grace. It would seem, indeed, as if Mr. Stearns had good reason to say of the old doctrine, both Lutheran and Calvinistic (for *his* repudiation of Sartorius excludes it in both forms), that it no longer suits the reigning faith of this country. The statement has called forth, so far as we have noticed, no contradiction or exception on the part of those who have noticed his book. His monstrous wrong done to Sartorius and to the theme of his book, on this plea, is suffered to pass without rebuke. Even the Lutheran Church, whose whole significance is here at stake and whose dignity and glory it should be to stand forward, especially at such a time, as the bulwark of the sacramental interest, has lost, unfortunately, to a great extent the power of entering any effectual protest in so grave a case. The

---

20. [See Nevin's extended discussion of what he termed "the modern Puritan theory" of the sacraments in his *Mystical Presence*, 92–137.]

Lutheran Observer,[21] which represents at present the reigning mind and life of that church, actually took notice of this mutilation of Sartorius, not long since, with a chuckle of delight, as a broad sign of the entire *antiquation* which has happily overtaken, here in evangelical America, the whole sacramental dream of the sixteenth century. The sympathies of this *organ* of Lutheranism fit it for making love ecclesiastically to the Cumberland Presbyterians, and other such sects, much more than for coming up to the help of its own proper faith in the hour of distress and danger. Could there well be, however, a more grinning irony on our existing sect system than is presented to us in such a spectacle—the creed of Luther, the faith of the Augsburg Confession, thus mortally wounded, in favor of the Baptists, in the house of its own professed friends!

It is all right, in this case, that the doctrine of infant baptism is made to share a common fate with the mystical presence in the Lord's supper, and the idea of sacramental grace generally. The baptism of infants can have no meaning for those who allow no objective value or force in the sacrament itself. Such may still hold fast to the rite, on the ground of old church tradition; but they do so with inward contradiction to their own faith; they are baptistic in principle, and to be at all consistent, should fall in fully also with the baptistic practice. This lies also necessarily in the christological theory, and their corresponding view they take of the Church. Only where the Christian salvation is seen and felt to be a fact, primarily made real, under a concrete form for the benefit of the whole world, in the person of Christ, can there be any proper consciousness of its enduring objective character in the Church, and its necessary relation in this form to the *whole* tract of our human existence, from the cradle to the grave. The idea of a Christ, whose life is not formed to take up into itself the entire fact of humanity (of which infancy is just as necessary a constituent as full age), is such a contradiction as no sound christological feeling, no true sense of the Church, can ever comfortably endure. But let all resolve itself into a mere outward and mechanical salvation, and the case is quite changed. The whole mystical, sacramental side of Christianity is given up as no better than superstition; and along with the loss of all faith in the grace

---

21. [The *Lutheran Observer* was founded in 1831 and was edited from 1833–1861 by Baltimore pastor Benjamin Kurtz, an advocate of revivalism and the Americanization of the Lutheran churches.]

of holy baptism, as well as in that of the holy supper, the right of infants to be comprehended in Christ, by any such laver of regeneration, is thrown into an unsubstantial unmeaning shadow.

J. W. N.

Article 2
"The New Creation in Christ"

(by John W. Nevin)

EDITOR'S INTRODUCTION

The occasion for this 1850 article by John Nevin was a brief notice in the *New York Observer* newspaper regarding an article by Nevin's Mercersburg colleague Philip Schaff that had appeared in the theological journal *Bibliotheca Sacra*. The *Observer's* writer had raised two objections to Schaff's piece: first, that Schaff's notion that "the Lord is perpetually born anew in the hearts of believers" was implausible and that it is not the teaching of the Bible; and second, that, contrary to Schaff, the Incarnation does not introduce any "new principle of light and life" into human history. The issues at stake here were the nature and implications of the Christian's union with Christ, the philosophical context within which such ideas are plausible or implausible, and the nature of the Bible's teaching on the matter. Nevin responds at length to both of these lines of objection and to the larger questions involved.

The *Observer's* writer had complained that Schaff's ideas "savor of the transcendental." Of course, the Mercersburg theologians were not New England transcendentalists in the tradition of Emerson and Thoreau, but they shared with the transcendentalists an idealist philosophical bent that favored organic unity over disjunction. Nevin correctly intuited that behind this charge of transcendentalism lay the popular metaphysic of Scottish Common Sense Realism with its focus on particularity and distinction, and he also knew that such thinking went hand in hand with a populist and individualistic biblicism.

But, as Nevin notes, others have read the Bible differently, and here he appeals first to the Gospel of John and especially to the discourse in John 6, which affirms "the real participation of believers in the life of Christ," before noting the pervasive presence of union-with-Christ language in the writings of St. Paul. In this context of the Pauline materials Nevin also defines the union that exists between Christ and the Christian—it is a "spiritual" union in that it is "wrought by the Holy Ghost," who brings the very life of Christ to the Christian such that "his life repeats itself in believers; their salvation is carried forward by a mystical reproduction in them of the grand facts of his history." Nevin also argues that such thinking "runs through the universal theology of the old Christian fathers," is characteristic of the medieval theologians, and "animates the faith" of Luther and Calvin. In short, Nevin implies that the sentiment expressed by the *Observer's* writer appears to be a recent novelty when measured against the scope of Christian history.

Turning to the second major objection—whether the Incarnation introduces a genuinely new principle into human history—Nevin immediately connects this criticism with a nominalistic understanding of humanity. If the human race simply consists of a "sand heap" of individuals with no larger principle of organic unity then Christ in the Incarnation will be seen as simply another individual with no relation to the whole. But, Nevin argues, this view implies that Christ is but a "passing theophany or avatar" with no real and lasting connection to the world. In response, Nevin contends that the human race is in fact an organic unity, and that Christ as the God-man and the Pauline "second Adam" has entered human history in a way congruent with that history but also going beyond it by introducing a new principle of life. Here, of course, we sense the powerful influence of Schleiermacher and the German mediating theologians.

But despite the totalizing language of the incarnate Christ as the salvation and goal of humanity, which certainly could tend in the direction of notions of universal salvation, Nevin was not a universalist affirming the ultimate salvation of all. Here his organic idealism was held in check by scripture, tradition, and a strong Christocentric ecclesiology with its emphasis on the real application of salvation through the means of grace. "The new creation," he says, "holds in the bosom of the Church and not beyond it; but it holds there, at the same time, as the inmost substantial sense of humanity itself, the form in which it is required to become universally complete." Thus the completion of humanity in Christ of which Nevin speaks is implicit rather than explicit. Thus we may say that Nevin's philosophical idealism was of a chastened sort that was disciplined by the biblical witness and the tradition of the church.

John W. Nevin, "The New Creation in Christ"[1]

"There are many valuable thoughts in the article of Prof. Schaff, though some of his declarations seem to us to savor of the transcendental. The affirmation he makes that 'The Lord is perpetually born anew in the hearts of believers,' sounds strangely to our ears. That his image is created there is indeed true, but that the Lord is born there, is not the teaching of the Bible. Again: 'The *commencement*,' he says, 'of Church History, is strictly the incarnation of the son of God, or the entrance of the new principle of light and life into humanity.' The incarnation of the Son of God is plain enough, but what is this 'new principle of light and life'? And what 'new principle' has there been in humanity since the incarnation, that was not in it before the event?"

—*N.Y Observer*, Sept. 8, 1848.

This paragraph occurs in a short notice of the *Bibliotheca Sacra* for August, the first article of which is a masterly Introduction to Church History from Prof. Schaff.[2] It is significantly characteristic of the system of thinking it represents, and furnishes fit occasion, in such view, for a few remarks.

Here is some approach to a determination of what we are to understand by that most ambiguous term "*transcendentalism*"[3] in the popular

---

1. [Originally printed in the *Mercersburg Review* 2:1 (January 1850): 1–12.]

2. [The reference is to Philip Schaff, "General Introduction To Church History," *Bibliotheca Sacra* 6:23 (August 1849), 409–441. Thus the date ascribed above to the quote from the *New York Observer* is incorrect. An expansion was later published in his *History of the Apostolic Church; with a General Introduction to Church History*, trans. Edward D. Yeomans (New York: Charles Scribner, 1853), 1–134.]

3. [The charge of "transcendentalism" was frequently leveled against the Mercersburg theology. With the New England Transcendentalists Nevin and Schaff shared a similar philosophical orientation toward intuitive idealism as well as a

vocabulary. It savors of the transcendental, we are told, to say that "the Lord is perpetually born anew in the hearts of believers," or that the mystery of the incarnation involves "the entrance of a new principle of light and life into humanity." Very well. Let us now look a little into the matter.

The first expression, says the critic, sounds strangely in our ears. The *image* of Christ is created in the hearts of believers, but not the Lord himself, according to the Bible. The image of Christ, then, as formed in believers, is something quite distinct, in the mind of the critic, from the living substance of Christ himself. It bears merely an outward resemblance to him, under a wholly independent form of being; it is the picture morally of his holy mind and character, but carries in it no participation whatever in his very nature. It is related to him, not as the branch to the vine, but only as a mechanical transcript or copy to the original object it is employed to represent. Christ stands in the world solitary and alone. He has made it possible, however, for men to obtain forgiveness with God, and then to be formed by the Holy Ghost and their own endeavors into a new religious life, the type of which is set before them in his person as an outward model. This process involves a new creation; for it is wrought in part, at least, by the creative *fiat* of God's Spirit; but in the end, it is a new creation that belongs in an immediate and exclusive way to each single believer for himself. It is no reproduction in him of the new creation already at hand in Christ; the Spirit calls into being within him, not the force of what is in Christ himself fontally for the salvation of the world, but the image or picture of this, simply under another form. This, we say, seems to be the meaning which underlies the criticism here in view. The opposite idea, which makes the new life in believers to hold in organic continuity with Christ's life, is set down as transcendentalism. To make it an abstraction, a thing of sheer thought, an abruptly miraculous *image,* is counted to be common sense; and the Bible, we are gravely assured, teaches no other view.[4]

---

negative reaction to the disjunctive empiricism of the Scottish Common Sense tradition. They differed, however, from the New England transcendentalists in their christocentric sacramentalism as well as their organic and developmental approach to history. See Clemmer, "Historical Transcendentalism," 579–92.]

4. [Nevin consistently challenges views of salvation that abstract it from the person of Christ, from the ongoing life of faith and obedience, and from the church. Here the influence of idealism, over against the Scottish Common Sense empiricism regnant in

[SCRIPTURE AND THE PROBLEM OF NAÏVE BIBLICISM]

Thus it is that the school here represented is ever ready to run away with the Bible in a wholesale way, as though it must of necessity be all on their side, just because with their *preconceived system of thought* it carries to themselves such sense and no other. Multitudes, in all ages, have read the sense of the Bible differently, but that weighs nothing with this school; no judgment is allowed to be of any force, in the case, against its own. "This is not the teaching of the Bible," cries the infallible critic; as though *his* dictum in such style must end the matter; and there it is made to stop. We should have been glad to see something more in this line of argument, a true appeal to the sacred oracles themselves. The subject is certainly deserving of such attention. It goes to the very foundation of Christianity. Is it a doctrine only or a fact? Is it a new creation in Christ, or is it a divinely wrought image of that only *out of Christ?* The question is worthy of something more than a magisterial wave of the hand, after the summary fashion of the criticism here in view.

The Bible as *we* read it, and as it has been read by millions of God's saints from the beginning, and we will add too, according to the most profoundly scientific exegesis of the present time, *does* teach broadly and clearly the very mystery which this critic proclaims to be transcendentalism, sounding strangely to his ears. The charge of disregarding it falls of right on himself and his widely influential school, and not on Professor Schaff. Has he never read the Gospel of St. John, in which, according to the judgment of the universal Church, the inmost and deepest sense of Christianity is revealed, and by which, accordingly, all the other Gospels are to be explained and made complete? Could it well be more explicitly affirmed, than it is here affirmed in fact, in the very beginning of this Gospel, that it is the *Life* of the Word which is the source of light and salvation to men, and that the Word became flesh to make room for its actual entrance into our fallen nature, as the fountain of a new creation? "Of his *fullness* have all we received" (John i. 16). We become sons of God by union with him in a supernatural way. Let Christ be apprehended as the central bearer of the new creation, whose universal *fullness* is made to reach over in the form of grace and truth (not law but life) into the souls of his people, and the sublime

---

America at that time, is evident. Thus there is, in Nevin and the Mercersburg theology more generally, a concern for integration and unity rather than disjunction, for the *a priori* and ideal over against the *a posteriori* and empirical.]

representation of St. John is simple and clear. Resolve the Christian salvation into an outward image only of Christ, wrought either with or without God's help, and the representation is blind as chaos. The beginning of the Gospel, too, is only in harmony with the idea that fills it throughout. It is not only a text or two, here and there, that admits the sense now urged, by violent and doubtful construction. Such men as Olshausen and Tholuck,[5] find this sense in every chapter; and it is only by the most forced and unnatural exegesis, that commentators of the Rationalistic school have been able at all to keep it out of sight. Everywhere Christ speaks of himself, or is regarded by the sacred writer, as the living fountain of the salvation he reveals. He is the resurrection and the life. To have the Son is to have life. The sixth chapter is as strong as words can make it in asserting the real participation of believers in the life of Christ. Except we eat his flesh, and drink his blood, we have no life; this involves eternal life, and a resurrection at the last day; it is to dwell in Christ, and have him dwell in us; to live by him, as *he* lives by or from the Father (John vi. 53–58). Is this simply to have his *image* formed in us, as something in no organic connection with his person? And what shall we say of his own beautiful emblem of the vine and its branches, employed John xv. 1–8, to represent this mystical union? Is the life of the vine not also the life of its branch? Is the last only *like* the first, a picture of it under a wholly separate form? Could any representation more forcibly show that "the Lord is perpetually born anew in the hearts of believers," that his life is reproduced in their life, that their formation into his image involves an inward adunation[6] also into the very substance of his mediatorial person? We might refer also to the startling language employed on this subject in his last prayer, John xvii. 21–23; but we forbear.

5. [Hermann Olshausen (1796-1839), a German New Testament scholar who taught successively at Berlin, Königsburg, and Erlangen. He wrote commentaries on much of the New Testament. Friedrich August Gottreu Tholuck (1799-1877) spent much of his lengthy career as Professor of Theology at the University of Halle, where he was instrumental in moving the school from rationalism to pietism. In addition to his biblical commentaries, Tholuck encouraged the mid-nineteenth century revival of interest in Calvin by publishing his New Testament commentaries and the *Institutes*. Tholuck's influence on American theology was substantial through his friendships with Schaff and theologians such as Edward Robinson, Charles Hodge, and Edwards Amasa Park. See the biographical sketches of both men in Schaff, *Germany*, 278-99.]

6. [I.e., the act or state of being united.]

Nor is this view of the new life confined to St. John. It comes before us also in the more dialectical thinking of St. Paul. No idea is more familiar with him than that by which Christ and his people are regarded as being joined together in the power of a common life; which, as such, of course, starts from him as its source, and is carried over to them by real organic derivation. He is the head, and they are the members, of the same mystical body. This image is ever at hand in his mind to express their union. Can it possibly mean less than an actual participation of one side in the living substance of the other? In this character of Christ's body, the Church is declared to be "the fullness of him that filleth all in all" (Eph. i. 23); which plainly signifies something far more than an outward merely moral relationship, however strict and close.[7] Everywhere again, and under all varieties of expression, believers are spoken of as being *in Christ*. One or two instances of such language might bear, possibly, to be resolved into a strong figure of speech; although we should feel it a strange hyperbole, indeed, to speak even twice or once of the patriots of the American Revolution as being *in General Washington*. But in the case before us, the instances are not one or two only; we meet them on every page; the very frequency and familiarity of their occurrence serves to blind us to the true and proper force of the phraseology. The foundation of the phraseology with St. Paul, and the sacred writers generally, is beyond all doubt the sense of such a union between Christ and his people, as actually inserts them spiritually into the substance of his life. They are a new creation (καινὴ κτίσις, 2 Cor. v. 17) in Christ Jesus; not a new creation out of him and beyond him, by the fiat of omnipotence, bearing some resemblance to him in a wholly different sphere; but a new creation, whose original seat and fountain is Christ's own person, and which conveys over to them, accordingly, with true reproductive force, the vitality which belongs to it in this form. This does not imply that the believer can be all that Christ is; much less that he can be thus complete in any separate view. Christ is the central person, in whom is the fullness of life for the whole world; his people are made complete only by being comprehended relatively in this fullness; as all the other points of a circle are made what they are by real dependence on the centre of it, and not by bringing the centre, as such, over into

---

7. [Here Nevin opposes the later New England Calvinism, which reduced the solidarity of the Christian with Christ to a "moral union" of shared sentiment and moral concern. On this development, see Evans, *Imputation and Impartation*, 113–37.]

themselves. The union here is indeed spiritual; it is wrought by the Holy Ghost; but the realness and inwardness of it are, on this account, only the more sure. It is the spiritual being of the believer, his personality, his intelligence and will (which in the end, however, must determine the quality of the entire man) that are poised on Christ as a perpetual living centre. "Christ liveth in me," says Paul, "and the life which I now live in the flesh, I live by the faith of the Son of God, who loved me and gave himself for me" (Gal. ii. 20). "In him dwelleth all the fullness of the Godhead bodily, and ye are *complete in him*" (Col. ii. 9, 10); your life, in other words, is made perfect, finds its true end and sense, in union with him as the universal centre of the vast spiritual organism of Christianity. It is, in truth, Christ's *image* that is formed in the souls of his people; but not a dead image, not an outward image, not such an image as is cut off in full from the object it represents, and comes before us as a quite different thing. It is "Christ in you, the hope of glory" (Col. i. 27); "Christ, who is our life" (Col. iii. 4); Christ that dwells in our hearts by faith (Eph. iii. 17); Christ formed with birth travail into our persons (ἄχρις οὗ μορφωζῇ, Χριστὸς ἐν ὑμῖν, Gal. iv. 19[8]); the very thought which the critic of the New York Observer pronounces transcendentalism sounding strangely to his ears. The image of Christ thus born into his people is like that of the vine in its branches, the power of his own life continuing itself over organically into their persons. He is the beginning of the new creation, the first-born from the dead; not as the outward cause of it simply, or its outward model; but as its principle and fontal spring; the whole flows forth really from his person (Col. i. 15–18). Thus it is that his life repeats itself in believers; their salvation is carried forward by a mystical reproduction in them of the grand facts of his history; he is born in them, suffers in them, dies in them, rises in them from the dead, and ascends in them to the right hand of God in heaven. This bold thought, as we all know, abounds in all Paul's writings. Our baptism buries us into Christ's death; our old man is crucified with him; we are risen with him through the faith of the operation of God who hath raised him from the dead (Rom. vi. 4–6; Col. ii. 12, 13). The sufferings of believers are the sufferings of Christ; they fill up that which is behind of these last, carry onward the sense and value of them in the world, for the sake of his body, the Church (2 Cor. i. 5; iv. 10,

---

8. [Trans. "until Christ be formed in you" (RSV). Nevin of course uses the Textus Receptus's ἄχρις for Nestle-Aland's μέχρις (trans. "until").]

11; Phil. iii. 10; Col. i. 24). In virtue of the living bond, which unites the members with the head, even that which is still future in their case is at times spoken of as past; they are not only called and justified, but are glorified also in Christ, as potentially secure of all that is comprised in his resurrection (Rom. viii. 29, 30). They are quickened, raised up, and made to sit together with him in heavenly places (Eph. ii. 5, 6). Their citizenship is in heaven; their life hid with Christ in God, and destined by its full relation hereafter to change even their present vile bodies into the glorious image of his own (Phil. iii. 20, 21; Col. iii. 3, 4). His spirit dwelling in them now shall in due time quicken even their mortal bodies into immortality (Rom. viii. 11). His resurrection is the guaranty and pledge of theirs, works itself out to its last result only in their recovery from the grave (Rom. viii. 23; 1 Cor. xv. 20–23, 45–49; 1 Thess. iv. 14).

But why should we go on to multiply proofs in this way, for what no unsophisticated reader of the New Testament surely will pretend to deny? What can the New Testament be said to teach at all, if it do not teach the fact of the mystical union, the true and actual formation of Christ's life into the souls of his people? Men may get rid of this teaching, if they choose, by wilfully turning the whole of it into barren metaphor and figure. But it is with a very bad grace they then turn round and say: *We* go by the Bible. The same system of interpretation, with less than half the same trouble, might set aside every text that is usually quoted in favor of the Trinity. The question of election, the question of the perseverance of the saints, and many other questions made to be of primary account in one orthodox system or another, are of far less clear representation in the Bible, than this view of the Christian salvation as involving "Christ in us the hope of glory." Nor is it, by any means, of new acknowledgment in the Church, however strange and transcendental it may now sound to *some* "evangelical" ears. It runs through the universal theology of the old Christian Fathers. It forms the key-note to the deepest piety of the Middle Ages. It animates the faith of all the Reformers. Luther and Calvin both proclaim it, in terms that should put to shame the rationalism of later times, pretending to follow them and yet casting the mystery to the winds.

[THE INCARNATION INTRODUCES A NEW PRINCIPLE]

We pass on to the second point presented in this criticism. The incarnation, we are told, is plain enough; but the critic is at a loss to make anything out of the "new principle of light and life," which it is supposed to introduce into humanity; and asks, what new principle has been in it *since* the incarnation which was not in it *before*.

His own idea of the incarnation is, plainly, that it did not enter into the organization of the world at all as a fact of permanent force. Probably he has no sense whatever of this organization, as a vast whole completing itself in man, and thus reaching forward as a single historical process from the beginning of the world to its end. *This* too, he would take to "savor of the transcendental." The world is for him neither organism nor history, but a vast sand-heap in which men are thrown together outwardly, to be formed for eternity as so many separate units, each perfect and complete by itself.[9] The incarnation, of course, in such view becomes one of these naked units only, the man Jesus mysteriously made God for himself alone, an abstraction that comes into no real connection with our general humanity beyond the limits of his person. He stands in the world a mere theophany, not of a few hours only, as in the days of Abraham, but of thirty-three years; a sublime avatar, fantastically paraded thus long before men's eyes, only to be translated afterwards to heaven, and continued there (for the imagination) in no real union with the world's life whatever. This, thus left behind by the transient apparition, pursues precisely its old course, including in its living stream nothing more than has belonged to it from the beginning. The incarnation, under such Gnostic view, is taken to be "plain enough"; while to conceive of it as a new principle of light and life for the world seems a flight clear over the horizon of common sense.

But now, in the full face again of all this abstract thinking, we affirm that it finds no countenance or support whatever in the Bible. According to the first chapter of Genesis, the world is an organic whole

---

9. [The metaphor of the "sand-heap" is one of Nevin's favorite images for depicting a nominalistic view of humanity as simply the aggregate of individuals. Such a view, he thought, fails to grasp both the deeper unity of humanity and Christ's organic relationship to it.]

which completes itself in man; and humanity is regarded throughout as a single grand fact, which is brought to pass, not at once, but in the way of history, unfolding always more and more its true interior sense, and reaching onward towards its final consummation. The Jewish dispensation had respect to the wants of the universal world, and was intended from the beginning to make room for the coming of Christ; which took place, accordingly, at last, when the "fullness of the time was come" (Gal. iv. 4), "in the wisdom of God" (1 Cor. i. 21), and "according to the riches of his grace, wherein he hath abounded, toward us in all wisdom and prudence" (Eph. i. 7–10). The incarnation, in this view, was no passing theophany or avatar. It was the form in which the sense of all previous history came finally to its magnificent outlet. This outlet, however, when it did come, involved a great deal more than was comprehended in the actual constitution of the world, the living human world, as it stood before; for it was brought to pass by the real union of the everlasting Word with our fallen life.[10] The mystery of the incarnation had been coming through four thousand years[11]; still the *coming* was not the presence of the fact itself; as little as the aurora which gilds the eastern heavens may be taken for the full orbed splendors of the risen sun. Christ is the sense of all previous history, the grand terminus towards which it was urged from the beginning; while in this very character, at the same time, he brings into union with it a new divine force which was not in it before, though required from the first to make

---

10. [Nevin affirmed that the Incarnation entailed a union of the Logos with fallen humanity. See "General Introduction."]

11. [Here Nevin appears to accept the conventional Ussher chronology regarding the age of the earth as created in 4004 BC. In his 1851 theological lectures edited by William Erb, however, he demonstrates considerable flexibility in his interpretation of the creation narrative, so long as humanity is viewed as the climax of the original creation and as setting the stage for the coming of Christ. In this sense Christology is foundational for anthropology: "The Mosaic account of the creation is descriptive rather than strictly historical and philosophical. It is a picture or representation of the process of creation exhibited to the mind of the seer in the form of a vision. It is not a report of the events themselves as they actually occurred, but a view of them, which is fully commensurate with the facts.... We cannot infer from the account what amount of time was required for the construction of the world as it now stands.... We are bound to believe, however, that man was strictly created at the beginning of our system. We must not regard his creation as a mere evolution. Man forms the climax of the world; yet there is introduced through him a higher principle, a new creation, which completes the process going on before. Christ was a new creation in the same sense." Erb, ed., *Dr. Nevin's Theology*, 166–68.]

it complete. He is the true basis thus of the period going before, as well as of the period that follows. Two conceptions, in this way, enter jointly into the idea of the incarnation as it challenges our faith throughout the New Testament. First, it is a fact which unites itself really with the living constitution, the actual concrete and organic history, of the world as it existed previously; it was no phantasm, no spectrum, no abstract symbol only played off to the eyes of men supernaturally for the space of thirty-three years. Secondly, however, it is in this form a new creation; not the continuation simply of the old, but the introduction into this of a higher life (the Word made flesh), which all its powers, as they stood previously, were inadequate to reach. Can there be any doubt, in regard to the scriptural authority of *both* these conceptions? They form the poles of the universal christian consciousness as it starts in the Apostles' Creed. They rule the whole process of theology in the Church, from the beginning, in opposition to Gnostic supernaturalism on the one hand and Ebionitic naturalism on the other.[12] Both are presented to us from every page of the New Testament. Christianity, shorn of either, falls at once to the ground. To make Christ an intrinsic result simply, or an extrinsic accident only, for the old creation, is to go full in the face of the whole Bible. He *must* be all or nothing here; the deepest and most central fact of the world, or no fact at all; the alpha and omega of humanity, or no part of humanity whatever.

To say that no "new principle of light and life" was introduced into the world by the incarnation, that the world carried in its constitution before Christ came all that is carried in it since, is virtually to deny the incarnation altogether; for it overthrows the historical centrality of the fact, and, indeed, thrusts it quite out of the process of history. The fact, in this view, ceases to be *immanent* to the economy of our universal human life, lies on the outside of it, comes to no real union with it in any way. Surely this is not Christianity. The Word, eternally with the Father, says John, became flesh in Christ, and so joined itself through him with our fallen nature. This he holds to be plainly the Fact of all facts, the *cardo* ["hinge" or "turning point"] of the world's life, the pillar that upholds at last the entire sense of the moral universe. "The law

---

12. [Nevin frequently uses these two early Christian heresies as foils representing contemporary tendencies to be avoided. The Gnostics were known for their docetic Christologies, which denied that Christ was truly human and that the divine had fully entered into history. The Ebionites contended that Jesus was but an inspired human being. Thus both denied the Incarnation.]

came by Moses; but grace and truth by Jesus Christ." I baptize you, cries the Baptist (himself greater than all the Old Testament prophets, and yet less than the least in the kingdom of heaven, Math. xi. 11) with water only; he that cometh after me shall baptize you with the Holy Ghost and with fire. So Christ himself everywhere claims to be, not the oracle simply of truth and life in force before, but the *principle* of truth and life made real for the world wholly and only by himself. The Spirit fell upon him at his baptism, in full measure, to find way through him and from him subsequently to the whole family of the redeemed (Math. iii. 16; John vii. 39; Acts i. 4, 5; ii. 1-4). He is the organ of living communication between earth and heaven, the central point where they are first fairly united into one (John i. 51). He is the real presence in the world of what had been proclaimed before in the way of shadow only and word (John i. 18; Math. v. 17, 18; Heb. ix. 8-12, &c., &c.). He is no moon merely to reflect, like the prophets before him, a simply borrowed light, but according to his own word, the very sun of the spiritual world (John viii. 12) and so, of course, a fountain and principle of light for it in his own person. He is the well of salvation (John iv. 14; vii. 37, 38), the manna of immortality (John vi. 49-51), the victory itself in which is swallowed up all the power of the grave (John v. 21-25; xi. 25, 26). He is the principle thus of *life,* as well as of light; the one indeed involving the other. He hath life *in himself,* fontally (John v. 26), for the use of the world. His life is the light of men (John i. 4). A new order of things is proclaimed, as coming into force especially with his resurrection and glorification. Cast into the ground, he becomes the seed of a vast harvest (John, xii. 24). Lifted up from the earth, he is the nucleus of a new humanity (John xii. 32). His entrance into glory opens the windows of heaven and allows free egress for the powers of his own higher life to go forth into the general stream of human history, by the Church, as never in all ages before (John vii. 39; Mark xvi. 15-18; John xiv. 16-20, &c., &c.).

Need we say that Paul again abounds everywhere with the same thought in his own way? Beyond all question, *he* saw in Christ a new principle of light and life for the human race. In no other view is his language at all intelligible. Christ is for him the "second Adam," more intimately related to the race, as its base and centre, than the first (Rom. v. 12-15; 1 Cor. xv. 21, 22, 45-49). He is in this character a "quickening spirit" (πνεῦμα ζωοποιοῦν)[13]; second in order of time, but first in the depth and inwardness of his representative life. He is the great mystery of humanity, hid from ages and from generations, but at last made manifest to his saints (Col. i. 26, 27); "that in the dispensation of the fullness of times, God might gather together in one all things in Christ, both which are in heaven and which are on earth" (Eph. i. 9, 10); "to the intent that now unto the principalities and powers in heavenly places might be known, by the Church, the manifold wisdom of God" (Eph. iii. 9, 10). He is our peace, the medium of our reconciliation with God, the source thus of a new order of consciousness in which all previous antagonisms are brought to an end (Eph. ii. 14–22). He is the universal solvent, through whose force the elements of the ethical world are subdued and constituted into new form (Gal. iii. 26–28; 1 Cor. iii. 21–23). Christianity in this view is a new creation, greater and more glorious than the first (Col. i. 16–18). All moral relations come, *in Christ,* to new significance and force. He is such a real fountain of freedom and power, as never was in the world before. What the law could not do, being weak through the flesh (Rom. viii. 3, 4), is accomplished by the mystery of the incarnation; the law of the spirit of life in Christ Jesus sets men free from the law of sin and death. He is himself our righteousness and life (1 Cor. i. 30), *in whom* we have redemption through his blood (Eph. i. 7), and *by whom* we have received the atonement (Rom. v. 11). He has abolished death, and brought life and immortality to light (2 Tim. i. 10). He is the foundation of the Church; it starts in his person; its whole, magnificent structure serves only to reveal the full force of the mystery of godliness here brought into view (l Tim. iii. 15, 16) the riches of the glory of God's inheritance in the saints, and the exceeding greatness of his power towards them that believe, according to the working of his mighty power which he wrought in Christ, when he raised him from the dead, and set him on his own right hand in the heavenly places (Eph. i. 18–20).

Again, however, we forbear. The difficulty is not to find proofs in the New Testament for the position here called in question, but to make room for them and set them in order. They crowd into view from every side. The idea of a new creation flowing from Christ, and actually lodging in the constitution of the world the force and power of a divine life which was not in it before, may be said to underlie, as a tacit assumption

13. [1 Cor 15:45.]

at least, every portion of the evangelical record. To *our* ears it sounds strangely, we confess, to hear this view of Christianity called in question by any who pretend to follow the Bible as their rule and guide. If the incarnation wrought no change in the spiritual posture of the world, but left it in its relations, capacities and powers, just what it was from the beginning, we may well ask with trembling anxiety: In what then did it consist, and what force has it for our salvation? *Could* the mystery be real if it brought no real difference into our life? Can we rationally admit at all the entrance of the Eternal Word into the organism of humanity if the fact be so taken as to involve no modification still of its previous state, no entrance into it at the same time of a new principle of light and life? The question is not, of course, whether the human world out of Christ remains what it was before; but whether that part of it which is comprehended in Christ, and which forms thus the true central stream of its history, has not come to be filled with new substance and sense. The new creation holds in the bosom of the Church and not beyond it; but it holds there, at the same time, as the inmost substantial sense of humanity itself, the form in which it is required to become universally complete. Christianity, so far as it prevails, is the actual elevation of our general life into a higher sphere of existence. History is made to possess contents by it which had no place in it before. The possibility of a real and full solution of the problem of man's life hangs on the actual coming of Christ in the flesh (1 John v. 4, 5, 11, 12, 20). By this, humanity is made complete. He brings into it light, life and immortality, is himself the principle, and fountain, and immediate ground of all this in the constitution it receives through his person. Just here is the broad chasm, which separates between all rationalism and the true christian faith. The Unitarian sees in Christ only an outward teacher, who accomplishes our salvation by his excellent doctrine and holy example. Does it, however, alter the case materially, to allow the mystery of the incarnation, and yet turn it into an outward *occasion* only in the service of the same end? If Christ be no *principle* of life for humanity, if he be not in truth the power of a new creation in its constitution, it follows necessarily that it needs nothing of this sort for its redemption. This is at once Pelagianism.[14]

---

14. [The fifth-century movement taking its name from the British moralist Pelagius, who taught that original sin was but the bad example of the first parents, that human nature is essentially good, and that obedience to God is possible apart from

Let us not be told, then, that it savors of the transcendental and contradicts the Bible to say that "the Lord is perpetually born anew in the hearts of believers," and that Christ is the "principle of a new creation" for the human race. It savors sadly of the *rationalistic* to have any other view; and we may well be amazed to find such skepticism placidly arrogating to itself the title *evangelical* as its own special distinction, and boldly underpinning its want of faith with the pretended wholesale authority of the Bible. Unitarianism plants itself too on the "teaching of the Bible," with quite as much reason, and full as good a grace.

J. W. N.

---

divine grace.]

Article 3
"Wilberforce on the Incarnation"

(by John W. Nevin)

EDITOR'S INTRODUCTION

This 1850 article by John W. Nevin reviews a volume on the Incarnation by prominent Anglican Oxford Movement figure Robert Wilberforce (1802–57). But it is in fact less a formal review than an explication and development of key Mercersburg themes, with Wilberforce's book as occasion for the exercise. As Nevin puts it, his "object is rather to call attention to what we conceive to be the immense practical significance of the general subject with which it is occupied." Given this aim, it is not surprising that Nevin downplays any disagreements with Wilberforce (over episcopacy, for example) and emphasizes their common ground.

In the opening section we find Nevin responding to the popular acclaim given Wilberforce's book, thought by some to be "the great production of the age." Nevin here comes across as a bit defensive and partisan as he acknowledges its importance but also offers an extended apology for the superiority of German theological scholarship.

The bulk of the article is developed in seven demarcated sections which, taken together, can be understood as a useful summary of the Mercersburg Theology. In the first Nevin develops the theme of the "Mediation of Christ." In contrast to the "outward view" of Christ as an "instrument or servant" who accomplishes a task in order to reconcile God and sinful humanity, Nevin contends that the Incarnation is not simply a means to the end of mediation. Rather, it is "the Mediatorial

Fact." From this flows the centrality of the Incarnation for all of theology—the Incarnation rather than Scripture is to be seen as the "principle of Christianity." In this Nevin challenged the biblicistic American Protestantism of his day.

Second, the Incarnation stands in continuity with human life and history as a whole. Christ is not a mere passing theophany or Gnostic apparition. Rather, he is the "Second Adam," the one who takes previous human existence into himself, and in elevating it becomes the root of a new redeemed humanity. Such thinking, of course, requires a more realist view of human nature than that which obtained in the prevailing Scottish Common Sense Realism with its nominalistic view of humanity. According to Nevin, Christ has taken unto himself "human nature objectively considered," a generic humanity consisting of "living law and power" which is thus brought into union with God. Here Nevin rather explicitly appeals to the recapitulation theme of the church father Irenaeus: "The race starts in Adam. It is recapitulated again, or gathered into a new centre and head, in Christ."

Third, the incarnate humanity of Christ is the locus of salvation. In this connection Nevin affirms that in the Incarnation Christ assumed a sinful humanity, that is, a humanity that bears the effects of the Fall (in speaking of "the nature of Man as fallen in Adam" Nevin is making more a metaphysical than a moral point in that this sinful humanity needed to be healed). In Christ sinful humanity has been healed and elevated into union with God. Christ as to his incarnate humanity has become the fountain of salvation, and salvation occurs though mystical union with Christ.

Fourth, because the transforming and reconciling benefits of Christ cannot be abstracted from the person of Christ, salvation hangs on "mystical union" with the humanity of Christ, a solidarity that occurs through the work of the Holy Spirit. Here Nevin takes pains to safeguard the uniqueness of the Incarnation—this union with Christ does not mean that the Christian is hypostatically united with God. Rather, because Christ carries a universal or generic humanity, Christians can receive his very life. Thus Nevin speaks of deification or theosis but in a carefully circumscribed sense—there is no "deification aside from Christ himself."

Fifth, Christ is now present with Christians in his humanity as well as in his deity. But this presence is by the power of the Holy Spirit rather than a local and material presence. Nevin contends that to say that Christ is only present with believers as to his deity (as many of Nevin's American contemporaries such as Charles Hodge affirmed) is effectively to deny the Incarnation.

Sixth, this presence of Christ with believers takes place "in and by his mystical body, the Church." Here Nevin insists in idealist fashion that the collective whole has priority over the individual: "single Christians accordingly have part in him only as they are comprehended at the same time in this whole." An important implication of this priority of the whole over the individual parts is that the Church mediates Christ to the Christian: "The Church, in this view, does indeed stand between Christ and the believer, but only as the body of a living man is between one of his limbs and the living soul by which it is quickened and moved."

Finally, this notion of the church as functionally mediatorial between Christ and the Christian implies visible organization or polity, worship, an ordained ministry, ritual or liturgy, and the sacraments. Such an understanding of the Church will recognize the necessity of means of grace, and here Nevin places particular emphasis on the sacraments, which "exhibit objectively the realities they represent." In this connection, Nevin decries the "evangelical skeptics" (doubtless the vast majority of American Protestants of his day) who denied sacramental grace.

Having used Wilberforce's volume as an occasion to present the Mercersburg Theology at some length, Nevin does recognize that Wilberforce was a "High Churchman" writing in support of episcopacy. But Nevin contends that Wilberforce places proper and primary emphasis on the Incarnation as the basis for his ecclesiology, and argues that the issue of episcopal government is secondary. Here Nevin argues over against his low-church American contemporaries that the key issue facing Protestants of the day is "Church or No-church," and that this important question must be settled on the basis of Christology: "We come to the true conception of the Church through a true and sound Christology (as in the Creed), and in no other way."

"Wilberforce on the Incarnation"[1]

The Doctrine of the Incarnation of our Lord Jesus Christ in its relation to Mankind and to the Church. By Robert Isaac Wilberforce, A. M., Archdeacon of the East Riding. First American from the second London Edition. Philadelphia : H. Hooker & Co., 1849, pp. 411. 12 mo.

We are not exactly prepared to pronounce this book, in the language of *some* of its admirers, the greatest theological work of the age. Our Episcopal friends are apt to be a little too fast in claiming credit in this style for the literature of their own Church, and a good deal too dull in perceiving or acknowledging the merit of any literature besides. They are quite too starched and pedantic especially in their bearing towards the theology of Germany. It is only ridiculous however to fancy the English Church or the Episcopal Church in America on any sort of parallel and level, as regards theological science, with German Protestantism under its better form. There is no doubt on the English side a vast fund of traditional orthodoxy and order, which at this time particularly cannot well be held in too high account; and there are errors and heresies too in the thinking of Germany, as we all know, that need to be guarded against with the most jealous and watchful care. But mere tradition can never be made to stand in the place of thought; nor are heresies to be cured by a declaration of war against all philosophy and science. Theology, to live, must be something more than a form of sound words. It must grapple with error, and overcome it. Its mission is to be scientific, as well as true to the faith once delivered to the saints. In this respect, Germany with all her errors stands far in advance both of England and America. She is the land emphatically of Protestant

1. [Originally printed in the *Mercersburg Review* 2:2 (March 1850): 164–96.]

theology. Not only is she entitled to the first rank in what regards the outward apparatus of the science, as most are now willing to admit; her primacy is equally clear in all that pertains to its true inward life and substance. We need her help not only in philology and history, but in the settlement and defence also of all christian doctrines. The theology of Germany, for years past, has been more wakeful, more profoundly earnest, more vigorously active, than that of all the world besides. The theology of this country, with all its pretension and cant, is for the most part mere schoolboy pedantry in comparison. This scientific activity may not save the German Church; at least not without help, under a different form, from some other quarter; but it cannot fail to prove at last of high consequence for the christian world. It belongs to the inmost power of Protestantism, and forms in some sense what must be considered the central stream of its life. The dangers which attend it are to be surmounted by its own resources, and not by refusing to look them in the face. If our remedy for error is to be found in mere outward authority, a faith that owns no fellowship whatever with science, it were better for us to fall back at once fully and wholly into the arms of Romanism. Admit this principle, and Protestantism stands convicted of falsehood from the start. It has no right to exist. Say that Protestantism has no power to take care of itself in following out its own law, but needs to be overruled and controlled in its course by a purely foreign authority, saying to it, Thus far shalt thou go but no farther; and we have the whole question of its legitimacy conclusively settled. It is for this reason, and in this view, that the problem of Protestantism may be said to be specially involved in the course of theological science at present in Germany. For whatever may be needed to make the Church complete in the end, it is clear that all other interests must be ruled sooner or later by the authority of ideas; theory must underlie all solid life and practice; and the heart of any movement is found consequently where its theoretic or ideal character is made most actively the subject of thought. The question whether Protestantism has a right to exist turns after all not so much on the practical working of Episcopacy in Great Britain, or of Puritanism in America, as it does on the results of theology in Germany. If the *idea* of the Reformation, its original and proper theory, be found unequal to the test to which it is here subjected, it is vain to imagine that it can command the faith and homage of the world lastingly on any other ground. Let it appear that Protestant theology, under its most free and active character, not only calls forth such terrible errors as have appeared in Germany, but has no power also at the same time to overcome them by a still more vigorous vindication of the truth, and the Roman controversy, as we take it, is fairly brought to an end. If Protestantism cannot think itself out to its last consequences without landing us in rationalism and pantheism, we need no other argument to set aside its claims from the beginning. It is proved at once to be a failure under its more respectable forms, as well as under those that are openly antichristian and false; and we are bound to save ourselves from its bad authority, not by allowing it wilfully only to a certain point, but by abjuring it altogether. It is in this view, we say, that Protestantism universally, whether the fact be perceived or not, has a deep and vital interest in the theological activity of modern Germany, notwithstanding its errors and heresies, more than in the thinking of any other part of the christian world. Let us be willing all round to do justice to its claims, and not affect to be independent of its co-operation and help. If we can go beyond its measure, well; but this we can never do by superciliously ignoring or overlooking the whole field of inquiry here offered to our view. The questions with which this German theology is occupied are questions that lie in the way of all true theological science, and challenge the respect of all really earnest and thoughtful minds. Nor is it easy to speak in too high terms of the learning and intellectual power with which they are discussed. If theology exist as a science at all, at the present time, it is in Germany. We are made to smile accordingly, when we hear a single English work, like that of Wilberforce,[2] referred to as *the* great production of the age in the department to which it belongs, without the least regard apparently to this fact. All who are acquainted with the later German theology know that the age abounds with great productions in this form. It would be easy to name many theologians not only of equal but of superior learning, and many works also of far more thorough and complete execution, which must be allowed largely to divide at least the theological credit of the age with *Wilberforce on the Incarnation.*

2. [Robert Isaac Wilberforce (1802–57) was an Anglican clergyman and son of the great abolitionist William Wilberforce. Prominent in the Oxford Movement, Wilberforce was, with John Henry Newman, a fellow of Oriel College, Oxford, where he taught from 1826 until 1831. He was received into the Roman Catholic Church in 1854. A portion of his *The Doctrine of the Incarnation* was reprinted in Fairweather, *The Oxford Movement,* 283–367.]

We have no wish however to disparage the merits of this book. It is in truth worthy of high admiration and respect. It deserves to be welcomed as a work of thorough independent learning, which may well be taken to form something of an epoch in the history at least of English theology. We only wish that it may be widely read and studied, both in England and in this country; for we are sure that it is suited to the wants of our reigning Christianity, whether theoretically or practically considered, and that it cannot fail to operate auspiciously, where it gains attention, in favor of truth and piety. Unfortunately it is not as well fitted as it might be for common popular use. The subject itself of which it treats is one that lies out of the range of ordinary thought; but there is a serious fault besides, as regards popularity, in the author's method and style. It is fashionable to speak of the darkness and vagueness of German writers; and we are willing to allow that a good many of them are well entitled to such reproach; but we must say we have found it more of an effort to keep the clue of thought steadily in this English book than to read understandingly some of the hardest German ones that come in our way. Wilberforce is for us decidedly a more *misty* writer than Dorner, for instance, or Rothe, or Daub, or even Kant himself in his Criticism of the Understanding.[3] The difficulty with these writers generally is in the arduous character of their thought, and in this alone; whereas in the work before us it lies often to a very considerable extent in the representation of the thought. The plan of the book, as a whole, is not sufficiently clear; it is put together somewhat clumsily and awkwardly in its several parts; a sort of continual haziness surrounds the progress of its argument; the language is often careless, and lacks throughout the transparency and vivacity that are needed for full popular effect.

---

3. [Isaak August Dorner (1809–1884), German mediating theologian who taught successively at Tübingen, Kiel, Königsberg, Bonn, Göttingen, and Berlin. Among his works was the *History of the Development of the Doctrine of the Person of Christ*. Seeking to reconcile the doctrine of the Incarnation with divine immutability, Dorner argued against the kenosis theories popular at the time and for a more dynamic, developing Incarnation in which the Logos was progressively bestowed upon Jesus. See the excerpts from his *System of Christian Doctrine* in Welch, ed., *God and Incarnation*, 105–284. For a contemporary account of Dorner, see Schaff, *Germany*, 376–380. Richard Rothe (1799–1867), was a German theologian and ethicist who spent much of his career at Wittenberg and Heidelberg. Karl Daub (1765–1836), was a German speculative theologian strongly influenced by Hegel. The last reference is to Kant's epochal *Critique of Pure Reason*, the definitive second edition of which was published in 1787.]

The work, with all its merits, is decidedly heavy and hard to read. We are sorry for this; as it may prove a bar in some measure to its favorable reception, where it might otherwise have found free passport and exerted a happy influence on the side of truth. The theme with which it is occupied is one of the very highest interest, lying at the foundation of all sound theology and carrying with it claims to attention, particularly for the present age, beyond perhaps any other that could well be named. It is handled here too, so far as actual substance is concerned, in a truly learned and masterly manner; so as to be everyway worthy of coming into respectful audience and consideration with all who take pleasure in divinity, whether in the Episcopal Church or on the outside of it. At the same time, as we have had too much opportunity to know, the theme, with all its vast significance, is for a large part of our reigning religious thought by no means palatable; for the reason precisely that it runs counter to many of its traditional prejudices, and is felt to involve practical consequences in the end, which it has become a sort of settled maxim with it to resist tooth and nail in defiance of all examination. The age, however tolerant it may be in other directions, has no toleration at all generally for the idea of the *Church* or for the mystery of the Sacraments; and is but too ready to turn away with impatient disgust from any theological inquiry that leads this way. With all its professed love for liberty and light, it is apt here to resent everything like free investigation, and to shrink from *science* as though its presence were only suited to give pain. In such circumstances, it is to be regretted that the work before us should not have every outward advantage along with it, to assist it in commanding for its great subject the homage, which this has a right to claim, but at the same time so little power with too many to enforce. We are apprehensive that it is not reaching any such circulation, nor gaining any such earnest attention as may be counted at all commensurate with its deserts. It seems to be received only with a sort of half-complaisance at best even in the Episcopal Church; while almost no notice whatever is taken of it among other denominations, for the simple reason perhaps that it is felt to move in a foreign sphere of thought, with which only *churchmen,* in the Episcopal sense, are regarded as having any sympathy or concern.

With all the prejudices of the age however towards the subject here brought into view, it is clear enough that this belongs notwithstanding to the proper religious life of the age itself, and that it is forcing itself more and more from all sides, in spite of prejudice, upon its consideration and regard. It is not uncommon, nor unnatural, for an idea or tendency to be at once resisted and responded to, in this way, by the life of an age whose inmost necessity perhaps it comes both to interpret and fulfil. A new spirit of thought plainly is beginning to prevail in regard to Christ's *person*. Even in New England, theology may be seen gradually waking to an interest, which a few years since was wanting altogether, in what may be called the Christological Mystery, with more or less apprehension of its living concrete relations to the constitution of the world and the course of history.[4] Questions which not long ago were considered fully settled and laid away as shelf abstractions, on the hypostatical union and its practical results, are now, whether men choose to be pleased with it or not, asserting their right to be re-studied and settled over again, with something of the same sort of interest that is given to immediately present realities of corresponding moment in the sphere of nature. It is coming to be widely felt that theology needs a regeneration as well as our christian life generally, and that this must turn on a clearer and more powerful apprehension of what is comprehended in the person of Christ himself, as the true centre and fountain at the same time of all truth and grace besides. Christology is acquiring, in this way, new significance as a world of truth within itself, from whose bosom only, fairly entered in the first place by faith, it can ever be possible to understand either the nature of God or the nature of man. In all such tendencies and indications, come from what quarter they may, we unfeignedly rejoice. They carry in them a promise of good for the future, while they serve to reveal also the ephemeral character of what is different or contrary in the present. The fashion of our present reigning theology, with all its affected self-sufficiency, is evidently doomed to pass away. The mind of the christian world is coming to regard it more and more with misgiving and distrust; and on all sides the persuasion gains ground that the Christological Question, embracing the true idea

---

4. [In his criticism of New England theology Nevin doubtless has in mind both Unitarianism, with its outright denial of the Incarnation, and their Trinitarian, albeit somewhat rationalistic, counterparts, who often reduced Christ to a moral example whose death on the cross made divine forgiveness of all possible. An example of this waking interest in "Christological Mystery" is Horace Bushnell, whose *God in Christ* had just been published in 1849. Bushnell shared Nevin's distaste for the empirical rationalism of the day, and, like Nevin, he viewed Christianity as a life rather than a collection of doctrines.]

of the Church and its relation to the Saviour's living person, is in truth the great question of the age, and carries in itself a power by which all the interests of religion are to be moulded hereafter into new shape.

We propose no formal analysis of Wilberforce on the Incarnation, nor any examination of its several parts in detail. Our object is rather to call attention to what we conceive to be the immense practical significance of the general subject with which it is occupied; which may be best done perhaps by singling out some of the leading aspects under which it is here made to challenge our regard, and holding them up to separate contemplation, without any particular respect to the author's plan. These will be found to agree substantially with views which are presented in our own book entitled *The Mystical Presence*; and we shall be glad certainly if the high authority by which they are now endorsed in this very able and learned English work, may serve to win for them in any quarter a more earnest consideration than they have yet been able to engage under a simply American garb.

[THE INCARNATION NOT MERELY A MEANS TO MEDIATION]

I. The *Mediation* of Christ holds primarily and fundamentally in the constitution of his person. With our current theology this is not admitted. The Mediatorial office is taken to be a sort of outward investiture, for which it was necessary indeed that Christ should have certain previous qualifications, but which is to be regarded still in this view as holding out of his person and beyond it; like the work assigned to Moses for instance, when he was selected and appointed to lead the Israelites out of Egypt, and to give them the Law at Mount Sinai. Two parties, God and man, are thought of as in a state of variance, and as needing reconciliation; a certain service is required for this purpose; it may be in the way of negotiation and persuasion simply, or it may be in the way of work, obedience, sacrifice, atonement; and to meet this requirement, under such purely outward view, Christ is regarded as assuming the character of a day's man or arbitrator, and as coming *between* the parties thus in order to bring them together. He may be considered a mere Prophet, in the Unitarian sense, who saves by his excellent doctrine and holy example; or he may be allowed to be far more than this, a Saviour possessed of truly Divine powers, according to the orthodox faith, by the mystery of the incarnation, who takes away sin by suffering the penalty of it in his own person; but still in either case, the thing done has its proper seat and substance in the relation of the parties concerned by itself considered, while Christ as the doer of it stands always as it were on the outside of the transaction, in the character comparatively of an instrument or servant to his own glorious work. Now every such view of redemption we hold to be more or less inadequate and false; and it is of the utmost consequence, we think, that attention should be fully fastened on the point, for the purpose of promoting a more just apprehension of this great mystery in its true nature and power. The Mediation of Christ, we say, holds primarily and fundamentally in the constitution of his person. His Incarnation is not to be regarded as a device *in order* to his Mediation, the needful preliminary and condition of this merely as an independent and separate work; it is itself the Mediatorial Fact, in all its height and depth, and length and breadth.

"His name of Mediator," says our author,

> is not bestowed by reason of any work, in which He was occasionally or partially occupied; it sets forth that office, which resulted from the permanent union in one person of God and Man. For the benefits which He bestows upon man's nature result from his being the link which binds it to Deity. The salvation of Adam's race depends upon the influence of that higher nature, which has been introduced into it from above. This gift was first bestowed upon humanity in the Person of Christ, that from Him it might afterwards be extended in degree to all His brethren.

He is accordingly not *a* Mediator, but *the* Mediator between God and Man; as Paul, 1 Tim. ii. 5, allows *one* only, in such way as to exclude all others. There may be a number of relative mediators between God and men, but there can be only one who is the absolute junction and union of the two parties thus distinguished.

> Christ is the real bond by which Godhead and humanity are united. And this arises not from any technical and artificial appointment; He bears this name, because He is what it expresses. His title follows from His nature, as effect from cause, as consequent from antecedent. He truly is what no other is, or can be beside Him, the Pattern Man, the second Adam; therefore no other can take his place among the generations of mankind.

The Mediation of Christ is his actually binding the nature of God and the nature of Man into one life, in his own person. "For this cause the Son of God consented to become the Son of Man: 'When Thou tookest upon Thee to deliver man, Thou didst not abhor the Virgin's womb.' Moses acted as mediator, Christ became one." The Christian faith, as set forth by the universal Church from the beginning, looks first accordingly not to our Lord's acts so much as to the mystery of his personality.

> It has sometimes been asked why our Lord's Atonement is not inserted in the Creed, in such express words as his Incarnation. The reason is that our Lord's Atonement may be admitted in words, although those who use them attach no christian sense to the doctrine which they acknowledge; whereas if the doctrine of our Lord's Incarnation is once truly accepted, His Mediation follows as its necessary result. So that the Church was guided by Divine Wisdom to make this article of our Lord's real nature the criterion of her belief, the *articulus stantis aut cadentis ecclesiae*[5]: it holds a leading place in the profession which in all ages has been required at Baptism; and the early believers gave a token of their reverence, when on declaring that He "was made man," they were wont, with one consent, to bow the knee and worship.

Christ's person is thus at once the centre and comprehension of all functions discharged on God's part towards man, or on man's part towards God. He is the sole channel of grace, and the only medium through whom our prayers can ascend acceptably to heaven. "This is the place wherein heaven and earth are connected ; the bridge which joins them together. He is the *door*, the *way*, the *truth*, and the *life*."—*P.* 170–173.

It makes all the difference in the world for our theology whether the Christian Salvation be apprehended as a living fact thus starting in the person of Christ, or as an arrangement or economy simply in the Divine Mind which Christ came into the world to serve in an outward and instrumental way. Every evangelical doctrine becomes different, as seen either from the one of these points of view or from the other. It is not enough that the articles of our faith may carry in any case separately an orthodox sound; all depends on the order in which they are bound together, the principle from which they proceed, their interior genealogy and connection as parts of a common whole. The most orthodox formula may be full of heresy, if abstracted from the real ground of

---

5. [Trans. "article of the standing or falling of the church."]

Christianity, and made to stand before us as a naked word or thought in some other form. The true order of the Christian faith is given in the Creed. All rests on the mystery of the Incarnation. *That* is itself Christianity, the true idea of the Gospel, the new world of grace and truth, in which the discord of sin, the vanity of nature, the reign of death, are brought forever to an end. Here is an order of life which was not in the world before, the Word made Flesh, God and Man brought into living union in the person of Jesus Christ, as the nucleus and fountain of salvation for the race. He is the Mediator, because God and Man are thus in a real way joined together and made one in his person. The primary force of his character in this view, the power which belongs to him to make reconciliation and atonement, lies in the fact that the parties between whom he mediates are in truth united first of all in the very constitution of his own life. He is in this way the actual *medium* of their conjunction. The mission of salvation which he came to fulfil was not indeed at once completed by the mystery of the hypostatical union; his Mediatorship involved a history, a work, the execution of prophetical, priestly, and kingly offices,[6] a life of suffering and trial, the atonement, the resurrection, the sitting at the right hand of God, from whence he shall come to judge the world; but all this only as the proper and necessary result of the first mystery itself, the entrance of the Divine Word in a living way into the sphere of our fallen Humanity. This brought heaven and earth together in the very heart or centre of the world's life, and carried in itself the guaranty that all which was required to make the union permanent and complete should in due order be triumphantly accomplished. Conceived by the Holy Ghost and born of the Virgin Mary, Jesus Christ must necessarily suffer also and die, but only that by doing so he might conquer death, and bring in everlasting righteousness and immortal life for the nature he came to redeem and save. Forth from this sublime Fact proceeds the presence of the Holy Ghost, the power of a new creation in the world, the mystery of the Church, one, holy and catholic, and the whole process of salvation from the remission of sins in baptism on to the resurrection of the last day. The sense of Christ's Person, as the true bond that reconciles God and Man, brings along with it all this faith; and no article, we repeat it,

---

6. [The Reformed tradition in particular has often discussed the work of Christ in terms of the threefold offices of prophet, priest, and king. See, e.g., Calvin, *Institutes*, II.15.1–6; Westminster Confession of Faith, 8.1.]

deserves to be considered part of the Christian Creed, which comes not to be of force in this order and on this ground. The early Church stood here on the true foundation. The Creed, as held from the beginning, forms the true and only legitimate basis of Christian orthodoxy. It needs, in this view, no condescending indulgence, no apology, no qualification, no surreptitious foisting of a new and better sense into its ancient phraseology. Any modern system which finds this necessary, however creditable and plausible it may appear in other respects, stands convicted by the very fact of being itself in a false position. No doctrine can be valid and worthy of trust in the world that comes from Christ, which is not inwardly rooted in the Christological mystery of the old Creed. As an *abstraction,* a thing of mere thought and notion, supposed to hold in the relations of God and man out of Christ, and beyond the power of the concrete Fact embodied in his person, all pretended orthodoxy is reduced at last to a mere empty sham. Even as it regards the nature of God or the nature of man separately taken, our faith and science become truly *christian,* only when they are conditioned by a lively apprehension of what has come to pass in Christ. Where sympathy with the Creed is dull, and inward sense for its grandeur gone, there may still be much talk of God's attributes and works in a different view, of election and reprobation, of man's natural depravity, of justification by faith, regeneration, and other such high evangelical themes; but there can be no really sound and vigorous theology at any point. We will not hear, in such case, those who pretend to plant themselves on the authority of the *Bible,* while they are guilty of such palpable falling away from the mind of the Church in the age when the New Testament was formed; for the very point here to be settled is the true sense and meaning of the Bible; and what we maintain is that the early Church is more to be trusted than they are in regard to what constitutes the primary conception of Christianity, which must serve as a rule to guide us in the proper study of the Scriptures. The Bible rests on Christ. Light is not more necessary for seeing the world than the idea of Christ is for reading the true mind of God in his written word. The indwelling Creed, in this view, must underlie our use of the Bible, if it is to be at all just and safe. To say otherwise is to subordinate the Bible to that which is *not* original Christianity, the thinking of this man or that, or the thinking of a sect in no union with the Fact of the Christian faith as it stood in the beginning; and surely when it comes to this there ought to be no great difficulty, one would think, in deciding which alternative it is the part of wisdom, not to say faith, to choose. However grating it may sound to some ears, the truth needs to be loudly and constantly repeated: The Bible is not the *principle* of Christianity, neither its origin, nor its fountain, nor its foundation. For the opposite imagination is not by any means an innocent or powerless error. It strikes at the essence of Christianity, which is neither doctrine nor law but living grace, and tends to resolve it into a mere abstraction, a theory, that has its being in the world in men's thoughts mainly, and not in any more substantial form; which, carried out to its legitimate end, is just what we are to understand by Rationalism. It is of the utmost account to see, on the contrary, that the principle of Christianity is the Lord Jesus Christ himself, the Word made Flesh, the Christological Fact underlying, as in the Creed, the new heavens and the new earth. With the sense of this old faith in the mind, no difficulty whatever is found in recognizing it as the true voice also of the Bible.[7] It springs into view from all sides; and the only wonder is how it should be possible for any, under the power of the uncatholic theory, *not* to perceive and acknowledge its force. Christ *is* always, in the New Testament, the sum and substance of his own salvation; the way, the truth, the life; the divine καταλλαγή, reconciliation or atonement, in whom God appears reconciling the world to himself (2 Cor. v. 18, 19); the victory over death and hell; the true ladder of Jacob's vision, by which the heavens arc brought into perpetual free and open communion with the earth. He is the Peace of the world, the deepest and last sense of Man's life, by which all its other discords are harmonized in the deep toned diapason of its real union with God.

[THE INCARNATION STANDS IN CONTINUITY WITH HUMAN LIFE AND HISTORY AS A WHOLE]

II. This conception implies that the sense and power of Man's life universally considered come to view only in Christ; on which account the

---

7. [In this extended paragraph we find a remarkable statement of Nevin's christocentrism. Here he stresses the priority of the person of Christ over truths about Christ (however valid those truths may be), and the role of the Apostles' Creed and the authority of the early church as guides for the reading of Scripture. Particularly striking is the description of Christ as the "indwelling Creed" which conditions the right reading of the Bible. Nevin further develops these themes in his essays on "The Apostles' Creed." On the Mercersburg approach to the interpretation of Scripture, see Dipuccio, *Interior Sense of Scripture*.

mystery of the incarnation, as revealed in his person, is no isolated portent or prodigy, but a fact that holds in strict *organic and historical continuity and unity with the life of the human world as a whole.* In no other view can the mystery be regarded as real. Christ is indeed the entrance of a *new* life into the world, the Word clothing itself with flesh; but he is this, at the same time, in the way of an actual, and not simply apparent, entrance into the world. He was no theophany, but a real and proper man, bone of our bone and flesh of our flesh. In this character however he could not be merely a common man, one of the race as it stood before. Such a supposition would belie the other side of his being. As the beginning of a new and higher creation, his entrance into the world must be of universal force, a fact of force for humanity in its collective view. In no other way can the mystery be apprehended as real. Make Christ either a common man, sharing humanity with Moses, David, Peter and Paul, or in lieu of this a man wholly on the outside of this humanity as it belongs to others; and in both cases the conception of his Mediatorial character is gone, lost in Ebionitism on the one side or lost in fantastic Gnosticism on the other. The person of Christ, as Mediator, is of universal human significance and force. So the Scriptures teach when they call him the *Second Adam*; a title plainly implying that he is to be regarded in some way as the root of the race, in a deeper sense even than this can be affirmed of the First Adam. It is accordingly a vast mistake, contradicting alike the letter and the spirit of the Gospel, and leading to consequences of enormous mischief, when the Christian Salvation is taken to be in its primary purpose and plan for a part of the race only, a certain number of individuals as such, and not for Humanity as a whole. It must terminate on individuals indeed, and this involves an "election of grace," but like all *Life,* it is universal before it becomes thus particular and single, and the single christian is saved only by receiving it into himself under this character. To conceive of Christ's redemption as having regard either to all men numerically and outwardly considered, according to the Pelagian theory, or to a given number only in the same outward view, according to at least one kind of Calvinism, involves in the end the same error; this namely, that Christ did not really assume our human nature at all in his Mediatorial life, but only stood on the outside of it and wrought a work beyond it, in the semblance of our common manhood, for the benefit of such as are brought individually and separately to avail themselves of his grace. This is to make Christ a mere instrument or means for the accomplishment of an end which is supposed to have its existence and necessity under a wholly different form; than which it is hard to conceive of anything more derogatory to the true dignity of his person. Gloriously above all this is the form under which he appears in the Gospel. He is himself there the Salvation of the world, not simply as a true mediation between heaven and earth is reached in his own life separately considered, but as this life also, on its human side, is found to be the comprehension in truth of Man's life as a whole, the actual lifting up of our fallen nature from the ruins of the fall, and its full investiture with all the glory and honor for which it was originally formed. Humanity, as a single universal fact, is redeemed in Christ, truly and really, without regard to other men, any farther than as they are made to partake of this redemption by being brought into living union with his person.

Archdeacon Wilberforce puts himself to some trouble, to show that there is such a thing as *human nature* objectively considered, in distinction from the mere thought or notion of a certain multitude of men regarded as having a common character.

> The objection brought against the actual existence of human nature is, that being only an abstraction formed by ourselves from a variety of examples, there can be no *real thing* intended by it; to give it actual existence is supposed to be the error of the Realists, who attributed an objective existence to those universal conceptions, which were only the creatures of their own minds. Hence, the reality of human nature, as a thing existing in the external world, is denied, because to assert reality for the idea of it in our own minds, would be contrary to the theory of Nominalism, which prevails in logic. But this is to abuse the principles of Nominalism on one side, as the opposite principle of Realism has been abused on the other. That many objects can be united by our classing them under a common idea, does not give them any real objective union; but neither does it take that union away, provided that by other means it can be shown to exist. Yet this is the argument of those who, on principles of Nominalism, deny the objective existence of human nature. They pass over the distinction between such classifications as men make for themselves by an inward act of reasoning, and such as have been provided in the external world by God's Providence. The one are only our own internal acts; the other have an external existence. The error of the Realists was

encouraged, according to Archbishop Whately, by observation of those organized beings, which are bound together by the unalterable laws of nature. That in these cases there existed a real, though unknown bond, which maintained the perpetuity of the class, led men to attribute an objective existence to their own abstractions. But if no real connexion had united these external objects, the sight of them would not have led any one astray. When we class together philosophers or physicians, we bestow a common name upon those who are associated by their dispositions or employments. There is no connexion between them, distinct from the thoughts and actions to which the individuals described choose to addict themselves. There is a real similarity in their doings, supposing the class to be happily designated; but it is a similarity only, and at their will they may cease to resemble one another. It would be a vicious Realism, therefore, to assert the existence of an objective connexion among these parties, because we can embrace them under a common idea; but it would be an equally vicious Nominalism to deny an objective reality, where an inherent law prevents the possibility of such rearrangement, and confines individuals to the peculiar classes to which they severally belong. The first would be to claim for our own mind the power of making its inward ideas into external realities; the second would be to deny the existence of external realities, because we have not the power of making them. We have no right, therefore, to deny the existence of a common nature in those who are derived from a common origin; whose union does not depend upon their voluntary combination, and cannot be dissolved by their own will.—P. 48–50.

With some, all this may be set down as so much mysticism and transcendentalism. They go on the common sense view, which turns the world into a sand-heap. We agree however fully with Stahl,[8] as quoted *p. 52*.

> The more superficial a man is, the more isolated will every thing seem to him, for on the surface all things are detached. In mankind, in the nation, even in the family, he will see nothing but individuals, whose actions are altogether distinct. The deeper a man is, the more conscious will he be of those inward principles of unity, which radiate from the centre. Even the love of our neighbour is only a deep feeling of this unity, for a man does

8. [Friedrich Julius Stahl (1802–61), German philosopher and jurist who taught at Erlangen, Würzburg, and Berlin, where he was part of the high-church evangelical "Gerlach circle" and an influence on Philip Schaff. See Nichols, *Romanticism*, 64–83.]

not love those to whom he does not perceive and feel himself bound. Unless sin could come through one, and through one atonement, there could be no understanding the command to love our neighbour.

Such a collective existence in the case of our race, not the aggregate of its individual lives but the underlying substance in which all these are one, is everywhere assumed in the Bible as a fact entering into the whole history of religion. The race starts in Adam. It is recapitulated again, or gathered into a new centre and head, in Christ.[9]

This is the fact declared, when it is stated that Christ took man's nature: it implies the reality of a common humanity, and His perfect and entire entrance into its ranks. Thus did He assume a common relation to all mankind. This is why the existence of human nature is a thing too precious to be surrendered to the subtilties of logic, because upon its existence depends that real manhood of Christ which renders Him a co-partner with ourselves. And upon the reality of this fact is built that peculiar connexion between God and man, which is expressed by the term Mediation. It looks to an actual alteration in the condition of mankind, through the admission of a member into its ranks, in whom and through whom it attained an unprecedented elevation. Unless we discern this real impulse which was bestowed upon humanity, the doctrines of Atonement and Sanctification, though confessed in words, become a mere empty phraseology. That "God was in Christ reconciling the world unto Himself," implies an actual acceptance of the children of men, on account of the merits of one of their race; as well as an actual change in the race itself through the entrance of its nobler associate. The work of man's redemption and renewal is a real work, performed by real agents. It is not only that the Almighty was pleased to save appearances, if we may so express it, by conceding to the representations of a third party, what He did not choose otherwise to yield or to acknowledge (as Queen Philippa prevailed over her harsher husband, Edward); but Christ's Incarnation was a step in the mighty purposes of the Most High, whereby all the relations of heaven and earth were truly affected. To deny, as is done by Bishop Hampden, "that we may attribute to God any change of purpose towards man by what Christ has done," would be to resolve this real series of acts into a mere technical juggle.

---

9. [Nevin's language here evokes the recapitulation theory of Irenaeus. See General Introduction.]

> But to the reality of this work, the existence of that common nature is indispensable, whereby "as the children were partakers of flesh and blood, He Himself took part of the same." Else, how would the perfect assumption of humanity have consisted with His retaining that divine personality, which it was impossible that He should surrender? Since it was no new person which He took, it can only have been the substratum in which personality has its existence. For His Incarnation was not the "conversion of Godhead into flesh, but the taking of the manhood into God." Or how could He have entered into a common relation to mankind in general, unless there had existed a common nature as the medium of union? This nature, which exists only in individual persons, He took for the earthly clothing of that divine personality, in which He must ever continue to exist.—P. 55–56

The universalness of Christ's life does not consist in the assumption of the lives of all men into himself, but in the assumption of that living law or power, which, whether in Adam alone or in all his posterity, forms at once the entire fact of Humanity, irrespectively of the particular human existences in which it may appear. These are always a finite *All*; the other is a boundless *Whole*; two conceptions, which are as wide as the poles apart. Christ, in this view, is organically and historically joined, we say, with the universal life of Man, as its only true ground, and centre, and end. The child, it is sometimes said, is father to the man; inasmuch as the first foreshadows the coming of the second; although, in truth, that which is second here, when we look to inward reality, must be counted first. It is only in full manhood that the tendencies and powers of childhood are made complete at last, through the actualization of their own sense. Analogous with this is the relation of our general human nature to the coming of Christ. It looks to this event from the beginning, as the proper completion of its own meaning; and in such view may be regarded as opening the way for it in the order of time; although as regards the order of actual being the mystery of the incarnation must be considered first, as that which lies at the ground of our whole human life in its true form. Christ thus is the deepest sense, the most urgent want of humanity, as it stood previously to his coming, or still stands where his coming is not owned. The universal constitution of the world looks towards him as its necessary centre. All the lines of history converge towards him as their necessary end. He is the "desire of all nations," the dream of the Gentile as well as the hope of the

Jew. If there be any wholeness in our human life whatever, any rational unity in history, and if the incarnation be at the same time a real putting on of humanity, a real entrance of the Word into the process of our existence, and not a mere Gnostic vision or Hindoo avatar instead, how is it possible to escape the truth of this proposition? Those who seek to cut off Christ from all organic, inwardly historical connection with the world in its natural form, as though his credit must be endangered by his being made to appear a true *birth* of mankind, the veritable *seed* of the woman which should bruise the serpent's head, know not surely what they are about. As an abstraction, in no natural union with the life of Man universally considered, how could his pretensions ever be legitimated or made sure?

[THE INCARNATE HUMANITY OF CHRIST AS THE MEDIUM OF SALVATION]

III. The *Humanity* of Christ is the repository and medium of salvation for the rest of mankind. The truth of this proposition flows inevitably from what has been already said of his Mediatorial nature, and its relation to the universal or whole life of the race. Christ has redeemed the world, or the nature of Man as fallen in Adam, by so taking it into union with his own higher nature as to deliver it from the curse and power of sin, meeting the usurpation of this false principle with firm resistance from the start, triumphantly repelling its assaults, and in the end leading captivity captive by carrying his man's nature itself, through the portals of the resurrection, to the right hand of God in glory. The process holds primarily altogether in his own person. In his own person, however, as the Second Adam, the bearer and root of our whole human nature, now lifted thus into actual union with the Godhead, and so made answerable to its true idea, as we find this labored after by its whole creation from the beginning. Thus perfected, he has become the captain and author of salvation for others, Heb. ii. 10, v. 9; and through his glorification, the way is open for the Spirit to carry forward the work of Christianity in the hearts and lives of his people, John vii. 39. Such is the order of the Creed; Manhood glorified first in Christ, then by the Spirit in the Church, which is his Body, the true fulness or completion of his life in the world. The beginning of the new creation then, the primary and original seat of our actual salvation, is the *Human Nature* of Christ;

for this is the real ground and foundation of the universal conception of Humanity in its highest form, the central orb through relation to which only this can ever change its character from darkness to light. True, the power of Christ to save rests in his person as a whole and falls back specially on his Divinity; it is the life of the Word which becomes the light of men. But it is this Life still only as it "comes into the world," and appears clothed in the habiliments of *flesh*; and so we say the Flesh of Christ, or the Word which has come in the Flesh, and not the Word out of the Flesh, is the door or fountain by which the whole grace of the Gospel comes to its revelation in the world. Starting in eternity, it finds here the only outlet for its entrance into time. As an accomplished fact upon the earth, in living union with Man's life, and not a mere decree or thought in the mind of God, the entire Gospel begins in Christ, and proclaims itself as something to be seen, felt and handled (1 John i. 1–3) in the power of his true Man's nature. Whatever of power there is in Christ for salvation, it is lodged for the use of the world in his Flesh, as the necessary medium of communication with the human race, the one only bond of his brotherhood and fellowship with those he came to save. To imagine any saving union possible with Christ apart from his Flesh, aside from that glorified Humanity by which only his Mediation stands in real contact with the world, is virtually to deny the mystery of the Incarnation itself by making it to be of no meaning or force. It is the mark of Antichrist, we are told [in] 1 John iv. 1–3, to place the coming of Christ *out of the flesh*.

This idea meets us everywhere in the ancient Church. "The mixture of Christ's bodily substance with ours," says Hooker, "is a thing which the ancient Fathers disclaim. Yet the mixture of his flesh with ours they speak of, to signify what our very bodies through mystical conjunction receive from that vital efficiency which we know to be his; and from bodily mixtures they borrow divers similitudes rather to declare the truth, than the manner of coherence between his sacred and the sanctified bodies of saints," *Eccl. Pol.* V. 56, 9.[10] So with the Church

---

10. [Richard Hooker (1553/4–1600) was by common consent the greatest theologian of the Church of England, and he played a decisive role in setting the tone for future Anglican theology in his *Lawes of Ecclesiasticall Politie* (1593–1600), a defense of the government and liturgy of the Elizabethan establishment against Puritan attacks. Although a firm opponent of Puritan excesses, Hooker stood broadly within the Reformed tradition, resembling some of his continental Reformed contemporaries in his retrieval of medieval scholasticism and interest in the doctrine of law. Hooker's

of the Reformation, the sense of the same mystery, as set forth in the Creed, wrought powerfully on all sides. Luther's faith and zeal here are well known. Calvin, in his way, is no less strong. With all his opposition to a crass Capernaitic view of Christ's flesh,[11] he insists continually on the great idea that the Christian Salvation starts from the Humanity of Christ in a real way, and that we participate in it only by entering really into the new order of life of which this is the fountain and seat. His language on this subject has been pronounced mystical and unmeaning; but it is so only for those who have become estranged in their thinking from the true and proper sense of the mystery with which it is concerned.[12] In itself it is uncommonly lucid and clear, and admirably answerable to the form under which the subject meets us in the Gospel. The Word is the source of life; to recover man, this has entered into union with his nature by becoming flesh; *in which form alone* Christ is now the author of salvation to all who believe in his name.

> The very flesh in which he dwells is made to be vivific for us, that we may be nourished by it to immortality. I am the living head, he says, which came down from heaven; and the bread that I will give is my flesh, which I will give for the life of the world (John vi. 48, 51). In these words he teaches, not simply that he is Life, as the Everlasting Word descending to us from heaven, but that

---

Christology and eucharistic theology have much in common with those of Calvin. For an interesting study of Hooker's complex relationship to Calvin, see David Neelands, "The Use and Abuse of John Calvin in Richard Hooker's Defense of the English Church, *Perichoresis* 10 (2012): 3–22.]

11. [An epithet applied to those affirming a local, physical presence of Christ's body and blood in the Eucharist, the term *Capernaitic* derives from Christ's Capernaum discourse on the bread of life in John 6:22–59 and the misunderstanding of it by some Jews in the audience.]

12. [Calvin's conception of realistic sacramental union with the incarnate humanity of Christ was subjected to severe criticism by a number of nineteenth-century Reformed federal theologians, most notably Charles Hodge and William Cunningham. See Nevin and Hodge, *Coena Mystica*. In Britain, William Cunningham, *The Reformers*, 240, wrote: "We have no fault to find with the substance of Calvin's statements in regard to the sacraments in general, or with respect to baptism; but we cannot deny that he made an effort to bring out something like a real influence exerted by Christ's human nature upon the souls of believers, in connection with the dispensation of the Lord's Supper—an effort which, of course, was altogether unsuccessful, and resulted only in what was about as unintelligible as Luther's consubstantiation. This is, perhaps, the greatest blot in the history of Calvin's labours as a public instructor." On these debates, see Evans, *Imputation and Impartation*, 223–227; Cunnington, "Calvin's Doctrine of the Lord's Supper."

in thus descending he has infused this virtue also into the flesh with which he clothed himself, in order that life might flow over to us from it continually.[13]

Calvin speaks, of course, not of Christ's flesh materially considered, but of his real human nature, through which only it is possible for this same nature in other men to be raised from death to immortality. The vivification of humanity begins in *his* manhood. His flesh is truly thus *life-giving,* not as the origin of life, but as its necessary and only medium for our fallen race. The manhood of Christ is the reservoir or depositary in which all grace dwells first (the Spirit without measure), for the use of the whole world besides. "*Christi Caro instar fontis est divitis et inexhausti, quae vitam a divinitate in scipsam scaturientem ad nos transfundit.*"[14] It would be hard to express the same thought more beautifully, or more clearly, in the same compass.

"Any school," Wilberforce tells us, "which denies the humanity of the Mediator to be the medium through which divine gifts are communicated to mankind (and such is the error of all Rationalists) is theologically allied either to Nestorianism or to Deism, in which Nestorianism results."—*P.*154.

[THE BENEFITS OF CHRIST CANNOT BE SEPARATED FROM HIS PERSON]

IV. The participation of Christ's benefits, in the case of his people, turns on a *real communication with his human nature* in the way of life. This is the idea of the "mystical union," which all evangelical christians are willing to admit; while they are too prone however, in many cases, to make it of no force by carefully excluding from it the very mystery from which it draws its name. Because it holds only through the Spirit or Holy Ghost, they will have it that it is altogether spiritual, in such sense as to have no relation to Christ's manhood whatever; pleasing themselves, under this name, with the fancy of a life union with Christ in his divine nature, as though this only might be regarded as the fountain of such high grace in a separate and independent view. But this would imply the very consequence from which they pretend to shrink, without reason,

---

13. [Calvin, *Institutes*, IV.17.8.]

14. [Trans. "the flesh of Christ is like a rich and inexhaustible fountain that pours into us the life springing forth from the Godhead into itself." Calvin, *Institutes*, IV.17.9.]

on the other side, an actual partnership of believers with Christ in the awful mystery of the incarnation itself; for what less is it, if every single christian be joined in the way of real life directly with the Word absolutely taken, and not with the Word only *through* the flesh which it has already assumed in Christ. There is but one Incarnation *(one* Mediator between God and man, the *Man* Christ Jesus), but he is of such constitution, carrying our universal nature in his person, that all men may be joined with God also through him by receiving into themselves the power of his life. This implies in their case no hypostatical union with Deity, no new theanthropy in the sense of Christ's person; but just the reverse, since the only medium of union with the Godhead is Christ's manhood, as something that must necessarily intervene between the Divine Word and all other men.

The law of such relation is by no means confined to this case, but finds analogies and exemplifications throughout the universal economy of our life; only we have here the absolute truth of what in all other cases comes before us relatively only and in the way of remote approximation. Men never stand separately, and with fully co-ordinate personality, in the union of society; but always in organic groups that cluster around some common centre, and find support in this as the bond or medium of communion with a life that is higher and more general than their own. Every *hero,* in the broad sense of this word as denoting one who is qualified and called to go before others in the mission of Humanity, stands actually between those who follow him and the superior world from which this mission proceeds; he is for them the real organ of its revelation; and through him, at the same time, they gain strength and power to master it as their own, although without such central support this would be wholly impossible. In this case the personality of every follower is completed, like that of the leader himself, by union with the higher life which fills his soul; but this only, let it be observed, not by taking his place as the primary organ of such communication, but by acknowledging rather his central position, and leaning upon him as the necessary medium of the benefit thus gained. Such is the universal law of our life. And what does it teach? Clearly this, that our human personality can never become absolutely complete, till it comes to be joined in a real way at last with the life of God itself, which alone needs no ground beyond itself; and that such conjunction requires (not a general deification of the race as the Hegelians dream[15]), but a Central Person, in whom Divinity may be actually united with Humanity, and who may be qualified thus to communicate the fellowship of the "divine nature" mediately to all who trust in his name. This is just the mystery which meets us in Christ. In him alone among men dwelleth the fulness of the Godhead bodily; and we are complete in him, as the head of all principality and power (Col. ii. 9, 10). Christ's person is the bearer of our persons. We are complete, as regards intelligence and will, only as we live not by and from ourselves, but through faith in him, as the centre and end of our whole existence.

There is no room then to object to the idea of the mystical union as now stated, that it implies a continuation of the hypostatical mystery over into the life of the Church. The ancients do indeed speak at times of our being deified in Christ, as sharers of his nature; but they mean not by this, of course, any deification aside from Christ himself.[16] Through the medium of his humanity, it is the privilege of believers, without losing their own separate individuality, to fall in on the fulness of his person as the true central ground of their own lives, and thus to participate in the grace of which he alone is the repository and fountain, and which is accessible to others only as they are joined to him in this way.

> The union of mankind with Christ is not a mere imitation—the following a good model—the fixing our thoughts upon One who has shown in the clearest manner, how God may be served and men benefitted—it is an actual and real union, whereby all renewed men are joined to the second, as they were by nature

---

15. [G. W. F. Hegel (1770–1831) affirmed that the idea of divine-human unity must come to expression in a single individual. See his *Lectures on the Philosophy of Religion*, 452–458. The left-wing Hegelian David Friedrich Strauss (1808–74; whom Nevin may have had in mind here), however, replaced the notion of a particular incarnation with the assertion that the unity of divine and human takes place in the human race as a whole. Strauss, *Life of Jesus*. 780, writes: "This is the key to the whole of Christology, that, as subject of the predicate which the church assigns to Christ, we place, instead of an individual, an idea; but an idea which has an existence in reality, not in the mind only, like that of Kant. In an individual, a God-man, the properties and functions which the church ascribes to Christ contradict themselves; in the idea of the race they perfectly agree. Humanity is the union of the two natures—God become man, the infinite manifesting itself in the finite, and the finite spirit remembering its infinitude."]

16. [See, e.g., Athanasius, "On the Incarnation," 107–8: "For he was made man that we might be made God; and he manifested himself by a body that we might receive the idea of the unseen Father; and he endured the insolence of men that we might inherit immortality."]

to the first Adam. This union cannot be explained away in the kingdom of grace, unless it is first explained away in the kingdom of nature. Unless "sin standeth" only "in the following of Adam, as the Pelagians do vainly talk" holiness must involve not the mere imitation, but the putting on, of the man Christ Jesus. By what means the relation is maintained, is in each case an inexplicable mystery; the natural alliance which takes place by descent being not less wonderful than that supernatural alliance which is brought by the regeneration. To analyze the law of family affinity is as much beyond our powers, as to understand how "as many as have been baptized into Christ, have put on Christ." The first is that transmission of the nature of our common ancestor which causes us to be what we are; the second is that spiritual Presence of the manhood of Christ, by union with which we become what it is given to us to be. The one of these is in Holy Writ set against the other, "for as in Adam all die, even so in Christ shall all be made alive." As the one has its influence both on soul and body, so has the other.—P. 229–230.

[CHRIST NOW PRESENT IN HIS HUMANITY AS WELL AS HIS DEITY]

V. As the medium of such living grace the *Human Nature* of Christ, and not simply his Divinity, is actively *present* always in the world. The Mediation of the Saviour, since his Ascension, holds towards God in his Intercession, while towards man it may be summed up in the single term of his *Presence*. This was his great promise, on going away: "I will not leave you comfortless, I will come to you."[17] The promise plainly regards the restoration of what was about to be lost, the presence of our Lord, namely, according to his human nature; only under a new and higher form. In this view, it is a spiritual and not a carnal presence; a presence accomplished not in the way of place and material contact, but by the intervention of the Holy Ghost; while however, as regards efficiency and force, it is not for this reason less real, but rather we may say more real than it could be in any other way. On this subject take the following extract.

> Neither is this Presence merely that He is an object to men's thoughts, as Jerusalem was present to David from the land of Hermon. The reality of Christ's presence depends on Himself,

---

17. [John 14:18.]

not on those He visits. It had been an unmeaning promise to His disciples, that His Presence should return to them through the power of the Holy Ghost, had He designed only that through the exertion of their mental faculties they might think of Him who was departed. In this sense how is Christ present more than any Angel in light? We are speaking not of men's actings towards Him, but of His actings towards them, since His Ascension into heaven. As He acts *for* them by intercession with the Father, so are we assured that He acts *towards* them by His Presence with power. What is meant by His office as Mediator, unless through the annexation of the Divine to the Human nature, the latter has in itself some real influence independently of our thoughts? And this is the answer to the assertion, that since a body must either be present in any place, or not present in it, therefore Christ's body must either be materially present in the consecrated elements at the Holy Eucharist, or that we must allow that His Presence is merely figurative. Doubtless it were so, if His body were a human body alone; but because He is Divine also, it has likewise that other medium of communication which does not depend upon local contiguity, but upon spiritual power. Even the sun, because its influence is more wide than its actual limits, while it is at rest in its place in the sky, is present upon earth by the effluence of its beams. But that Sacred Manhood which was created for the service of the Mediator between God and men, in which were stored up the "treasures of wisdom and knowledge," that from it "grace and truth" might flow forth into the whole race of man, has a real medium of presence through the Deity which is joined to it: so that it can be in all places and with all persons—not figuratively, but in truth—not by material contact, but by spiritual power. And while its material place is among the armies of heaven, its spiritual presence is among the inhabitants of the earth, when, how, and wheresoever is pleasing to its own gracious will.—*P.* 221–222.

The Mediation of Christ, then, is not something past and gone, nor yet something that lies wholly beyond the actual order of the world, with which we are to communicate only in the way of memory or thought; it lives always, with perennial force, in the actual Presence of Christ's Manhood in the world. This thought reigns throughout the Epistle to the Hebrews. His *one* sacrifice is once for all, not as a transient event, but as an ever during fact in the power of his indissoluble Mediatorial life. His intercession is going forward *now* in real union with the daily course of the world, as truly as the sun enters into the same economy from day to day.

> Our Lord's acts of Mediation towards men, as well as his Intercession with the Father, are a present fact in the world of life, and not a mere fictitious representation. To be accounted the bond of union between different natures is to discharge the part of a Mediator; to be their real bond of union is to *be* one. Christ did not undertake this office as a legal fiction; he is the "One Mediator," because in him Godhead and Manhood were really united. And if he has still the same character, it must be in fact and not in name—Godhead and Manhood must still be connected by his actual intervention. While he is one by nature with the Everlasting Father, he must be one also by grace with those inferior members to whom he has vouchsafed to become Head, that he might be the "Saviour of the body." For the gifts of grace do not become less necessary through the lapse of ages: every generation of Adam's children has equal need of that external principle of supernatural renewal, which flows from the humanity of the Son of God into his brethren. The acts of his human must continue therefore as certainly as those of his Divine nature, and consequently that Presence of his manhood, whereby "we are members of his body, of his flesh and of his bones."—If Christ be still Mediator, there must be the perpetual presence among us of his man's nature, whereby he who is one with the Father becomes one also with his brethren.—P. 238–239.

To separate the action of Christ in the world now from his man's nature, and to refer it only to his Divinity, is just to say that he no longer *acts* as a man at all, in other words *is* no longer really man, as in the days of humiliation.

> And what then must be thought of that body which suffered on the Cross, but that either it was a created substance, invested by God's mercy with more than mortal power and goodness, that it might accomplish that sacrifice which was needed for mankind—which is the Arian hypothesis; or else that the Father of all displayed himself in man's form by a transient and occasional manifestation, and (that work being over) has again retreated into the abyss of his unapproachable Godhead—which is the more subtle heresy of Sabellius.[18]

18. [Wilberforce, *Doctrine of the Incarnation*, 239–40. Arianism denied the deity, or *homoousios*, of the Son, and was condemned at the Councils of Nicea (AD 325) and Constantinople (AD 381). Sabellianism or modalism was the ancient heresy which

The Incarnation cannot be held as real if the being and working of the Mediator in the world be not apprehended as the presence in it still of the living power of his true Human Life. This should be plain to all.

[CHRIST PRESENT IN THE WORLD THROUGH THE CHURCH]

VI. Christ's Presence in the world is in and by his mystical body, the *Church*. As a real human presence, carrying in itself the power of a new life for the race in general, it is no abstraction or object of thought merely, but a glorious living Reality, continuously at work, in an organic and historical way, in the world's constitution. Christ communicates himself to his people, and lives in them, not by isolated favor in each case, but collectively. His relation is at once to the whole family of the redeemed, and single christians accordingly have part in him only as they are comprehended at the same time in this whole. To be in Christ, is to be a member also necessarily of his mystical body, as dependence on a natural centre implies comprehension in the universal orb or sphere holding in the same relation. This is the idea of the Church. It comes from within and not from without. It grows out of the mystery of the Incarnation, apprehended as an abiding fact, and comes before us in the Creed accordingly, not as a notion or speculation merely, but as an article of *faith*. So too it has its attributes from itself and not from abroad. It is by an *a priori* necessity, it claims to be one, holy, and catholic. To deny or question this necessity is at once a heresy, which strikes in the end at the very foundation of Christianity itself. "That the Church is one body results from organization, not from enactment," much less from human policy and agreement. "Neither is the profession of the Church's unity the mere admission of an external appearance, but the belief of an inward verity"[19]; facts may or may not accord with it at any given time, but it still remains unalterably certain in its own nature, until Christianity itself be found to be false. Christ's *one* mediation, as related to men and reaching them through his glorified humanity, always present for this purpose in the world by the Spirit, is carried forward through the intervention of the Church, his Body Mystical, the fulness of what he is otherwise by distinction only in its single members. The Church, in this view, does indeed stand between

held that there is but one divine person who assumes different roles.]

19. [Wilberforce, *Doctrine of the Incarnation*, 247.]

Christ and the believer, but only as the body of a living man is between one of his limbs and the living soul by which it is quickened and moved.

[IDEA OF THE CHURCH IMPLIES VISIBLE ORGANIZATION, WORSHIP, CLERGY, LITURGY, AND SACRAMENTS]

VII. The idea of the Church, as thus standing between Christ and single christians, implies of necessity visible *organization,* common *worship,* a regular public *ministry* and *ritual,* and to crown all especially grace-bearing *sacraments.* To question this is to give up to the same extent the sense of Christ's Mediation as a perennial fact; now and always taking effect upon the economy of the world through the Church as his mystical body. Let it be felt that the Incarnation is a mystery not simply past, and not simply beyond the world, but at this time in full force for the world, carrying in itself the whole value of Christ's sacrifice and resurrection as an undying "Once For All"—the true conception of the Mediatorial Supremacy, as the real headship of Christ's manhood over all in behalf of the Church and for its salvation; let it be felt, at the same time, that this mystery touches men in and by the Church, which itself is made to challenge their faith for this reason as something supernatural and divine; and it becomes at once impossible to resist the feeling that the "powers of the world to come" are actually at hand in its functions and services, with the same objective reality that attaches to the powers of nature under their own form and in their own place. To see no more in the ministry and offices of the Church, in this view, than a power of mere outward declaration and testimony, such as we might have in any secular school, betrays a rationalistic habit of mind, which only needs to be set free from the indolence of uninquiring tradition that it may be led to deny altogether that Christ has ever or at all come in the flesh.

It sounds well, and falls in well too with *natural* reason and popular sense, to magnify what is called spiritual religion as compared with a religion of outward ordinances and forms, and to make Christianity turn on individual exercises transacted directly with God in the sanctuary of the mind, aside from all regard to sacramental or other intervening media. But it ought to be borne in mind that Christianity is not mere nature, and that to throw ourselves here on simply natural conceptions and impulses is in truth to substitute for it another theory of religion altogether. It comes to us as a system of redemption and salvation by a Mediator. It is throughout a mediatorial economy. The grace it reveals is offered in Christ, not from a different quarter. It is offered in Christ again as Man; by the intervention of his flesh; through the door of his humanity, in the most real and true way. Under this form it is not something to be thought of merely, with however much devotion, on the part of the believer; the case calls for an actual participation in its life and power. Christianity is so constituted accordingly as to be dependent always on means, which have for their object this union and communion in a real way. Salvation in these circumstances is still a personal and inward or spiritual interest; *mere* relations and forms save no man; but it is made to hang on the medium of a special economy in the Church as the mystical body of Christ, serving to bind the subject in living union with his natural flesh or humanity; which is embraced and rested upon by faith accordingly for this purpose. Not to acknowledge this, but to insist on having access to God independently of any such special economy, by virtue simply of the relation in which all souls stand to him as the "Father of the spirits of all flesh," is not Christianity but Rationalism under the christian name.

> To assert the truth of Christ's presence—the reality of that union which binds the whole mystic body of His Church to the manhood of the Incarnate Word—is to maintain the reality of His Mediation, and the absolute necessity of that bond by which heaven and earth are united. For it is a necessary result of the cardinal truth of the Christian system—the truth, *i. e.*, that all gifts and blessings are introduced into our race through the intervention of that nobler member, who connects it with the Almighty. And herein is the Christian scheme of Mediation opposed to that theory of Rationalism, which rests upon the capacities of nature. The principle of Rationalism is, that man's improvement may be effected through those gifts which God bestowed upon him by creation, inasmuch as sufficient means of intercourse with the Supreme Spirit were provided by the law of his nature. Whereas the Church deals with man as a fallen race, whose original means of intercourse with God have been obstructed, and which needs a new and supernatural channel for the entrance of heavenly gifts. And this channel has been provided through the Man Jesus Christ. In His person did Godhead enter manhood, that through this one perfect type of humanity, it might "leaven the whole lump." Thus does the law of grace supersede the law of nature. If man had never

fallen, to inherit the nature of the first Adam had been a sufficient means of communion with God. But because the natural means of communication have been cut off, that supernatural union is requisite which we obtain by participating the nature of the second Adam. Now, it is for the diffusion of this renewed and renewing manhood, that those media have been provided, whereby the Son of Man communicates Himself to His brethren. All the ordinances of the Church, its hallowed things, places, and persons—its worship and sacraments—are a series of instruments whereby the sanctified manhood of the Mediator diffuses itself as a life-giving seed through the mass of humanity. Thus does He continue to effect that work through His man's nature, which He avowed to be the very object of His earthly being: "For their sakes I sanctify Myself, that they also might be sanctified through the truth." And for this office are external media as requisite, as were body and limbs to the truth of His human being. As He could not be a man without that substantial existence which revealed Him to the senses of mankind, so He could not be the Head of the Body Mystical, without the use of those actual media of intercourse, whereby He unites His living members to Himself.—P. 249-251.

There is no opposition between Christ and the Church, or between individual piety on the one hand and sacramental grace on the other; but just the reverse. Christ becomes full only in and by the Church; and personal experience is made solid and real, only as it rests on grace offered and appropriated from abroad.

> To maintain that the outward means of grace, whereby we are united to the manhood of Christ, are not less necessary than those emotions of our own which have their seat within, is not to put the Church instead of Christ, but to protest against men's putting themselves in the place of their Redeemer. To speak of inward seriousness as necessary, is only to testify the truth of each man's separate responsibility; but to speak of it as superseding outward means, is to do away with the office of the "One Mediator." The individual life of each man's spirit, as opposed to the carelessness of a thoughtless walk, is the very treading down of Satan under our feet; but to contrast it with the value of Gospel ordinances, is to deny Christ, to depose him from his office of a Mediator, and to set up idols of intercession in our own hearts.—P. 270.

With this view of the significance of christian worship generally, the peculiar sense and power of the holy sacraments are apprehended as a necessary consequence, the rejection of which must do violence to the whole Creed. They are "not only badges of profession" but also "certain sure witnesses and effectual signs of grace."[20] They exhibit objectively the realities they represent. So we have it asserted very distinctly in the New Testament. Such was the faith, from the beginning, of the universal ancient Church. Such also is the original Protestant faith, as held by the two great confessions, Lutheran and Reformed on the Continent, as well as by the Episcopal Church in England. Our author closes his view of this subject with the following paragraph, which we commend specially to the consideration of all *evangelical* skeptics, who make a merit of sneering at the idea of sacramental grace, whether in the case of baptism or in the case of the Lord's supper, as though it were the same thing with the "*opus operatum*"[21] itself in the worst sense of Rome.

> It remains only to recall that which has been already stated, as applicable to both the sacred ordinances which have been considered. The reality of both of them has been maintained: it has been affirmed that Baptism is not merely the expression of a charitable hope; that the Lord's supper is not a bare act of pious recollection. The essential principle of each of them has been shown to be union with the perfect manhood of Christ Our Lord. Let it be remembered only in conclusion, that to deny their reality is to assail the great principle of the Mediation of Christ. For the Doctrine of Our Lord's Mediation does not rest only on the Divine power of Christ, as a partaker in the nature of self-existent Godhead; it implies also that, by associating man's nature to His own, He has made created being the channel of His gifts. Now, as the media through which these gifts are dispensed to His brethren; as the ramifications, whereby His Divine nature distributes itself on the right hand and the left, these two Sacraments go together—their importance is equal—their effect alike—and to disparage them is to derogate from that principle of action which the wisdom of God has seen fitting to adopt.

20. [A quotation from Art. 25 of the Thirty-Nine Articles of the Church of England.]

21. [Trans. "the work performed," a term associated with the *ex opere operato* ("by the work performed") conception of sacramental efficacy. According to Roman Catholicism, the performance of a sacramental action communicates saving grace except in such cases as the recipient presents a spiritual obstacle or "impediment" to that reception.]

Every attempt to explain them away, every contrivance for extenuating the real import of what they effect, is a virtual detracting from the reality of that objective and actual influence, which Christ the Mediator is pleased to exert. Its tendency is to resolve His actions into a metaphor, and His existence into a figure of speech. His specific and personal agency as the Eternal Son, who in the fulness of time conjoined Himself to man's nature for the recovery of a fallen race, is merged in the general action of that ultimate Spirit, whom none but Atheists professedly reject. For the real objection against the Sacramental system does not arise from any deficiency in its Scriptural authority, which has been shown to be ample, but from the abstract improbability that external ordinances can be the means of obtaining internal gifts. Now, this improbability rests on the circumstance that the *natural* mean of connexion with God is the intercourse of mind with mind, and consequently that the intercourse through Sacraments is *supernatural.* The connexion with God, *i. e.* which man received by creation, and which Rationalism affirms to be sufficient for his wants, is more compatible with men's natural position, than that new system of Mediation which has been revealed in the Gospel. But let the doctrine of mediation be admitted, and it ceases to be an argument against the Sacramental system that it does not accord with that scheme of nature, which the Gospel professes to supersede. And the Rationalistic argument against these means of grace, is of equal avail against that whole scheme of Mediation upon which they are dependent. If the natural intercourse of mind with the unembodied mind of the Creator supersedes the necessity of Sacramental ordinances, does it not supersede equally the humanity of Christ? If man has still that immediate communion with God, of which Scripture affirms that the Fall deprived him, what need is there of a Mediator between them? Thus does the objection mount up from earth to heaven—from Christ feeding men below through Sacraments, to Christ mediating above by His Atonement and Intercession. For "if we have told you earthly things, and ye believe not, how shall ye believe if we tell you of heavenly things?" If the Sacraments be thus emptied of their meaning, it is because the present actings of Christ as the Son of Man are not appreciated; and the purposes of His Incarnation are forgotten. And this forgetfulness again may be traced to unbelief in that real diversity of Persons in the Blessed Trinity, in which all creaturely existence has its ultimate root. Thus does a practical Sabellianism respecting Christ's Person coincide with that Rationalistic theory, by which the reality of His Sacraments is disputed. And their surrender is fatal to the true Doctrine concerning Himself, even as the true doctrine of His nature sets the importance of these instruments in a proper light.—P. 346–348.

Archdeacon Wilberforce is of course a High Churchman,[22] and his whole work is designed to be in favor of Episcopacy as established in the Church of England. At the same time however, he knows very well how to distinguish between the form of Christianity in this view and its true interior life and substance. There are two sorts of high churchmanship. One starts with a certain system of outward order, as though it were the first thing, the main thing, settled and sure by divine appointment in and of itself, and made to inclose thus externally all truth besides as its necessary boundary and hedge. In this way, too often, we find Episcopalians laying all stress on their favorite system, as of divine right and obligation apart from its own contents altogether; as though Christ had been pleased to provide by such an outward institute in the first place for the safe-keeping of his truth and grace, and it were possible now by simply historical evidence, or in the way of ecclesiastical tradition, to make sure of this always as the necessary condition and medium of reaching what lies beyond. Episcopacy, with this way of thinking, is taken to be the primary interest of Christianity, an indispensable stepping stone at least, or threshhold, to all that constitutes its interior sanctuary. It is to be accepted first as the necessary inclosure and platform of the Church. Vast pains are taken to establish its claims in this abstract view, on grounds and reasons that have nothing to do whatever with the inward constitution of Christianity itself; and vast affectation follows, in

---

22. As noted earlier, Wilberforce was an important figure in the Oxford Movement in Anglicanism. The earlier Anglican "High Church" party designated those Anglican churchmen after the Restoration (1660) who were committed to divine-right episcopacy and elaborate liturgical ceremony, less interested in fellowship with continental Reformed churches, and generally staunchly supportive of the monarchy. While sharing the patristic interests of the earlier High Churchmen, the Oxford Movement associated especially with John Henry Newman, Hurrell Froude, John Keble, E. B. Pusey, W. G. Ward, and Isaac Williams (in addition to Wilberforce), was also motivated by deep concerns regarding governmental intrusions into the life of the church, a desire to defend traditional doctrine over against Enlightenment-influenced liberalism, and concerns about the subjectivity of evangelicalism. Their strong clericalism and doctrine of apostolic succession represented something of a break from the older High Church tradition (see Sykes, *Old Priest and New Presbyter* for a good history of High Churchism and the Oxford Movement's relation to it). For treatments of the relationship of the Oxford Movement and Mercersburg, see Nichols, *Romanticism in American Theology*; and Littlejohn, *Mercersburg Theology*, 88–123.

parading such merely outward prerogative as a substitute for everything else, and a sufficient apology for overlooking and despising all earnest thought under a different form. This is pedantry, and so far as it prevails tends naturally and of right to bring the Church theory, with which it is associated, into discredit and contempt. But there is another way of holding and asserting the claims of the Church. It is to begin, not with the circumference of Christianity, but with its centre, the mystery of the Incarnation as we find it set forth in the Creed, and so to proceed to what flows from this for faith by necessary consequence and derivation. In this way the *idea* of the Church comes first; and what its actualization may be found to comprehend subsequently is apprehended and accepted in such living inward connection, not as something external to the proper christian life, but as the very form and expression of this life itself. It is in this order that Archdeacon Wilberforce presses the claims of his subject. He sees the danger of substituting the Church as a formal system in place of its Head, and finds the only right security against it in the sense of their inward relation to each other as it springs from the christological fact itself.

> So long as the Church is regarded as an external system, based on certain laws and administered by certain leaders, it can never fail to enlist a measure of that party spirit which belongs to man's nature, and thus to draw away attention from the holy purposes for which it was instituted. The only safeguard against this danger is the due subordination of its external frame-work to its internal principle; and the constant recognition that its life depends, not on the gifts of government, but on the gifts of grace. If the essence of the Church's existence be that certain men have a right to rule, and teach, and minister, whether they be chosen by the free voice of the congregation, imposed by government, or delegated by the Apostles, there is such large opening for cabal and dispute, that love and peace and Christ's presence will soon be lost in the din of party strife. The Presbyterian platform offers as good footing to the spirit of partisanship as the system of Episcopacy; and the Pilgrim Fathers of Massachusetts were as ready to persecute as Boniface or Hildebrand.[23] But let the essence of the Church's existence be felt to be Christ's

---

23. [Two medieval Popes who sought to extend the power and authority of the papacy. Hildebrand (Pope Gregory VII, 1073–1085) is best known for his humiliation of German emperor Henry IV at Canossa. Boniface VIII (1294–1303) issued the Bull "Unam Sanctam," which proclaimed universal papal sovereignty.]

presence—let it be remembered that His manhood is the true seed of the renewed race, and that through spiritual presence it bestows its life-giving power on all the members of His mystic body—let every other question be dependent upon these—let them take their place, as of subordinate importance, and as merely contributing to this great result—and what room is there for discord between Christ and the Church, when the Church is Christ Himself manifest in His mystic body? "For no man ever yet hated his own flesh, but nourisheth and cherisheth it, even as the Lord the Church." The theorist may be unvisited by the sun's warmth while he discusses its nature, or the poet while he describes its brilliancy; but how can we loose sight of his glorious beams by going forth to walk in the sunshine? And so long as this Divine principle is kept fully in view, it can hardly fail to soften and elevate those whom it influences. So that if the harshness of party-spirit be not cured, it may at least be abated.—P. 268–269.

High Churchmanship, in this view, is everywhere entitled to respect. The Creed owns it in distinct terms, and it meets us from all sides in the faith of the early Church; to such an extent indeed that without it there can be no power to understand or appreciate this faith fully in any direction. The inferences which some feel authorised to draw from the idea of the Church in favor of Episcopacy, or farther still in favor of Romanism, are another thing. We have nothing to do with them here, in the way either of favor or opposition. They are at all events not what can be considered first and foremost, either as to evidence or importance, in this great question of the Church. There is a wide field of theological truth beyond them, and back of them in the order of faith, which it is quite possible for us to enter and possess intelligently before coming to their settlement and resolution at all, and which indeed we *must* possess with such preliminary occupation, in order to be at all qualified for this secondary work. For what is a man's faith worth in Episcopacy for instance, as a divine institution, who has not in the first place, as the root and ground of this a firm faith in the idea of "one, holy, catholic Church" as necessarily flowing from the idea of the Incarnation, and whose mind is not led from this centre out to the other supposed necessary peripheral interest of Christianity, rather than in the reverse order from what is the circumference merely to the centre? And so on the other hand what is a man's rejection of Episcopacy worth, or his rejection we may add of Romanism itself, if it be not supported from behind by any true acknowledgment of the mystery of Christ and his Church, as we find it proclaimed from the beginning in the universal christian Creed? A controversy about Episcopacy between those who have not in their minds the sense of the Church as a divine mystery in the world, under the form of an *a priori* necessity starting in Christ, must ever be a waste of words more or less, on both sides. As such an *a priori* object of faith, then, the idea of the Church offers wide scope for contemplation and inquiry back of this controversy altogether; and in the circumstances of the present time especially, it is of the utmost account that this preliminary ground should be properly regarded and fairly taken into use under its separate character, without embarrassment from any such relations, which after all are of secondary rather than primary account, and even if taken in this view to be absolutely necessary, must still be held to be so in the way of derivation only from what goes before and not as its ground and cause. We like this book of Wilberforce on this account. However much it may aim to serve the cause of Episcopacy, that is not made the front at all of its argument. It starts with the beginning, and not with what at best should be counted only as the end. It plants itself on deeper ground, and throws itself back on the substance of Christianity as something older than Episcopacy, something that must of necessity underlie all its pretensions and claims if they are to be found in any case worthy of respect. It is an argument for the idea of the Church, as founded on the glorious mystery of the Word made flesh and its perennial force in the world, which all who call themselves christians are bound to own and confess, whether such acknowledgment be felt to involve Episcopal conclusions or not. We may resist these, if it seem fit, and yet allow in full the force of what is involved in the idea of the Church as their supposed foundation. The inquiry here offered to our view, though in Episcopal hands, belongs in truth to Christianity in its most comprehensive character and form; all denominations, that have not formally or informally renounced the Apostles' Creed, may meet here as on common territory; for the question of the Church, as an article of faith, is one in which they are all alike bound to take interest, whatever may be their difference of view in regard to the outward form and order of the Church.

  This deserves to be well understood and considered. The question with which we are first concerned in this great case has nothing to do directly with Episcopacy or any other outward constitution as such; it regards the being of the Church, and its primary attributes, as an article of faith, in the sense of the ancient world. Is the faith of the ancient Church on this subject, as we find it uttered among the supposed fundamentals of the Creed, to be accepted as something still in force, or is it to be rejected as an empty dream and idle superstition? Is the Holy Catholic Church, as it once filled the soul of Christendom, a "figment," or is it still as in the beginning a divine fact on which men are required to lean as the very "pillar and ground of the truth" that starts in Christ? The misery of much of our modern religion is not just that it differs from this or that particular form of church life, which may be supposed to have distinguished the early Church, but that the Church itself is taken to be a wholly different thing. It is notorious that the Church, according to the universal sense of the ancient christian world, was held to be the repository actually of superhuman powers among men, the medium not metaphorically but really and truly of grace lodged in its very constitution, from Christ its head, for the salvation of sinners. In such view only was it regarded as an object of *faith*. It was identified with the idea of Christ's Mediation, as a perennial fact in the world. The foundation of the christian life was held to be objectively at hand in its institutions, for the use of all who might lay hold of it by their means. Prophetical and priestly functions were felt to belong to it, as the Body of Christ. Its sacraments were regarded as vehicles, by the Spirit, of the high and solemn realities they were framed to represent. The idea of a mystical supernatural force going along with the activity of the Church, was acknowledged in every sort of way on all sides. All this is notorious; and it is just as notorious, on the other hand, that for much of our modern evangelical thinking this whole conception of the Church has gone entirely out of authority and date. A painful chasm holds here between much of our modern religious habit and the religion of the ancient Church. It becomes accordingly a great question, and the *first* we need to settle in relation to ecclesiastical order (without clear and full answer to which it is vain to agitate any other questions in regard to it), whether in this issue the ancient faith, or the modern variation now noticed, is to be taken as the true sense of Christianity. Church or No-church; that is the point which first requires to be settled. And to do this, it is not necessary to proceed empirically, or in other words to be ruled by mere outward observation. Back of all *Lo here,* or *Lo there,* in this case is the necessary constitution of the Church itself as an article, not of sight, but of faith. That starts in Christ; and according to the view we have of Christ, in the end, will be and must be our view also of the Church. We come to the true conception of the Church through a true and sound Christology (as in the Creed), and in no other way.

J. W. N.

Article 4
"Liebner's Christology"

(by John W. Nevin)

EDITOR'S INTRODUCTION (TO JOHN W. NEVIN, "LIEBNER'S CHRISTOLOGY" AND "CUR DEUS HOMO")

The next two works included in this volume address the question of whether the Incarnation would have occurred even apart from the fall of humanity into sin. Though the question had been raised before at various times in the history of Christian theology, it was posed with particular insistence and acuity by the idealist-influenced theologians of the early and mid-nineteenth century. According to this way of thinking, the Incarnation is the goal of creation, as the always-implicit idea of divine-human unity is explicitly realized in the God-man. Thus the Incarnation is often seen as a metaphysical necessity rather than a contingent response to human sin.

Nevin addressed this larger question in three extended reviews published in the *Mercersburg Review* in 1850–51. In the first, Nevin reviewed Richard C. Trench's *Christ the Desire of All Nations* (1846), in which the Anglican theologian affirmed that the Incarnation was more than just a response to sin.[1] In the second and third (printed here) Nevin presented lengthy reviews of a volume by Lutheran mediating theologian Karl Liebner and of two articles by Julius Müller critiquing Liebner. In both of these texts Nevin summarizes the German works in question but without taking a definitive stance on the question.

1. John W. Nevin, "Trench's Lectures," *Mercersburg Review* 2 (1850): 604–619.

Early on in his synopsis of Liebner Nevin notes Liebner's dependence upon the progressive theology and philosophy of the period. While acknowledging problems in Hegel and Schleiermacher, Liebner sought to build on their contributions, and with Hegel he recognized a close relationship between theology and philosophy.

Liebner's work, Nevin notes, was divided into two parts—the first explicating the christological problem and the second offering a solution. According to Liebner, the christological problem is dominated by three factors with attending issues: Divinity (and the problem of "pantheism"), Humanity (and a "false doctrine" of human freedom or "ethicism"), and Nature (with the problem of "a false naturalism"). Moreover, two key questions have been posed with special urgency in the contemporary period—the necessity of the Incarnation even apart from sin, and proper framing of Christological doctrine so as to avoid both pantheism and dualism. With regard to the latter, Liebner argued that the Reformed tradition tended to emphasize the humanity of Christ and so tended toward Ebionitism, while Lutherans emphasized the divine and so approached Docetism. As a solution to such problems, Liebner offers an "ethical theanthropology" in which the unity of the God-man is seen in terms of a Trinitarian ethical focus on divine love. Interestingly, at this point Nevin comments on the difficulty of Liebner's book: "it is by no means as clear in its style and form as the richness of its content deserves."

Not surprisingly in light of Nevin's interest in the rationale for the Incarnation, much more space is given to the question of whether the Incarnation would have occurred even without the Fall. This is developed especially in connection with Nevin's summary of two 1850 articles by Liebner in response to criticisms of Liebner's book by the Erlangen Lutheran theologian Gottfried Thomasius. Here Nevin explains how Liebner cleverly sets up a dilemma in order to argue for the necessity of the Incarnation apart from sin. In brief, Liebner contends that, properly understood, the Christian doctrine of sin requires the necessity of the Incarnation apart from sin. Both human freedom and the "unity of God's plan for the world must be preserved." The goal of creation (i.e., the divine plan) is "full communion with God himself," which is realized absolutely and unconditionally in the God-man, Jesus Christ. But if the Incarnation is not the center of God's plan but rather a contingent response to the fact of sin, then nothing is absolute and unconditional about God's plan. Liebner then argues that two responses to this difficulty in turn create more problems. First, there is the solution of Calvin with his emphasis on divine sovereignty, but this is to make God the author of sin. Second, there is the approach of idealist anthropology such as that of Hegel, which makes sin an "anthropological necessity," which in turn compromises human freedom. The only way to evade these consequences, it is argued, is "the theory which includes in the conception of creation itself the idea of the Incarnation, as the last necessary sense of the world."

In the second of the two articles, "Cur Deus Homo," Nevin examines the arguments of Julius Müller in response to Liebner. Müller, of course, was the great champion in nineteenth-century Germany of the hamartiological argument for the Incarnation—the Incarnation as a response to human sin. In his summary of the first installment of the article, which deals with the relevant historical theology, Nevin notes that Müller finds "traces" of the non-hamartiological argument in the church fathers (especially in Irenaeus), but that the issue was more generally discussed in the medieval period. Anselm and Aquinas reject it, but it was adopted by some, especially Duns Scotus and his followers, and Müller sees the argument as meshing well with the "Pelagianizing anthropology" (with its minimizing of the problem of sin) of the nominalists. Moving on the Reformation, the non-hamartiological approach was decidedly rejected by the magisterial Reformers, though it found advocates among the Socinians. Thus Müller contends that the non-hamartiological argument for the Incarnation "fell everywhere with the older Protestant theology into the reproach of heterodoxy."

Müller then turns to more recent speculative approaches of "pantheistic systems," and his rejection of Hegel's "logico-metaphysical blasphemy" is firm—Hegel makes the Incarnation "the completion of God himself," thus compromising both divine freedom and immutability. If Christian orthodoxy is to be maintained, Müller argues, the question of the necessity of the Incarnation must be decided on anthropological grounds. In this context Müller also argues that Schleiermacher is not an example of the non-hamartiological argument in that "the system of Schleiermacher implies that the mystery of the Incarnation is conditioned by the imperfection of the world as it now stands."

Müller's second installment examines whether the non-hamartiological argument for the Incarnation can be sustained in a way consistent with the existence and freedom of a holy and personal God, the goodness of the original creation, the Fall as the result of human decision, and the necessity of Christ's atoning death. Here Müller repeatedly suggests that the idealist Christology undercuts both the seriousness of sin and the need for redemption. Needless to say, the argumentation is dense, but Nevin's summary of it is reasonably clear. Müller begins with a summary of the biblical materials, noting that Scripture consistently presents the Incarnation as a response to human sin and that the problem of overcoming sin involves "the whole view that is taken of Christ's person." Even participation in Christ's life through faith, repentance and the work of the Holy Spirit involves "the supposition of sin."

But if one assumes that the Incarnation is not a response to sin, what is the point of it? If one argues that the human race has no telos and unity apart from Christ, if Christ is indeed the head of the race in a concrete sense, then the relationship of Christ to the church is applied to all of humanity, and no redemption from sin is really necessary. Also, on this way of thinking the death of Christ is no more than a demonstration of divine love and the propitiatory dimension of the atonement is lost.

Müller also explores other entailments and problems of this idealist Christology. Suggestions that Christ is the head of the race lead to universalism, the position that all are ultimately saved, and attempts to make the Incarnation a necessity grounded in the structure of humanity end up collapsing the ethical into the metaphysical. Furthermore, why should this ideal of divine-human unity be expressed in a single individual rather than in the human race as a whole? Keying off the idealist preoccupation with consciousness, Müller also notes that on these grounds the Incarnation cannot be restricted to humanity but should also include angels and other conscious beings, thus leading to "a succession of personal unions."

Finally, Müller addresses these issues by distinguishing between the role of the Logos before the Fall and the work of the Incarnate Christ and the Holy Spirit after the Fall. Prior to the Fall into sin, the preincarnate Logos was "bearer of the Divine idea of the world, which comes to its focus in the conception of created personality," but with the Incarnation and the need for redemption through the atoning work of Christ, "all true elevation, in the case of man, springs from the Holy Ghost."

"Liebner's Christology"[1]

Christologie oder die christologische Einheit des dogmatischen Systems, dargestellt von Dr. Th. A. Liebner. Erste Abtheilung. Göttingen, 1849.[2]

This volume is introductory to a system of dogmatic theology, which it is proposed to construct from the christological principle. The author assumes that the true heart and core of all religion is the great fact of the incarnation, the living person of Jesus Christ, through which the life of man is restored to harmony with the life of God, and so redeemed at the same time from the curse of sin. To understand and represent properly then the glorious economy of the gospel, it is necessary to start with the idea of the incarnation, to make this the principle or foundation of the whole scheme of thought it is found to embrace. The doctrine of man on the one side, a sound and sufficient anthropology, and the doctrine of God on the other, a sound and sufficient theology, must both be conditioned in the nature of the case by a sound and sufficient christology, rightly setting forth the conjunction of these two forms of existence in the awful and mysterious personality of Him who is at once both God and man. If this conjunction be at all natural and normal, and not a fantastical abnormity violently forced on the nature of man to serve a purpose, it must follow that the full sense of humanity is brought out finally only by its means; and that this becomes fully intelligible of course only as the survey of its parts and proportions is made to begin here, and is carried forward subsequently with continual reference throughout to the fundamental or principal fact,

1. [Originally printed in the *Mercersburg Review* 3:1 (January 1851): 55–73.]
2. [Th. A. Liebner, *Christologie oder die christologische Einheit des dogmatischen Systems* (Göttingen: Vandenhoeck and Ruprecht, 1849); trans. *Christology, or the Christological Unity of the Dogmatic System*.]

which is found to underlie thus at last the universal truth of man's life. And so we may say in like manner, that if the mystery of the incarnation be in real harmony with the nature of God, and not a mere docetic vision on this side as pretended by the old Gnostics, it must follow that the full sense of God's relations to the world—not of course his essential being, but the manifestation of what he is in the process of creation—is also reached at last only in this mystery, and becomes fully intelligible accordingly only by its means. That must ever be a false and mutilated view of the nature and history of man, which rests not on a firm apprehension of his true relationship to God, as this comes out ultimately in the constitution of the Messiah. That must ever be a false and defective view of the nature of God, as related to the world, which stops short of the theanthropy, as the true and necessary central sun that serves to irradiate and complete all other revelations by which he is known.

[GERMAN IDEALIST INFLUENCES]

The system of theology to which we are here introduced by Dr. Liebner,[3] is governed throughout, he tells us in his preface, by the thought that Christianity is the absolutely last and highest form of religion, the system of all systems, the full and real end which all other forms of religion only reach after in the way of nisus or endeavor, and in which alone accordingly is to be found their proper truth.

> This thought is one that is necessary to the Church, and one cannot partake truly in her life without coming under its power. For just as certainly as the Church carries in herself the consciousness of possessing the highest and richest life, even the holy and blessed life of Christ himself, and feels that the one thing needful is the full communication of this life through all the veins of the body of which he is the head; the very same assurance must she have intellectually, that she is in possession also of the absolutely highest, all comprehending and all controlling truth, or of the entire fulness of reason, to which all that

---

3. [Karl Theodor Albert Liebner (1806–71), Lutheran theologian who studied at Leipzig and Berlin (where he sat under Schleiermacher and Hegel) before teaching at Göttingen, Kiel, and Leipzig. His writings sought to integrate the christocentrism of Schleiermacher, the speculative idealism of Schelling and Hegel, and the ethical concerns of Kant.]

> may claim to be reason besides can stand related at best but as a fragmentary preparation.[4]

Such assurance in substance the mind of the Church has carried in itself, through all ages; and we find it frequently proclaimed, in terms more or less clear, by the proper representatives of this mind in the sphere of theology. Still the assurance is not itself a clear insight at once into the construction of the fact which is thus firmly felt to be true; and we need not be surprised to find accordingly, that down to our own day the problem of a full and adequate representation of the central significance of the mystery now in view as being the real heart of all truth and reason besides, has never yet been brought to a conclusively round and complete solution. This however affects not at all the certainty of the fact itself, nor the reasonableness of the assurance by which it is held to be true; it belongs only to theology as a science, to the theory of Christianity as the understanding seeks to master it in harmony with the knowledge it has of the world in other forms. At the same time theology as a science is itself part of the living process of Christianity, and needs continually to be advanced more and more in its own direction in order that this last may come to its full and perfect triumph. The theory of religion here, and the power of it in the actual world, what it is for the understanding and what it is for the life, must go forward hand in hand together; and it is vain to look for the last universal success of the gospel under the second form, without a corresponding progress also under the first. It may be regarded then as a fact of much meaning and promise, that at the present time a new and more than usually active interest seems to be drawn on all sides towards the christological question, as one which is felt to lie at the root of all right theology, and to condition by its proper scientific solution the prosperity of all other christian interests. Liebner admits that much of the speculation which has been turned in this direction in modern times has been actuated by a spirit more or less hostile to the true sense of Christianity, and that even in its best character it has labored too generally under a false philosophical tendency, which has served materially to mar and vitiate its results. But this, he thinks, forms no reason for calling in question its significance, or refusing to make account of its endeavors and deeds. There is no good reason why the thinking even of Schelling or Hegel,

---

4. [Liebner, *Christologie*, vii.]

though in no fellowship whatever with the christian faith as such, should not be acknowledged as of real weight for theological science, where it has to do even in a false and insufficient way with interests and relations which it is the province of such science to set in proper light. Theology can never be dissociated from the general progress of human thought. This moves with organic necessity in one direction always, as a single whole; and it belongs to theology to move along with it, as the only power that can furnish a right response in the end to the vast and mighty interrogations with which it forms still the inmost burden of the age. In this way however it is quite possible that the impulse to such new openings of thought, rendered necessary by the previous course of theology, may spring not immediately from the sphere of faith as such, but from the sphere of philosophy, and in this form seem even to carry an unfriendly aspect towards christian truth. Still in such case if the thought thus set in motion belong in truth to the actual philosophy of the world's mind at the time, it may be entitled notwithstanding to the earnest regard of those who take an interest in theology, as an indirect contribution at least to its service and benefit. Such merit beyond all doubt must be allowed to the later German philosophy, in its relations to the better German theology of the present time. It has served to force attention and inquiry towards questions which had not been rightly answered before, and to which a full and fair answer is now required as the last sense of Protestantism and the innermost want of the age. Both Schelling and Hegel have struck in this way on more than one chord of thought, demanding and deserving universal regard in the bosom of the Church.[5] In particular, the christological ideas of this last are very significant and full of instruction; for however monstrous they are in their own nature, and contrary to the truth as it is in Christ, they still bear striking testimony to the great central fact of the gospel by seeking to solve in another way the problem with which it is concerned; whilst they make it necessary for christian science to go more deeply into its own truth, for the very purpose of bringing out clearly its superiority to the false speculation so plausibly presented in its place. And if we are bound to allow this much in favor even of Hegel, who will pretend that

---

5. [Friedrich Wilhelm Joseph von Schelling (1775–1854), idealist philosopher and contemporary of Hegel. He viewed sin as an ontological necessity, a fall away from the One into particularity. On the idealist Christology of Schelling and Hegel see General Introduction.]

a still greater regard is not due to the professedly christian speculation of Schleiermacher, and others following more or less his theological influence, as occupied with the same profound and deeply interesting themes? It comes to nothing, that such deep earnest thinkers are found to deviate here and there from the established orthodoxy of their time, that they are chargeable with great and serious errors, and that it is not safe to follow them blindly in their theological speculations. We know well enough that it is not safe to follow any leader blindly, whether he be an original thinker or an easy traditionist who never thinks at all. That is not the question. We know too that Schleiermacher has fallen into serious errors.[6] But what then? Was he not still the theological Origen[7] of his age? And is there no use whatever to be made of the activity of such a mind long and earnestly exercised on the deepest problems of religion, no profit at all to be expected or sought from his keen dialectical intelligence and vast armory of learning turned towards their solution? Alas for the misery of such a judgment as that. Say that he has answered all questions wrong; yet who will pretend that he had not tact enough at least to know what questions actually lie in the way of theology as it now stands, and most loudly crave an answer at its hands; or that the endeavors of such a man to find the right answer deserve not the regard of inferior (even though more orthodox) minds, as instructive hints and helps at least by which they may be profitably guided towards something better? This only rational view of the matter we find taken by Dr. Liebner. He is not satisfied by any means with the christological efforts thus far of the modern time. He is not satisfied with the theory of Schleiermacher, nor with the light in which the subject is exhibited by

---

6. [On the Christology of Schleiermacher see General Introduction. Though F. D. E. Schleiermacher (1768–1834) is often today regarded as the "father of liberal Protestant theology," in the mid-nineteenth century he was viewed by many as a bridge from rationalism to orthodoxy. For example, Philip Schaff, *Germany; Its Universities, Theology, and Religion*, 320, remarked, "Schleiermacher first built a bridge over the abyss that divides the dismal swamp of skepticism from the sunny hills of faith, and kindled again the flame of religion and of the Christian consciousness."]

7. [The analogy is apt. Origen of Alexandria (c. 185–c. 254) was a remarkable theologian, exegete and textual scholar, whose Platonizing theology had a powerful and yet diverse impact on subsequent Eastern theology. His influence is often evident on multiple sides of later controversies.]

Göschel,[8] Dorner, Fischer, Martensen,[9] or Lange.[10] But he is not led by this to undervalue and slight the labors of such men on this field; much less to set down the field itself as a waste of metaphysical thorns and briars, unworthy of culture. On the contrary, he finds in these manifold efforts of the great minds of the age, all looking in the same direction and grappling with the same profound questions, full evidence and proof that the general problem with which they are concerned lies in truth near the inmost heart of theology at the present time, and that all the interests of religion as well as those of philosophy call loudly from all sides for its right solution. However speculation may have failed, in one case or in fifty, to bring out such a solution in full satisfactory form, it has lost none of its force for this reason as constantly accumulating testimony to the reality, weight, and importance of the fact it seeks to explain; whilst it must be taken also to determine conclusively at least some of the points and positions that are necessarily comprehended in the subject as a whole.

Professor Liebner's work, now before us, falls into two parts. The first is occupied, at some length, with "the posture of the christological problem at the present time." The second, making up the main portion of the volume, is devoted to its general "theological and theanthropological solution."[11]

[THE CHRISTOLOGICAL PROBLEM]

In setting forth the present posture of the problem, the author directs attention, in the first place, to "the ecclesiastical and theological crisis

---

8. [Karl Friedrich Göschel (1784–1861), German speculative philosopher and legal scholar. See his *Beiträge zur speculativen Philosophie von Gott und dem Meschen und dem Gottmenschen* (Berlin, 1838).]

9. [Hans Lassen Martensen (1808–84), Danish Lutheran bishop and theologian. Especially influenced by Hegel, he sought to combine speculative theology with mystical interests. Martensen's synthesis of Hegelian philosophy and Christianity prompted Søren Kierkegaard's *Attack upon Christendom*. On Martensen, see Curtis L. Thompson, *Between Hegel and Kierkegaard: Hans L. Martensen's Philosophy of Religion*.]

10. [Johann Peter Lange (1802–1884), German biblical scholar and theologian. He taught at Zurich (where he filled the position to which D. F. Strauss had been briefly appointed) and Bonn, and wrote an extended response to Strauss's *Leben Jesu* (his *Life of the Lord Jesus Christ*). For a contemporary account of Lange, see Philip Schaff, *Germany*, 381–88.]

11. [Liebner, *Christologie*, xvi.]

now passing, and its relation to christology in general"; and then brings into view what may be termed the "church and school christology as it now stands."[12]

Theology, he tells us, may no longer shun the consciousness that the Church is at this time passing, by as great a crisis as she has ever heretofore met, into a *new* order or state. The new in this case at the same time can come in properly only as it is actively produced or brought to pass by waking mind. No mere tradition will now serve the purposes either of life or thought. The new must be positive in its nature; it is not found therefore in any merely negative or destructional tendencies of the age; these must be regarded at best but as signs of its approach, or solicitations inviting its presence. Still with such positive character, it must not be absolutely new, but a new stadium simply of the life of the Church, in strict historical connection with all that has gone before. No unhistorical movement in this form can ever deserve confidence. All real progress is conditioned indispensably by a full acquaintance with the previous course of theology and a just reverence for its authority, as well as by a proper regard to the speculations of philosophy in the widest view.

> Without a thoroughly comprehensive sense of this vast ecclesiastical back-ground, without a home familiarity with the past theoretical development of the Church, without having faithfully accompanied her sufferings, conflicts and victories in the working out of her principle thus far, so as with true churchly sensorium to live them into himself as part of his own experience, no man can possibly lay hand anywhere with real effect to the theological work demanded by the wants of the present time; nay, no such man can have any right inwardly to lay his hand upon the work at all. It is impossible indeed to denounce too severely the folly, which pretends to bring help in such a case from abroad only, from any and every quarter as it may happen, and not from the bosom of the Church herself.[13]

This however implies no disregard for the resources of philosophy, but requires rather that they should be diligently studied and turned to account. These are part of the material which true christian theology is bound to take up and employ for its own higher ends.

12. [Ibid., xvii.]
13. [Ibid., 3.]

> It is truly astonishing to see, in a retrospective view of the modern philosophy generally, how all its great heroes, partly without their own knowledge or will, have been forced to render even *positive* service to the christian cause; as it would seem indeed universally that no great man, no genius, can be born and baptized in the church without paying tribute in this way to Jesus Christ.[14]

It is high time, in this view, that theology should learn to look on all spheres of thought as rightfully tributary to herself, and show her proper supremacy, neither by blindly following nor by blindly rejecting what they offer, but by appropriating out of it in a free way all that is capable of being assimilated to her own more powerful life.

> The theology which refuses to give heed to the mighty questions that have been set in motion by the modern philosophy in its vast wrestlings and endeavors called forth by the progress of the Protestant epoch (questions indeed which only the full sense of Christianity can ever answer—but this also only as wrought out into the form of science), must be set down as utterly unequal to the necessities of the age.[15]

All other theological questions belonging to the general crisis of the age, in the judgment of the author, gather themselves up centrally at last in the sphere of *christology*. Here ultimately are to be referred all difficulties and perplexities in the science of religion, and to this deep ground we must trace them in order to their proper answer. The first grand question accordingly regards the possibility of a christology at all in the sense of the Church, in some such form as this: Has the Church in the substance of her christology, that is, in that with which she must stand or fall, in the fundamental idea of the true and real God-man, rightly apprehended the nature of christianity?

To be of any real force, this idea must be more of course than an empty sound or notion. It must be such as to meet and master fairly the contradiction with which it is encountered in all the factors that enter into its constitution. This has become more profound and comprehensive in our age than ever before. The factors in question are Divinity, Humanity, and Nature. On the ground of these severally we find pantheism, a false doctrine of freedom, and a false naturalism arrayed

14. [Ibid., 5.]
15. [Ibid., 6.]

in opposition to the whole truth and possibility of the christological mystery. To retain then firm hold of her own faith here, the Church is required and urged to dissolve the force of these most hard and difficult issues, by setting them in full harmony with the sense of this faith, as the true ground where they all come finally to their proper meaning. In other words, to surmount scientifically the false tendencies of the age in the several directions now noticed, she is called, as the processor of all truth, not to ignore them with suicidal self-will, but to satisfy rather in a true way the problems they are seeking to satisfy in a false way. Over against the antichristian pantheism, ethicism, and naturalism of the age, the case needs a truly christian pantheism, in the sense of Paul's ὁ θεὸς τὰ πάντα ἐν πᾶσιν,[16] a corresponding scheme of humanity, and a corresponding theory of nature also, in which full justice may be shown to each sphere, while all come together in Christ. All this the possibility of a christology in the sense of the Bible, the realness of the great fact of the incarnation as it has entered into the faith of the christian world through all ages, is felt to involve; and the leading thought of the time accordingly, in the estimation of our author, that which more than any other stirs the inmost depths of its life, is the verification of the full sense of the evangelical mystery through all its length and breadth just in this form.

> Christianity demands practical acknowledgment as being in truth the absolute religion, and seeks to show itself as the highest divine-human power in the world, at once commensurate in force with its universal life and being; a power, in which consequently not merely all truly ideal forces are hid, all treasures of wisdom and knowledge in the form of thought, but that contains also the real force by which the world is carried forward toward its absolute end, the full harmony namely of nature, humanity and God—humanity the organ of God and nature the organ of man in such divine union—the kingdom of God fully come; a power, through which thus what appears in the creation of nature and man in the first place under a potential form only, is made to receive the principle of its absolute actualization. Such a system of the absolute involves necessarily for its centre the *christological,* Christ the God-man, as the personal medium and support of the whole. The absolute religion and Christ the *personal absolute religion,* imply one another; or the

---

16. [From 1 Cor 15:28, "God may be all in all" (NRSV).]

> first without the second would be a periphery without centre. In its more general form, as referring to religion at large—humanity the organ of God and nature the organ of man in union with God—the thought before us is most immediately accessible, and has been frequently brought out, or at least felt after, in the latest times, even in the sphere of philosophy; its necessary relation to the christological idea is less seen, although it is an oversight of endless consequence to think of constructing the other without this. To understand both now in their true inward union, and so to set forth the whole world-moving and world-mastering power of Christianity in the strictest sense, forms at present the highest problem of theology, in the solution of which it must find its deepest self-satisfaction, the key for the right understanding of the age, and that intellectual energy which is needed for all true church activity.— P. 10–11.

Two great points, according to Professor Liebner, are pressing towards new determination particularly at this time, in the movement of the christological question. The first is "the idea of a theanthropology independently even of sin and its removal; or the idea that God's incarnation stands in an original essential and necessary relation to humanity, and so to the creation itself, as their completion." The second is "the necessity of advancing, on purely christian trinitarian grounds, and in a way that may surmount all pantheistic and Ebionitic views, to such a unity of the true divine-human person, or of the person in which God has really become man, as may leave *no longer possible* the consequence of a personal disruption of Christ, a dualism involving finally again the going asunder of the two factors, the divine and the human, in his constitution."[17]

"We are well aware," the author remarks,

> that the first point, in its most general expression, the *necessity of God's taking flesh*,[18] is still offensive to many, in view especially of its having of late been urged mainly in a form at variance with full christian truth. It has been made to carry in part a pantheistic aspect, or avoiding this it has been directed against the right view of the Trinity, or it has been used finally to corrupt the true doctrine of man's nature as regards sin. All these

---

17. [Ibid., 12.]

18. "Of course under the supposition of the creation. *Freedom* characterises God's relation *as a whole* to the world; it is a system of *free* divine revelation, which includes the stages of creation and the incarnation."

phases however have no necessary connection with it, but are only a foreign garment thrown around it, or misrepresentations we may say through which the idea but seeks to reach its own right sense. In its proper truth, which was not unknown to the earlier ages of the Church, it belongs rather to genuine christian theism, standing in full agreement with the doctrines of the Trinity, of the creation, and of human freedom, and not at all presupposing the original necessity or inevitableness of sin; nay, in this true character it claims to enter essentially and indispensably into the very ground of Christianity itself, and to be in the heart of it the actual key of the universal christian system, with which only its absolute fulness can ever be fairly unlocked and revealed.—In virtue of the absolute unity of the eternal purpose of divine love toward the world revealed in Christ, the idea of the world in the christian theistic sense, humanity appears christologically determined and disposed even in its creation itself, forms in its essence and teleology an organic system which has its principle in Christ, the *God-man.* Christ, even without regard to sin, which belongs not to the conception of man, is the divine-human head of humanity as his σῶμα ["body"]; both are inseparably joined together as *one* organism. God creates humanity to communicate himself to it as his personal creature, in the way of real revelation, and so to bring it into perfect communion with himself, which is the full idea of religion. This real self-manifestation, self-communication of God to humanity, completes itself and finds perfect satisfaction only in the central and universal *person of the God-man,* which forms accordingly the completion of humanity itself. The purely hamartological, soteriological method of accounting for the incarnation (man sinned and *therefore* only the eternal Son of God became man), which in the age of the Reformation acquired prominence over against a corrupt theory of sin and salvation, is no longer sufficient. To overcome the more general and deeper contradictions of the latest times, it is necessary to descend more profoundly into the ground of Christianity itself, which is just the idea we have here in view; so that this, in union with the true doctrine of salvation, alone contains full power over these contradictions, and in particular the most perfect and decisive corrective for antichristian pantheism, which well knew what it was about in seeking to master the idea in its own sense.—Sin served only to bring in this modification, which indeed reaches far and deep, that now Christ appears also as a Redeemer and Sacrifice. This sense moreover, when we eye it sharply, will be found to lie in the whole depth of the Protestant (scriptural) principle of justification by faith. For since Christ not only takes away sin or guilt, but also positively gives his whole personal divine-human being to mankind for their positive righteousness (humanity in every case righteous before God only through faith in Christ, its theanthropic head, all loved only in One, on whom rests the absolute favor of the Father), this doctrine requires under such positive aspect the acknowledgment, that aside from sin even Christ is the all fulfilling principle of perfection for the race. The whole weight of the soteriological view (which in the scriptures of course stands out in strong relief), loses nothing in fact by this idea, but rather finds in it first its proper support; nay, even the *O felix culpa Adami*,[19] retains its truth; since that is certainly a new depth of love, which challenged by sin engages the God-man to humble himself even to the curse of death for the redemption of the nature he was pleased to assume.—P. 13–14.

The second point named, we are told, the bringing of the hypostatical mystery to a fully satisfactory expression between the opposing rocks of pantheism and dualism, has never yet been successfully gained; although it has always been kept steadily in view by the faith of the Church, as an object never to be surrendered to any pressure whether to the one side or the other. This is confirmed by proper historical notices, including particularly the later efforts both of the Lutheran and of the Reformed theology on this field. Account is taken also in a general way of the several speculative christological schemes which have been brought forward in modem times (by Göschel and others), which are found to fall short of what is here required, though offering indispensable elements for the right solution finally of its problem.

"That this right solution of the problem here in view," says Schoeberlein,[20] "still remains a desideratum for theology, is not to be denied. Neither the Lutheran[21] nor the Reformed sections of the Church

---

19. [Trans. "O happy fault of Adam," an expression associated with the theodicy that God allows sin as a means to a greater good.]

20. In an able review of Liebner's work, approving and endorsing its main substance, in *Reuter's Repertorium* for September 1850. [Ludwig Friedrich Schöberlein (1813–81), Lutheran theologian who taught at Erlangen, Heidelberg, and Göttingen.]

21. It is hardly necessary to remark, that the reference here is to Lutheranism in the sense which the word carries in Germany, where account is still made of the old distinction between the two great Protestant confessions as something real and important. As for our so called "*American* Lutheranism," which is another thing altogether, a system after the order of Melchisedeck, without genealogy or history, or like the men of Cadmus purely autochthonic—it is not to be supposed, of course, that it should

have yet been able to represent the *theanthropic person in true unity.* The onesided theological leaning of the Lutheran confession has run into docetic consequences, while the onesided anthropological tendency of the Reformed has run into Ebionitic consequences. And the middle view of Zinzendorf and others,[22] which supposes a transformation or letting down of the Logos into a holy man, is no real medium, but leaves the christian consciousness unsatisfied in both directions."[23]

[THE CHRISTOLOGICAL SOLUTION]

The second part of the work, as already said, is devoted to what the author holds to be the right method of answering the great questions which he thus brings into view. The God-man, he tells us, must be *ethically* apprehended. All other modes of representation give only a transient show of knowledge.

> A truly *ethical theanthropology*, if it can be reached, must furnish the key at the same time for all christological questions. Such an ethical theanthropology presupposes inwardly however, not only a truly ethical anthropology, but most of all a theology also, in which as the culmination of ethics is given the possibility of a true confluence of the anthropological and the theological in the theanthropological. *All this forms then the proper christian system.* Christianity is essentially an ethical system. The ideas of moral personality, freedom and love, which go far beyond the merely logical and physical, are its inmost marrow. In these it rests, and this universally—in its doctrine of God, no less than in its doctrines of man and of the God-man. It is just for this reason that the christian system is the highest, the system of all systems.[24]

---

take any interest in this christological question, or in any other bearing directly on the heart of the original Lutheran theology. [Here Nevin refers to the efforts of Samuel Schmucker (President of the Lutheran Seminary at Gettysburg, Penn.) and Benjamin Kurtz (Editor of the *Lutheran Observer*) to accommodate Lutheranism to American evangelicalism by dispensing with sacramental efficacy.]

22. [Nikolaus Ludwig von Zinzendorf (1700–60), German Pietist and bishop of the Moravian Church. Zinzendorf studied at Halle, where he was influenced by August Hermann Francke, and later founded the pietist community at Herrnhut. His Christology is understood by some to anticipate nineteenth-century kenoticism.]

23. [Liebner, *Christologie*, 280.]

24. [Ibid., 65–66.]

Thus it becomes necessary, for the construction of a right christology, to fall back on its ultimate grounds in a true christian theology or right doctrine of God. The three spheres, Man, Christ, God, throw light continually on each other; but it is in the last only we are to seek finally the full sense of the whole.

> That is, we must follow the grand objective course of the christian system itself, as it goes forth from the idea of God. The highest truth of this idea however is the christian doctrine of the Trinity, which is itself in truth but the idea of God in full ethical form. The ethical idea authenticates itself here in this, that by its means the doctrine of the Trinity (what has always been its greatest difficulty), can be carried out so as to avoid truly both tritheism on the one side and subordinationism on the other. Within the doctrine of the Trinity is to be found then the principle which lies immediately at the foundation of the ethical idea of the human and the divine human, Man and Christ. This will sum up the whole sense of the christian doctrine of the Logos; whilst it brings out at the same time also the true christological scheme of the world, which is the unity of creation and the incarnation.—P. 66.

What the author proposes thus is to bring out the proper *ethical* foundation of the christian mystery (in contradistinction to the insufficient grounds, more or less logical or physical merely, which have been rested upon too generally in the previous christological theories, which he finds occasion to reject for this very reason), by getting back to its true original and only sufficient seat in a corresponding view of the Godhead, under its christian eternal distinction of Father, Son and Holy Ghost. This leads him through a profound speculative inquiry into the constitution of the Trinity, in which the text, "God Is Love," is taken as a guiding pole-star, to be kept constantly in view in the criticism and rejection of what is false as well as in the determination of what is held to be true. The only right order here is to begin at once not with the abstract, but with the concrete, not with the conception of God in its lowest and most general character, but with this conception as it meets us in its full ethical force in the New Testament. In the way of preparation however for this, it is found well to pass in review the several theories by which it has been attempted to construct the idea of God speculatively from a subordinate and incomplete stand-point, commencing with the extreme abstraction of the Eleatic philosophy, and taking other schemes afterwards in the order of their approximation towards the proper fulness of the idea in its perfect form. This criticism sets aside as unsatisfactory the schemes of Schleiermacher and Hegel, and also the metaphysics of the older Protestant theology (in which God is defined as *mera et simplicissima essentia*[25]), as well as the "absolute substance" of Spinoza. Having brought this task to a close, the author finds the way fairly and fully open for the positive presentation of his own scheme or system, and to that object accordingly the latter part of his work is mainly devoted.

In this we shall not pretend to follow him here, even with the most general sketch; for our limits forbid anything like a satisfactory report of his argument in this form; and it would not be right, in the case of so deep and difficult a subject, to hazard either the credit of the book or the claims of truth on any merely cursory and fragmentary representation, in which terms and propositions must be continually in danger of being taken either in a wrong sense or it may be in no sense at all. Our chief purpose has been, in connection with the book, to call attention to the deeply significant interest of its subject; and with its help to set forth in a general way the nature of this subject, the character and sense of the christological question or problem, as it now enters particularly into the very life of the Church, practical as well as theoretical, and from all sides loudly claims due audience and response.

There can be no doubt but that this work of Professor Liebner forms a most valuable addition to modern scientific theology. It is the fruit of most profound and vigorous thought, upheld and replenished throughout by the most comprehensive learning. It is not for the superficial, or for such as take no earnest interest in theology; for whom all severe thinking in this direction is a burden, who will have it that all theology is at an end, and who are ready to cry down for this reason as transcendental mystification whatever goes ever so little beyond the poorest commonplace categories that happen to have become lodged in their own brain; caring not to see, and in their blindness having no power to see that these same easy categories involve at bottom the very essence of rationalism itself. Liebner's book, we say, is for no such readers; nor are such ever likely to travel far into its pages. But theology,

---

25. [Translation: "pure and simple essence." The phrase is associated with the scholastic doctrine of the simplicity of God, that God's essence and attributes are one and the same.]

thank God, is not yet given up to the mercy of this lackadaisical school. It is still with many a living science, as religion also is for them not merely a dead mechanical tradition, but the most concrete and earnest among the interests of life. Such will be prepared to hail the appearance of this great work, as well as of every other, which seeks under the guidance of a truly evangelical spirit to carry the torch of science into the farthest depths of the kingdom of God. It is to be regretted at the same time, that the work is by no means as clear in its style and form as the richness of its contents deserves. It is far enough from being loose or unscientific in its method; it is pervaded with principial unity and rigid logical connection throughout; but still the method is a good deal involved, and such as it costs more effort than the case necessarily required to keep steadily in sight. The style moreover is a good deal cumbersome and hard, abounding in long complicated sentences, with all sorts of parenthetic interruption—making it necessary for the reader to keep his attention continually on the stretch, and often to read backwards as well as forwards, in order to get with safe intelligence at all to the end of the tangled labyrinth of words with which he finds himself surrounded. A better literary form, in the general view now noticed, would serve materially to assist the influence and credit which it so well deserves to carry with it on other grounds.

[LIEBNER'S RESPONSE TO GOTTFRIED THOMASIUS]

We find in the August and September numbers of Reuter's *Repertorium*, published in Berlin, an additional contribution to the literature of this great subject from the pen of Professor Liebner, in reply to some strictures made on his book in another journal by the distinguished Lutheran theologian, Dr. Thomasius[26]; of whose labors in the same department (for he also has written a special treatise it seems on the constitution of Christ's person) Liebner in his book speaks with the highest respect, though he calls in question their full success. The difference and controversy turn on the view taken of the *Trinity*, on the question

---

26. [Gottfried Thomasius (1802–75), German Lutheran theologian who taught at Erlangen, and who was known particularly for his work on Christology. A portion of his *Christi Person und Werk* (1853–61) was translated and published in Welch, ed., *God and Incarnation*, 24–101.]

concerning *the necessity of the Divine Incarnation,* and on the way of carrying out the doctrine of the κένωσις or *Inanition* of the Logos.[27]

Liebner takes up first the second point, which he considers of primary account for the present state of theology, and towards which the main stress of objection from the other side would appear to be directed. He complains however, that Thomasius enters but little into the real merits of the question; which indeed is hardly allowed even to come into view clearly in his criticism.

> The question relates to the proposition that Humanity is *made* with reference to Christ; or in other words that the free act of creation draws after it with necessity the mystery of the incarnation; that these two facts go to make up one whole self-revelation of God in the world: an idea, whose germ is presented to us in the Bible, particularly by St. Paul, and which has had its patrons in a whole succession of church divines in ancient, middle, and modern times. Thomasius however thinks it enough to bring forward one single formula, employed by me to express the thought, which he finds not to his mind, and then dismisses with the vague charge of pantheism—in the style of too many of our otherwise respectable theologians, who are accustomed to dispose summarily of all that squares not with their own habit by some similar dogmatically sweeping note.[28] All the rest of my book bearing on the point, the pains in particular that are taken to show that the idea in question is grounded in the constitution of Christianity, and in full harmony with the christian conceptions of God, of the creation, and of the moral liberty of man forming indeed the key that is necessary to unlock the inmost sense of the whole; all this, I say, he hides from the eyes of his readers as well as from his own. This is a grief to me, I say it honestly, not so much on my own account, as for the sake especially of those *Lutheran* readers, who look mainly to the

---

27. [The Greek word κένωσις (*kenosis*) means "emptying," and is related to the word Paul uses in Phil 2:7 ("emptied himself," RSV). As nineteenth-century theologians wrestled with how infinite deity and finite humanity could coexist in a single person, some concluded that the Logos had "emptied himself" of some or all divine attributes in the Incarnation. Kenoticism was particularly popular at the University of Erlangen, with proponents such as Thomasius. Kenotic Christologies were criticized on the grounds that they threatened the doctrine of divine immutability and implied an interruption of the intra-trinitarian fellowship. See Welch, *Protestant Thought*, 233–40.]

28. The fault of some respectable theologians also in our own wise and free America, as well as of some who are not very respectable.

excellent journal here in hand for information, but in *this* case must be led wholly astray—in regard to a book which to *them* especially would fain not continue unknown.

It may be worth while here to follow the article briefly in its attempt to show particularly "that the *christian doctrine of sin* can not be carried out rightly on all sides without the idea of the necessity of the incarnation, and so of the original and essential relation of Christ to humanity, even in its first creation, and without regard to sin or its removal."

Two points require to be secured in the christian doctrine of sin, the freedom of man on the one side, and the fact that God is not the author of it on the other. But now the unity of God's plan of the world seems to require that sin, which opens the way for redemption, the centre of all God's counsels in regard to the world and the end of all his revelations, should for this very reason enter into this plan and be included in the aim and purpose (divine teleology) of the world as a whole. Here arise vast difficulties, from which there can be no full escape without the intervention of some new principle that may serve to set in harmony the seemingly discordant views from which they spring. This help is found actually, according to Professor Liebner, in the idea just stated, and nowhere else.

The end of man's creation is full communion with God himself. This is religion in its highest and most absolute form; which thus becomes the end of the whole creation, whose last sense is man. A failure in this object must be taken then as a failure of the whole creation, so far as this world is concerned. To an *unconditional* realization of such absolute religion however, man's life is conducted only in the incarnation of the eternal Son of God, that is in the central and universal person of the true and real God-man, who just in this way completes the process of God's self-communication, the sense of all his revelations, as the completion of humanity itself; he is the personal absolute religion. The incarnation becomes thus the absolute and unconditional centre of God's free purposes of love towards the world; or which is the same thing, the real centre and hinge of all history. This hinders not the entrance of sin, by the free act of Adam, and its settlement in the general life of the race; but however the billows of that awful curse may triumph in every other quarter, on this rock in the end they must break. The membership of the race might fail in the necessary exercise of its own freedom; there was security still in the *head*, that in such contingency the whole ethical idea of the world, as this lay in the mind of God when he called it into being, should not fail, but be carried forward notwithstanding to its triumphant conclusion. The destiny of man stood safe in the coming Second Adam, though all might seem to be lost for a time by the fall of the First; only it became necessary in this case, that his appearance in the world should be that of a suffering, atoning Redeemer; a result that has served however to bring in a more glorious dispensation of grace, according to Rom. v. 15–21, than all that could possibly have been reached in any different way.

> Christ, the God-man, the personal absolute religion, is and remains still the essential end and scope of the whole creation (Coloss. i. 15–16—τὰ πάντα δι' αὐτοῦ καὶ εἰς αὐτὸν ἔκτισται[29]), and so far has his end originally in himself, but in the fulness of his love makes himself at the same time the means of redemption for sinful humanity. Thus have we a perfect theodicy, in which the freedom of man is saved in harmony with the full stability and unity of the Divine world plan.

If on the other hand the incarnation of the eternal Son be not taken into the original scheme of the world, be not thought of as its centre according to Coloss. i. 15–16, but only as a contrivance to destroy sin, the bad fruit of man's freedom, which being free thus *might not have been at all;* or if the complete revelation of God and the proper consummation of humanity stand not unconditionally sure in Christ, if the crowning sense of all here be not *absolutely predestinated,* if the Son of God be not, as eternally in the Trinity, so also in History, the one whole and full object of the Divine complacency, and all besides acceptable only in him and through him, all partaking of his fulness as the Head:—if this be not the original and necessary order of the creation itself, but only an after thought brought into it by the tremendous accident of sin, the whole economy both of Nature and of Christianity is indeed thrown into hopeless confusion, as being throughout at the mercy of chance. There remains nothing that is unconditional, necessary, and absolutely eternal, either in God's plan or in his actual work. All becomes a sea of uncertainty, where in fact the end falls out in no harmony whatever with the beginning. The rescue of man's freedom at such cost is too dear.

---

29. [Trans. "all things have been created through him and for him" (NRSV)]

Two ways have been fallen upon by deep thinkers, pressed with the sense of this difficulty, to uphold the interest of God's sovereignty thus brought into danger—which however soon run into equal difficulty on the opposite side.

The first is that of Calvin.

> A great truth undoubtedly enters into his system, to which it owes its power, and in view of which only it is possible to understand or explain its far reaching influence. Here, if anywhere, the proposition holds good, that an error is strong only through the residue of truth it still contains. God's sovereignty must indeed be *unconditionally* secured. But this can be done truly only in another way. If that be not found, if it be not seen how the Divine idea or decree stands unconditionally sure of its own end in the God-man, whether the Adamitic probation lead the life of the race through sin or not, there can be no possible escape for strict thinking from the Calvinistic consequence, as among others Schleiermacher also has so strikingly shown.
>
> The second false way, which however only carries out the full meaning of the first, the one view at bottom involving the other, consists in resolving sin into an *anthropological* necessity—such as serves at last in truth to throw it back on God. Man is taken to be so *made*, in the relation of his lower and higher powers, nature and spirit, that with his development sin takes place necessarily, the higher part of his nature being bound by the lower, which rightly it should rule. Sin thus has not come *into* man, but grows forth from his original constitution, as part of God's work.

In exemplification of this view, which he takes to be so closely related to that of Calvin, Liebner refers to the theories of Schleiermacher and Rothe, as well as to the speculations of Fichte and Hegel on the idea of sin.[30]

From these plausible schemes, which draw their strength for thoughtful minds from the great interest of the Divine sovereignly, the only adequate deliverance is found, he thinks, in the theory which includes in the conception of the creation itself the idea of the incarnation, as the last necessary sense of the world. Grant this, and there is no

---

30. [Immanuel Hermann Fichte (1797–1879), German idealist philosopher who taught at Bonn and Tübingen. The general tendency of such idealism was to view sin as a necessary moment in the dialectic resulting in self-knowledge rather than as a contingent moral disaster.]

longer any reason or temptation to resolve sin into an anthropological necessity, the fault of man's nature, or to lay the burden of its origin on God. It falls on the freedom of the human will, where it is made to fall in the Bible. We recognize no necessity in its introduction into the sphere of man's life.

> On the contrary, we see a necessity rather of a wholly different sort; namely this, that if humanity have not the character of goodness in its original constitution, as this comes from God, by no possible human act can it ever *become* really good; it must remain forever involved in the contradiction of wrongly balanced and adjusted powers with which it has been doomed to start. Even a *true* incarnation in this case, a sinless Christ, must be impossible. In other words, if sin be not something brought *into* humanity, as no proper part of it, it can never be brought *out* of it even by redemption itself. With this falls to the ground the whole puzzling system of Schleiermacher in regard to sin and redemption, in which neither sin is sin properly nor redemption properly redemption. And even Rothe's masterly and classical exposition, which goes beyond Schleiermacher's physical categories in its view of freedom and proper personality, has truth for us only as an uncommonly acute delineation of the actual development of man's sinful nature as it now stands, not as a speculative construction of its sinful development as it stood in the beginning.

It amounts to nothing here, according to Liebner, that Thomasius and others standing on the same general ground are ready to say: "We are not in this fault, we do not make sin necessary." That is only to their private benefit; the case however regards the *doctrine of the Church*; which needs to be so set forth, that these theories of the original necessity or unavoidableness of sin may no longer be able to uphold themselves as logically indispensable. It must be counted ever a poor interest for church orthodoxy, which simply closes its eyes to the difficulties that surround it, and so quarrels with every effort that is made to meet and solve them on the part of others.

In this general way Prof. Liebner vindicates the view he takes of the necessary relation of Christ to the world. The subject is to be taken up in its soteriological relations fully and specially, he tells us, in the second part of his work, the appearance of which we anticipate with no small interest. Our business at present has been simply to bring it before our readers in the way of report, without pretending to pass upon it any judgment of our own.

In the second part of his article in reply to Thomasius, our author takes up the charge of pantheism, and shows very satisfactorily as it seems to us that it is in this case, as employed against his book, a mere empty sound without any force whatever. There is much more room, he thinks, for urging this very difficulty on the general view of Thomasius himself. It needs at all events to be well considered and kept in mind that the danger of pantheism can never be fairly avoided by simply falling over into the arms of an abstract deism. And most especially must that be counted a poor and shallow conception here, by which the idea of Christ's central posture as the Son of Man, in and by whom only our entire humanity can become complete, is taken to imply the falling away in any measure of the grand original and eternal distinction that must ever hold between Himself and the persons of his people. But this point we are not called to take up at the present time.

J. W. N.

Article 5
"Cur Deus Homo?"[1]

(by John W. Nevin)

"It is oftentimes considered the chief purpose of Christ's Incarnation," says Trench *(Huls. Lect., p.* 218),[2]

> that it made his death possible, that it provided him a body in which to do that which merely as God he could not do namely to suffer and to die; while some of the profoundest teachers of the past, so far from contemplating the Incarnation in this light, have rather affirmed that the Son of God would equally have taken man's nature, though of course under very different conditions, even if he had not fallen—that it lay in the everlasting purposes of God, quite irrespective of the fall, that the stem and the stalk of humanity should at length bear its perfect flower in Him, who should thus at once be its root and crown.

This passage we have quoted before, in our notice of the work from which it is taken, as one of significant interest in relation to the great subject to which it refers.

In a later article we have called attention to a more full and formal presentation of the same view by Professor Liebner of Germany,

---

1. [Originally published in the *Mercersburg Review* 3:3 (May 1851): 220–39.]

2. [Richard Chevinix Trench, *Christ the Desire of All Nations, or the Unconscious Prophecies of Heathendom* (Cambridge: MacMillan, Barclay, and MacMillan, 1846). The quote in question is found on pp. 63–64 of this 1846 edition. Richard Chevinix Trench (1807–86), Anglican clergyman and biblical scholar who taught at King's College, Cambridge and later served as Anglican Archbishop of Dublin. His Cambridge Hulsean Lectures for 1845 and 1846 were reviewed by Nevin in his "Trench's Lectures."]

who makes it in fact the foundation thought of his recent work on Christology.³ The view is adopted also by Dorner, and has called forth as we have seen the direct approbation of Schöberlein,⁴ in an able recension of Liebner's work published in Reuter's *Repertorium*. Liebner himself has appeared again, as we have also seen, in the same Journal, in opposition to Dr. Thomasius, a distinguished Lutheran divine, who it seems has entered the lists with him on the opposite side. This may serve to show the interest which is taken in the question here brought into debate, and how intimately related it is felt to be to the very heart of theology at the present time.

We find now a new writer on the field, Dr. *Julius Müller*, the author of the widely celebrated treatise on Sin.⁵ His mere name is sufficient of course to command attention and respect. He is not a man to take up any subject lightly, and what he writes is sure to carry with it the weight both of extensive learning and profound thought. This credit is well sustained by his dissertation on the subject before us, in two articles contained in Schneider's *Deutsche Zeitschrift* for October 1850, under the title: "The Question examined, Whether the Son of God would have become man, if the human race had continued without sin."⁶ The occasion of the discussion is in large part at least the work of Professor Liebner. It is not however a review of this in any strict sense, but addresses itself to the inquiry with which it is occupied in a general way. The investigation is exceedingly calm, but at the same time exceedingly searching and deep, and the conclusion reached by it is a full negative answer to the question that forms its theme. The author allows a large merit to Liebner's work, and considers it an important contribution to theological science, especially in its view of the deep and difficult doctrine of the Trinity; but he rejects as unsound and unsafe the thought

---

3. [See "Liebner's Christology" in this volume.]

4. [Ludwig Friedrich Schöberlein (1813–81), Lutheran theologian who taught at Erlangen, Heidelberg, and Göttingen.]

5. [Julius Müller (1801–1878), Lutheran theologian who taught at Göttingen, Marburg, and Halle. As his nickname, "Sünden-Müller" ("sin Müller") suggests, he was particularly known for his work on hamartiology (the doctrine of sin), and especially for his *Christian Doctrine of Sin*. For a contemporary account of Müller, see Schaff, *Germany,*, 340-46.]

6. [Julius Müller, "Untersuchung der Frage: Ob der Sohn Gottes Mensch geworden sein würde, wenn das menschliche Geschlecht ohne Sünde geblieben ware," *Deutsche Zeitschrift für christliche Wissenschaft und christliches Leben* (1850): 314-20, 333-41.]

on which it rests throughout, that the necessity of the Incarnation lies primarily not in the fall of man but in his creation. Liebner of course, as we have before seen, does not call in question the soteriological design of the mystery, its relation to sin as the only possible means of redemption and salvation; he simply maintains that this is not to be viewed as the exclusive or primary reason of the mystery, that there was a necessity for it on the contrary back of this, and of a far broader and deeper nature, in the original idea of humanity itself, in virtue of which only it was possible for the special need created by the fall to find its remedy and cure here under any such supernatural form. But Müller refuses to acknowledge any necessity for the Incarnation, beyond the existence of sin and the idea of redemption. The soteriological interest forms in his view the ultimate and whole reason of the stupendous mystery; so that if the first Adam had not fallen there would have been no second Adam to take his place, if sin had not entered into the world the Son of God would never have assumed human flesh.

[HISTORY OF THE NON-HAMARTIOLOGICAL VIEW]

Some traces of the other view, according to Müller, are to be met with in the Patristic Period, particularly in the writings of Irenaeus; but it is among the Schoolmen of the middle ages that it first comes distinctly and formally into view. Anselm of Canterbury, in his celebrated tract *Cur Deus Homo?*, excludes it by referring the Incarnation wholly to the necessity of an atonement for sin; and Thomas Aquinas rests in the same conclusion, as most in harmony with the authority of the Scriptures, although he seems occasionally to look a different way, and has been quoted in fact by some as the patron of the other opinion. On the other hand a certain abbot Rupert,[7] a theologian of decidedly biblical rather than scholastic turn, appears in the 12th century as the open advocate of the view, setting it in what he conceives to be necessary connection with Augustine's theory of predestination. After his time, a number of the schoolmen are found answering the question, *Cur Deus homo?*,[8]

---

7. [Rupert, Abbott of Deutz in Germany (d. 1135).]
8. [Trans. "Why the God-Man?"]

in the same general way; as for instance Alexander Hales,[9] John Duns Scotus,[10] and his school.

> With this last his Pelagianizing anthropology may have come here somewhat into play, inclining him to detract from the weight of sin as a determining influence on God's counsels; but the immediate reason he urges in favor of the view is that the happiness and glory to which Christ's soul has been predestinated is a Divine purpose which in the order of dignity goes before the purpose of salvation towards other souls, on which account the Incarnation, as being the necessary condition of its realization, cannot in the order of God's purposes depend on the fall of man absolutely as its cause. Were this the case, it would seem to follow that Christ must be regarded as a *bonum occasionatum*,[11] something which Duns Scotus takes to be wholly derogatory to the proper glory of his nature.[12]

We find the same view earnestly maintained again by the celebrated John Wessel, and still also under the same general regard to the dignity of Christ's person, as infinitely transcending even in his human nature the worth of all human beings besides.

With the Reformers of the 16th century the sense of sin was so active, and along with this the idea of redemption so prominent and strong, that the question, Whether the Son of God would not have assumed flesh even if man had never fallen, may be said to have had no power even to engage their serious attention. At all events they could have for it but one answer. The mystery of the Incarnation depends for them on the tragedy of Sin. If pressed with the difficulty of upholding the absolute sovereignty of God's decree they are ready in favor of this view to take refuge even in supralapsarianism, and to include the fall itself in the decree as the condition of redemption. So Calvin, as we all know, without any sort of qualification or reserve.[13] But Luther when

---

9. [Alexander of Hales (c. 1186–1245), Franciscan scholastic theologian who taught at Paris and helped to popularize the *Sentences* of Peter Lombard.]

10. [John Duns Scotus (c. 1265–1308), medieval scholastic theologian and philosopher who taught at Cambridge, Oxford, Paris, and Cologne. Known as the "subtle doctor," Duns Scotus was an important figure in the rise of voluntarism.]

11. [I.e., a good occasioned by other considerations rather than excellent in and of itself. On this, see Dorner, *Person of Christ*, I:365.]

12. [Müller, "Untersuchung der Frage," 316.]

13. [Under the influence of the idealist historiographies of F. C Baur, Alexander Schweizer, and others in the mid-nineteenth century, it became popular to view classic

necessary looked at the matter in the same light. Even in his Larger Catechism he says: "*Ob id ipsum nos creavit Deus, ut nos redimeret*,"[14] God created man in order to his redemption—a proposition which implies that the act of creation must have carried in it a provision for that which makes redemption necessary, in other words must have involved the necessity of sin. A public representative indeed of the other view of the necessity of the Incarnation comes before us in this age in the person of the Lutheran Osiander.[15] But this advocacy stood connected with what was considered an unsound theology on the subject of justification, which caused it of course to have more weight against the view in question than in its favor. The case was made still worse for it by its gaining the approbation of Faustus Socinus[16]; though with him again the reason for receiving it lay in a particular peculiarity of his own system which the hypothesis happened to fit, rather than in the older theological speculation. "Thus it happened," says the writer before us,

---

Reformed theology as logically conditioned by predestination as a "central dogma," with supralapsarianism (the view that the divine decree of election logically precedes the decrees to create and permit the fall) often the result. Schweizer's contemporary Heinrich Heppe, however, drew a distinction between this predestinarian Calvinism and the German Reformed tradition, which he viewed as Melanchthonian on the decrees of God. The Mercersburg theologians, who felt compelled to choose between Calvin's sacramentolgy and Calvin's predestinarianism, adopted this interpretation. For an extended statement of this perspective, see Wolff, "German Reformed Dogmatics." On Heppe's thesis regarding the distinctive character of the German Reformed Church, see Kennedy, "Reformed Orthodoxy Redivivus," *The Reformed Review* 33 (1980): 150–157. It is now generally recognized that Calvin did not view predestination as a central dogma and that he was not a supralapsarian (though his Genevan successor Theodore Beza was), and that supralapsarianism historically has been a minority viewpoint among the Reformed. On these matters more generally, see Muller, *Christ and the Decree*.

14. [Trans. "God created us in order that he might redeem us." This phrase is not found in Luther's Larger Catechism and is also wrongly attributed by some nineteenth-century writers (e.g., Schneckenberger, Heppe, Lindsay) to Calvin's "grösseren Katechismus" or his "Geneva Catechism."]

15. [Andreas Osiander (1498–1552), German Lutheran theologian of the Reformation period. Opposing Melanchthon's view of imputed righteousness, Osiander maintained that justification is the communication of essential righteousness in that divine substance indwells the believer.]

16. [Faustus Socinus (1539–1604), founder the anti-trinitarian Socinian movement who spent much of his career in Poland.]

that a theological opinion which had been considered in the middle ages open for free discussion in the schools,[17] fell everywhere with the older Protestant theology into the reproach of heterodoxy. The orthodox divines of the Lutheran confession, so far us they touch the question, declare themselves with one voice against it. Still this has not prevented the later theology from looking favorably on a view, which is felt to be recommended especially by the consideration that the highest act of Divine love, bringing with it the greatest exaltation of man, cannot be regarded as dependent upon man's wilful selfperversion, and so on something accidental, but must rest on the original pure idea of the creation in the Divine mind, or in other words on the *essential relation between God and man*.[18]

[THE INFLUENCE OF SPECULATIVE "PANTHEISTIC" SYSTEMS]

The investigation here in hand has to do with its subject, only as presented on the ground of the true Bible doctrine of a personal God. Pantheistic systems, which resolve the activity of God's love into a metaphysical process of absolute self-consciousness, made complete at last through the speculative thinking of the human spirit, have also appropriated to themselves the thought now in question; but their meaning is simply that man is formed by his nature to become divine or theanthropic, in which view the entire history of the race is to be regarded as a so called eternal incarnation of the Deity. All such logico-metaphysical blasphemy is here left entirely out of sight. Supposing the Incarnation to be necessary even for a normal development of our human life, it is regarded as flowing only from an *ethical* principle or ground, from an act of the personal God; in the case of which any *necessity* it may have must rest wholly on the freedom of the Divine will, the disposition of God's love to reveal itself under such form.—So also no regard is had to those theories of an original necessity for the Incarnation, which shrink not from making it to be the completion of God himself, the higher

---

17. So Bonaventura speaking of the two different theories says: "*Quis autem horum (modorum) alteri praeponendus sit difficile est videre pro eo, quod uterqae modus catholicus est et a viris catholicis sustinetur.*" [Müller, "Untersuchung der Frage," p. 317. This inexact quotation is from *S. Bonaventurae Opera Omnia* (Paris, 1855), IV:23. Trans. "But which of these ways is superior, it is difficult to see, for in fact both are Catholic and are supported by Catholic teachers."]

18. [Müller, "Untersuchung der Frage," 317.]

unity, as they say, in which the contradiction of the pretended abstractions, Deity and Humanity, is brought to an end (*aufgehoben*).[19] Such a view gives the mystery indeed the character of absolute necessity, not for man only but also for God; but it completely destroys in doing so the true idea of the absolute, and gives us under the name of an eternal Divine incarnation the absurdity of an *absolute coming to pass*. This excludes too the conception that the Son of God or the Logos became flesh; the assumption is that *God became flesh*; an idea which implies a rejection of the Christian doctrine of the Trinity, and resolves the whole being of God into a process. Christian science should be on its guard thus against even the sound of anything like an agreement with such a view; a caution, Müller thinks, which has not been sufficiently observed in certain quarters of the later German theology, where a disposition has been shown to transplant not merely the sound but the actual substance of the false idea in question to the historical field of the Bible. The idea of course has the whole voice and spirit of the New Testament against it; while it inevitably subverts besides the conception of God and that of the creature both at once.

> The being of God would in this view fall fully into the course of time; up to a certain point in time he could not have been true and perfect God; and so could not be this either after such date; for an absolute which has come to pass is no less a contradiction, than one eternally coming to pass. Since moreover there could be no incarnation of the Logos without created existence, it would follow that God needed the world in order that he might truly be God; he creates it accordingly, to bring himself into full reality—that is, he does not create it at all, for the idea of creation implies essentially freedom over against the world, which is here supposed to be wanting; in the world, which all sound theism owns to be the creature of God, he must at the same time see the *condition of himself*, and Angelus Silesius would be right with his impiously bold word:
>
> *Gott ist so viel an mir, wie mir an ihm gelegen;*
> *Ich helf sein Wesen ihm, er hilft mir meines hegen.*[20]

---

19. [From the German verb *aufheben*, which means both to "annul" and "lift up." This is a key term in the philosophy of G. W. F. Hegel, for whom the dialectical process involves both abrogation and raising to a higher level of synthesis. On the Hegel's Christology, see Yerkes, *Christology of Hegel*.]

20. [Trans. "God is as concerned for me, as I for Him; I help Him to His being, He helps me to cherish mine," in Müller, *Christian Doctrine of Sin*, (1852), I: 118.]

> Propositions such as the necessity of God's becoming man to complete his own nature, and the consequences that flow from it, may have some intelligible meaning on the platform of pantheism; but when transplanted to theistic ground they lose all sense and force, and deceive with a mere show of depth that comes only of the dim uncertain twilight in which they involve the mind. If they cannot satisfy it they at least put it into a state of confusion, and that itself is for many a sort of inward satisfaction.[21]

The question then regards properly no conception of this kind, as the ground of the necessity for the Incarnation; but supposes the case to be that such necessity is referred only to the *human side* of the transaction; in the sense namely, that it is *man* only who could not truly fulfil his own idea, the sense of his own nature, without the entrance of the Logos in a real way into the organism of his life.

Here comes into consideration the posture of Schleiermacher's theology with regard to the point in hand. Thomasius makes this the source in fact of the modern form of the proposition, that the Son of God would have become incarnate even if man had not sinned. But Müller shows very clearly that it has no root in Schleiermacher's theory whatever. According to this theory, Christ is the completion of human nature, the second stage of man's creation as distinguished from the first in Adam (*Glaubenslehre* § 89).[22] The first creation is imperfect, through a want of full harmony in the nature of man between his conscience and will, the consciousness of God not being strong enough to give the spirit its proper supremacy over the flesh; in Christ first this consciousness with its corresponding power appears in full force; and from him, through the action of faith directed towards him by his people, it is brought to extend itself to the race generally, completing thus the original sense of our human life, and setting it free from its previous imperfection. Creation and redemption here are only different parts of one work. In this view, it is plain that there is no room for the question, whether the Incarnation would have been necessary if man had not sinned. For what the system takes for sin is in truth a mere natural

---

21. [Müller, "Untersuchung der Frage," 318.]

22. [Schleiermacher, *The Christian Faith*, 367, writes, "As everything which has been brought into human life through Christ is presented as a new creation, so Christ Himself is the Second Adam, the beginner and originator of this more perfect human life, or the completion of the creation of man."]

defect in the first form of man's being itself, which from the first looks forward to the higher consciousness of Christ as its own needful complement and end; and this itself must be regarded of course then as the only normal order which the case allows. Or if it should be imagined that there might have been, according to the theory, such a progress of the first imperfect life of the race as would not have been attended with that inward contradiction and disturbance which we now experience under the notion of sin, it is easy to see that in such case there could be no room for the introduction of a higher order of existence in a single personal Christ as the means of redemption for others. In every view clearly, the system of Schleiermacher implies that the mystery of the incarnation is conditioned by the imperfection of the world as it now stands, and knows no ground beyond this or aside from this on which to speak of it as necessary.

[ANALYSIS OF THE NON-HAMARTIOLOGICAL POSITION]

We come thus to Müller's second article, with the question disentangled from all false connections, and reduced to its proper theistic and truly christian form. Admitting the existence of a personal holy God, the perfect freeness of his acts, the original sufficiency of the first creation, the awful reality of the fall as something made necessary only through man's will, and the need of a real redemption by Christ's death, the thesis under consideration still asserts that the mystery of the incarnation does not depend absolutely on this abnormal course of things, but would have had place also on the supposition of a normal or sinless development of man's life. It is allowed that the entrance of sin rendered it necessary for the mystery to take the special soteriological character under which it now appears; but the idea is that back of this particular need there lay a broader and deeper necessity for it in the original creation of man's nature itself, which would have required it to make this in full what it was designed to be even if it had remained true to its first state. This is the thought to be examined and tried.

The older advocates of the opinion endeavored to rest it on direct scriptural proof. Its modern friends however see and acknowledge that the Bible everywhere refers the fact of the incarnation to sin and the necessity of redemption. In other words it proceeds throughout on the simply soteriological theory, without any distinct regard to the other. It is not necessary to quote particular texts in proof of this. They meet us on all sides; while only three or four, such as 1 Cor. xv: 45–47, Eph. i: 21–23, Col. ii: 10, l Peter iii: 22, and as more plausible than all the rest Col. i: 16–17, are made to look by circuitous and doubtful interpretation the other way. But why, it is asked, may we not admit along with this direct biblical view, another also of more comprehensive character, growing forth from the power of legitimate and necessary speculation exercised on the vast scheme of Christian truth as a whole? Thus related the two theories do not exclude each other. Rather the biblical representation is to be taken simply as a determinate phase of the truth, which is embraced in the other more general construction. The first proceeds analytically, planting itself on the fact of man's state as it now is; the other moves synthetically, in just the opposite direction. The last has to do with the general or universal substance of the relation in question; while the Bible, answerable to the actual condition of the world, brings into view a *specific mode and form of* its realization, namely the Word made flesh in order to the exhaustion of man's curse by suffering and death.

But this imagination of the possible harmony of the two theories, according to our author, is attended with great difficulties. Take first, for instance, that which starts from the *need of redemption*. The theory involves not merely single biblical texts, but the whole view that is taken of Christ's person, and of its relations to the world both before and since.

> Our earthly human life as it now stands is directly and unavoidably subject to suffering; the soteriological view of the incarnation affirms of course that the entrance of the Son of God into this whole form of existence presupposes sin, and by it alone becomes intelligible. The same theory presses the consideration moreover, that in assuming flesh the Logos has been born as a member of the Jewish nation, and in subjection to its law, while the whole Israelitish economy resulted certainly from the fact of the fall. Only in view of sin again, it is urged, does it become intelligible why the incarnation took not place at the beginning of man's history, but at a later time; sin must first ripen, and humanity show what it was able to do of itself after the fall, before the Son of God could appear as the author of redemption and the dispenser of a higher life. And who can doubt, the soteriological theory is ready to add, but that all this is according to the sense of the Apostles, and particularly of that one among them,

who alone has left us in his writings the outline of a general view of the world with Christ for its centre?[23]

The mode too in which we are brought to participate in Christ's life is such as to involve in its very nature the supposition of sin. Not only is this the case with repentance, but also with faith in the sense of Paul and John. Suppose no opposition between the natural and spiritual, the world of sense and the invisible world in man's soul, and what room would there be for the idea of faith as the power that breaks through the one to embrace the other? What room would there be for the conception of that agency of the Holy Ghost, which is represented to be now the medium of Christ's life and work in the world since his return to the Father? But how can we think of any such opposition between the two worlds in question, the soteriological theory asks, without the entrance of the disturbing power of sin into the process of man's life?

As regards the *work* of Christ again, the soteriological view will not consent of course to hold itself simply to the idea of the priestly office; as though the prophetical and kingly offices were to be properly cared for, as some have pretended, only by the other theory. It finds full scope for both these last in its conception of the kingdom of God, which is based on the fact of the fall and destined to end as a new creation in the glories of the resurrection. The three offices are in truth subordinated throughout to the idea of *redemption*.

> Thus it is that the theory which finds the cause of the incarnation in sin and the need of salvation spreads itself out over the entire compass of the fact as it appears in history, over Christ's person and work, beginning and end, mode of revelation time, national sphere, all going before as preparation and all following after as consequence; no room is left anywhere for any other principle to appropriate to itself any part or portion of the fact; the actual incarnation is taken up by its explanatory account at all points, so as completely to thrust aside that other theory of an original general necessity for it as a purely vague and empty abstraction.[24]

The same want of inward agreement between the two views will be felt if we reverse the order of consideration and start with the opposite

---

23. [Müller, "Untersuchung der Frage," 338.]
24. [Müller, "Untersuchung der Frage," 338.]

principle, that namely which places the christological necessity back of sin in the general nature of man.

The idea is that if the development of humanity had gone forward in a perfectly normal and sinless way the Logos would still have become flesh. But for what end? Not for show merely, or to please the imagination. It must be thought of under an ethical view, as Liebner himself is careful to allow; it must be regarded as an act of *love* on the part of God. To whom? Of course to the human race. What would it communicate then; what want of the race would it propose to supply?

Here the ground is taken that the race could have no true unity or wholeness without the God-man, that if its parts are not to fall asunder atomistically it must have a *personal head*, in whom the human nature is joined with the divine. This cannot mean merely that Christ is appointed for all mankind as their ruler, and all mankind for him to submit to his government, that they belong of right to him and he to them; for so much the soteriological view itself allows, which is taken to fall short of the principle here in hand. Christ's headship over the race then must be understood of an *actual relation* holding between it and himself; as the New Testament also in truth refers the sense of κεφαλή ["head"] only to a relation of this sort. Thus then a predicate, which is used of Jesus Christ commonly in his relation to the *Church*, is here transferred to the relation he bears to mankind in general, an application it never has in the Scriptures. But what does it signify in the first relation? Nothing less, certainly, than that he is joined in real life union with his Church, so as to be its ruling and actuating principle, filling it with his presence, and using it as the organ of his will, by the power of the Holy Ghost. But now extend this conception to the race as a whole, and what becomes of the reference of the incarnation in any view to the idea of sin? Humanity then, sin or no sin, as being already in union with the divine-human life, needs no redemption. It has by this real relation all that it requires, and it becomes idle indeed to speak of sin as in any sense a fall from God; since in the midst of it all the race still stands, through its actual head, in full fellowship with God, and in full possession also of eternal life. What room can there be in such circumstances for the idea of redemption, or for making it in any way the object of the incarnation?

Each of the views in question then, it appears, goes actually to exclude the other. They refuse to stand together. It follows that to maintain itself at all the idealistic theory, which pretends to resolve the mystery into a deeper general ground back of the soteriological view, must quit this abstract position, and come forward as the only sufficient key for the explanation of the whole fact.

In this case however one feature of it at least must still be excepted, the Saviour's *death upon the cross*. Not to refer this wholly to sin would be to contradict plainly the whole sense of the Scriptures. But it is not easy to uphold the propitiatory signification of this death if we are to retain steadily the thought that the God-man is the real head of the whole human race. It seems the most ready course to say that the intervention of sin made it necessary for the head of the race to appear under such a form as should include, in addition to the requirements of the idea under its normal character, the provision of an atonement for the removal of the guilt belonging to men by means of suffering and death. But to say nothing of the isolated position the atonement is thus made to take in the general revelation of Christ, the force of it as a real condition of reconciliation with God cannot stand where it is firmly held that Christ is the actual head of all mankind, and so still less of course the necessity of the incarnation for any such end. The death of the Son of God then must be taken as having a declarative value only, suited to assure men that their original and essential relation to their ever living head remains good notwithstanding their sense of guilt. Such a declaration might have been given by word alone; but it is rendered more expressive through the real symbol thus exhibited in the transaction of the cross. How every such view tends to sink the central mystery of faith into the form of a mere accommodation to human fancy and conceit, stripping it of all objective necessity and so of all real inward power, it is not necessary here to prove. It falls in truth into the sphere of certain well known rationalistic theories, which are fairly exploded on the field of true theology.

Will it be said, to avoid this difficulty, that the idea of Christ's natural headship of the race anticipates and presumes of course a real appropriation of his atonement on the part of men, by repentance and faith, and so cannot be regarded as having force till this condition is at hand? But if the thought in such form is not to lose itself in the mere conception of Christ's destination for the race at large, which belongs to the other theory, it must imply evidently the restoration of all men to communion with God as the metaphysically necessary end of all human development, and so along with this the overthrow in full of the ideas of freedom, accountability, guilt, punishment and pardon; and what becomes then of the real appropriation of the atonement through repentance and faith?

Or may it be supposed perhaps, that a part of mankind by its wilful resistance to the attraction of the head sunders itself from the body that belongs to it? So Liebner would seem to think when he speaks of the loss of the wicked as "compensated" by the head, in which is realized the full idea of humanity. But this in one view is plainly to fall back into the scriptural thought that Christ is the head of the *Church*; for the system of humanity as such is made to give way in favor of the body of the redeemed, to which only, and not to the race at large, the term σῶμα ["body"] is applied in the New Testament. In this way the idealistic account of the incarnation would yield in truth to the soteriological. In another view however one cannot see why the supposed capacity of Christ to compensate for the loss of a *part* of the race should not be sufficient also to compensate if need be for the *whole*—a result certainly as anti-soteriological as possible. Then the last sense of his revelation would be not his love towards actually existing men, but the perfect realization of the full idea of humanity in himself! But what becomes then of the *ethical* motive already acknowledged, as lying at the ground of the mystery? The thought besides dialectically destroys itself; for a head in which the whole idea of the body is already realized, so that it can by itself make good any deficiency in this whether partial or total, is by such character raised above the relativity that belongs to the very conception of the head.

Paul found all the treasures of wisdom and knowledge in Jesus Christ *crucified*. If the theory before us is to be more than an empty abstraction, as before said, it must be able, aside from this idea of the cross, to explain the other aspects and connections of the historical incarnation, as related to the world both before and since. Can it do this? Liebner seems to think so; for on the ground that the idea of humanity is supposed absolutely to require a perfect realization in one central individual, free from all the onesidedness that must attach to other individuals as such, he bases the conclusion that mankind *in any case*, that is even without sin, could be righteous before God only by faith in Christ, their divine human head.

But now when Liebner himself expressly says at the same time, that this absolutely universal individual cannot belong originally to humanity, but must proceed from a higher sphere, how shall we understand it in the first place that the race should be found from the start, not by its own apostacy from God but by God's creative act, in a condition of perfect inability to meet the Divine requirement, without the implantation of a new principle higher than the nature of humanity as such? How again is the consequence to be avoided that God in the first act of creation purposely made the world bad, in order to make it better in the second? And if we attend to it, this unavoidable insufficiency of all human individuals aside from the God-man as their universal centre, this want of righteousness in virtue of which they *cannot* be the objects of the Divine complacency, rests on no other ground than this, that as abstractions of the true ideal unity which is reached in Christ they are of course onesided and partial representations only of the real generic conception, and so necessarily inadequate examples of humanity. This itself then unfits us to stand before God in our natural state, that we are only *individuals* in the common metaphysical sense of the term! We have here a questionable mixing of the ethical and the metaphysical, from which it is only a step to the error current among the disciples of the Nature-philosophy of Schelling, that individuality is itself the principle of evil, the original fall from the absolute or God.[25]

All goes indeed to subvert the very idea of sin. For if the abstract singleness of the human person taken by itself is itself evil, since the whole creation besides looks to this as its end, it follows that evil is identical with the conception of a finite creation; or rather in place of a creation the ground of relative existence is made to be, as in the old Gnostic systems, a falling away from God; whereby at last the ethical force of sin is wholly swallowed up in theosophico-metaphysical dreams. Or without this, if it be assumed in any view that the world as it came originally from God could not please him, how must the idea of sin suffer and along with it the whole view of salvation! It can hardly be taken at best to signify more than an aggravation of defects previously inherent in the creature as such. The relation between normal and abnormal becomes one of difference, not in principle, but only in degree. How easily thus may the sense of our own sin mingle itself

---

25. [Müller, "Untersuchung der Frage," 314–315.]

with the sentiment of mere natural insufficiency before God, and in this lose itself altogether! Such is the mischief always of trying to fix ethical predicates on metaphysical relations which are independent of will and freedom, with the view of thus transforming them into an ethical character; the transformation strikes unavoidably the other way, the ethical notions are lost in the simply metaphysical.

The origin of Liebner's confusion here is carried back by our critic to a metaphysical thought, which has captivated others also too far, he thinks, on the same ground; this namely, that the relation of *genus* and *individual,* and the postulate from it of one representing in metaphysical sense the life of the whole, is made the point of departure for the speculative construction of the christology. The thought, in the opinion of Müller, is only a delusive phantom, with associations and tendencies besides that may well cause it to be regarded with distrust. The adequate actualization of humanity in the person of the Son of Man did not require that he should include in himself all particular talents and properties of the race, any more than it required that he should enter into all human relations and connections. His life was revealed under natural limitations, as of sex, nationality, family, &c. True, these particularities, essential to the truth of his human nature, were at the same time surmounted and as it were set aside by the greatness of his vocation and spirit. But this is something very different from the supposed concentration metaphysically of all the constituents of the total race in him, as the central individual and microcosm of humanity.

But now taking the thought in its true sense, that the moral idea which humanity carries in itself requires its adequate realization in the form of individual life, how will it bear on the proposition that the Son of God would have become incarnate if there had been no sin? The thought itself contains nothing that looks to the realization of this ideal only in one single individual. Rather it requires it of all; for not to strive after it would be a positive falling away from morality, and the imagination of an endless striving that can never reach the end, a vain *progressus in infinitum* ["infinite progression"], is a contradiction that destroys itself. It lies however in the very nature of the *moral idea,* that the nisus in question should be directed towards the *whole* realization of this idea if it is to have place in the mind at all; for the idea is based on man's relation to God, and is for this reason superior to all conditions and circumstances besides. Artistic, scientific, political ideals have quite another character. Their realization calls everywhere for a division of work into different spheres; even the most prominent minds here are the bearers and organs only of some distinct part of the idea. So the greatest musical genius may have no sense whatever for works of sculpture and painting, or the reverse. But in the realization of the *moral* idea, there is no room to speak of any such division of tasks in the service of the whole. The aim must be all or nothing. The object of redemption accordingly, now that sin has turned the race aside from its original destination, is to bring to pass the adequate realization of this idea in all that are gathered by it into the kingdom of God. But suppose sin had not occurred; then the idea must have actualized itself to the full in all human individuals—which is indeed implied also by the hypothesis of a normal development; and thus the thought before us by no means leads to the necessity of the incarnation for the realization required.

[OTHER DIFFICULTIES ATTENDING THE IDEALIST CHRISTOLOGY]

New difficulties in the way of the theory under consideration come into view when we take into account the existence of other created intelligences besides men, either angels or the inhabitants of other planets.

> If it lies in the conception of created personality universally, that its complete destiny can be reached only through the real union of the Logos with its nature, we must assume (against Heb. ii: 16 indeed) that such a mystery has had place also in favor of the angels. But it belongs to the very idea of a true incarnation that the Logos enters as subject into the process of an individual human life throughout; and if he is not to lose his personal unity in thus going out of himself this can have place only in one individual. United with two or more, he would not be truly in any with his actual self, but the union must be thought of merely as a sort of prophetical inspiration—the Logos simply working upon the created consciousness, without identifying himself with it and so without personal conjunction. Or else we must imagine a succession of personal unions—like the Hindoo avatars of Vishnu for instance, in which the deity takes the forms of different creatures and drops them again one after another. But this conception also plainly destroys the truth of the incarnation; for to this the permanence of the union is indispensable, since the

truth of man's being implies continued existence. Pantheistic systems indeed, if they admit the hypothesis of other orders of personal beings beside men, can easily enough extend to them *their* idea of the incarnation, the process by which God takes form in the world; this however, just because they allow no real incarnation in the Christian sense, as a free act of love on the part of the Son, emptying himself of his glory for the purpose, but turn this thought into a vague shallow generality that has no power to bring man an inch nearer to the living God. Christian knowledge owns only one incarnation of the Logos in the person of Jesus Christ alone, and must reject with like decision every transfer of the conception, whether it be to other human persons or to beings of a different race.[26]

But how now is the restriction of this condescension to the case of the *human* race to be explained? According to the soteriological theory, by its special need of redemption; it is the lost sheep, over against the ninety and nine which are left behind for its rescue, Matth. xviii: 12; the good angels are supposed to require no similar grace for their perfection; while the fallen angels are regarded as too deeply lost to be capable of any redemption. But take the other view, by which the incarnation is supposed necessary without sin; what reason then can be given for this restriction? No other it would seem than this, that the human nature in itself considered stands nearer to the Divine nature, to the Logos, than all created intelligence besides. It is preferred thus, not for its moral misery and want, but for its metaphysical excellence and worth. The transaction serves not so much to magnify the riches of Divine grace, as to illustrate the comparative dignity of the human race.

Unless however we reason in a circle from the mere fact of the distinction itself, which it is pretended to account for by its means, this fancy is found destitute of all biblical proof. The angels are styled also sons of God; they stand in near union with him, more close at present certainly than that to which man is admitted; they excel man in knowledge; the state of the resurrection is even described expressly as being "like unto the angels."[27] In the view of the Bible thus, the image of God in which man is said to have been created is not peculiar to him, but belongs to all personal beings; as indeed the idea of their personality itself implies. Nay, the deeper fall of the lost angels would seem to show that

26. [Müller, "Untersuchung der Frage," 337-338.]
27. [See Mark 12:25 and parallels.]

their first state was higher than the original condition of man; which in fact the whole Christian world has always believed.

The human race, we may believe, has indeed a great and wide end to serve in the general economy of creation; not however as standing higher than other personal intelligences, but as standing comparatively lower. According to our author, the very extremity of the case, and the difficulty of the conditions involved in it, would seem to be that which invests the work of redemption here with its special significance and interest. Sin itself becomes thus the occasion of such a display of Divine love as could not otherwise have place. This redounds to the distinction of the human race; and as it is the *human nature* that is glorified by its union with the Logos in the work of redemption, he is to be regarded as standing to this nature in a relation of special intimacy and appropriation; in such way that the glorification of the redeemed is always a process of conformation to the image of the God-man, a partaking of his glory, the entrance into them of Christ's being and life. Redemption is more than the simple restitution of man's primitive integrity; what we gain in Christ is something incomparably greater than what we have lost in Adam.

[THE DANGER OF PANTHEISM]

Here however we are bound to use great caution, that the relation in question be not so taken as to break down the conception of the true and proper boundary that must ever hold necessarily between the nature of the creature and that of the Creator. The principle of man's union with God is *love*; which implies full personal distinction, and here also distinction of substance or essence. If such union overthrew the substantiality of the creature, causing it to lose itself in the Divine substance, it would be in truth no union but only destruction. God's love then would be in its action like hatred, absorbing or annihilating its object. The view which assumes the necessity of the incarnation independently of sin, Müller thinks, is particularly exposed to the danger of falling into this unethical apprehension of the nature of our relation to Christ; according to which man is to be regarded as coming to a sort of deification, an actual unity of *essence* with the Logos, in virtue of his humanity. Every such imagination of course, whether it be open or latent only and disguised, reduces the existence of the creature to a mere unsubstantial show, and ends necessarily in the yawning gulph of pantheism.

But, now, if according to all that has been said the theory of the original necessity of the incarnation cannot be maintained, what view must we take of the *idea of the God-man*, beyond which certainly no higher idea is to be thought of as the τέλος ["end" or "goal"] of the Divine scheme of the world, and which therefore must necessarily be the central idea around which all the other parts of creation revolve, as they find in it also their union and end? Does not the Apostle Paul say expressly in this sense, Col. i: 16, 17, that the universe is created in Christ, and for him, and that by him all things consist?

Here different points of view are usually blended together which need to be kept distinct.—So much the soteriological theory of the incarnation also must hold for settled, that Christ is the turning point of history, that the cross on Golgotha is the boundary where its centrifugal tendency became centripetal. Was the first Adam the commencement only of a process of natural life, which through the force of sin became a constantly growing departure from God; the second Adam is the author of a process of spiritual life, which rests in no end short of complete fellowship with God, 1 Cor. xv: 45f. But the thought before us goes beyond this; it means that humanity, and so the world at large, has been originally formed with reference to the God-man and to union with him and under him as a head. Here also there is at bottom a deep truth, which is only half misunderstood. The end of all created life as it lies in God's mind, ideally viewed must be placed in such a free union of the personal creature with him, as shall cause it to be in full the organ of God, filled and glorified with his life, and as shall enable it, in virtue of the perfect holiness and bliss to which it is thus raised, to raise the rest of the creation also, after its way and measure, into a participation of the glorious liberty of the children of God. This world of personality, however, thus united with God, is in his eternal idea viewed as a whole, made up of manifold individuals joined together complementally as its members, and so as a kingdom of created intelligences, which as such remain substantially distinct from God, while he is in them still as all in all. The Logos now, as the absolute image of the Father and the hypostatical principle of his self-revelation *ad extra*,[28] stands with all beings created in the image of God, that is with all personal

---

28. [Trans. "toward the outside." I.e., Gods's self-revelation to creatures.]

creatures, in deep specific correspondence. As this principle he is the bearer of the Divine idea of the world, which comes to its focus in the conception of created personality; and in such view he is also the Mediator of all these intelligences as actually existing, Mediator in a universal sense that must be carefully distinguished from the soteriological, the Revealer of God for them in a purely inward way and by virtue of his dwelling in their spirit, and the sovereign king who conducts their history to its absolute end and completion; for only in communion with God can man, or any personal creature, rise to communion with God, whether directly or in the way of return from sin. Here we have in view the normal development of created personality, and in this sense it is undoubtedly true that man in his very origin is formed for Christ, namely as the Logos. The human nature is primitively disposed for the incarnation, just as all created personality is so in being made for communion with God. What since the fall the Holy Ghost is now for humanity in the sphere of redemption, and what before this redemption took place the Logos never ceased to be for the same humanity, though only as a light shining in darkness, that he would have been for it entirely and in full if it had gone forward without the disorder of sin; so that in this sense also the Holy Ghost is the representative of Christ (John xiv: 16, xvi: 7), here of course as the Logos. And thus all that is truly noble and great in antiquity, in which a higher inspiration comes into view pushing aside for the moment the narrow interests of selfishness, is to be referred to the immanent operation of the Logos as its source; some sense of which indeed we have even in that memorable word of the earnest Roman philosopher: *Nemo vir magnus sine afflatu divino unquam fuit.*[29] Now however, since the entrance of redemption, all true elevation, in the case of man, springs from the Holy Ghost, and so stands inseparably connected with the pursuit of holiness, with the consciousness of personal sin and strenuous endeavors to be delivered from its power.[30]

The passage, Col. i: 15–17, refers to this primitive relation to the Logos, and not to what he is for the world by the incarnation. This is implied by the title πρωτότοκος πάσης κτίσεως, the first-born of the whole creation. In this view it is also that Christ in his state of exaltation,

---

29. [Trans. "No man was ever great without divine inspiration." Hannis Taylor, *Cicero: A Sketch of His Life and Works*, 2nd ed. (Chicago: McClurg, 1918), 497 (the quote is from Cicero, *De Natura Deorum*, II.66).]

30. [Müller, "Untersuchung der Frage," 338–339.]

having again the glory which he had with the Father before the world was, John xvii: 5, is described by the apostles as Lord and Head, not only of the Church, but also of the angels in their various classes and orders; comp. Eph. i: 21, Col. ii: 10, 1 Peter iii: 22, and the ἀνακεφαλαιοῦν ["comprehending," "bringing together"], Eph. i: 10.

If this view of the ideal order of the world in the Divine mind be correct, all else becomes *means* for carrying it out to its appointed end. These are conditioned, in the everlasting omniscience of God, by the vast and mighty disorder which has been brought into the world by sin. The reality of this is so fearful, the catastrophe it involves so great, that to meet it properly required on the part of Divine love not merely a slight modification of its plan as arranged to proceed without sin, but the introduction of a new provision, the most wonderful invention of this love, the awfully glorious mystery of the incarnation. This takes its place thus indeed among the *means* which God employs to carry out the plan of the world, the centre in which all means meet that have for their object the overthrow of sin; a thought which loses its difficulty just in proportion as we are brought to look into the abyss of evil and at the same time into the depths of Divine love.

It is only the fact of sin in truth, apprehended in its world-vast solemnity and significance, that furnishes an adequate reason for the highest act of God's love. The sense of this fact therefore must lead the way in every effort that is made successfully, to understand or interpret the christological mystery.

The distinguished writer, whom we have been trying to follow in this article in the way of free synopsis, is careful to tell us that he has no idea of charging the perilous consequences, which he is led to point out as apparently flowing from the theory he reviews, on such excellent men as Liebner and others who have stood forward in its defence. He regards them rather as fellow laborers with himself on the same platform of evangelical freedom, and has no doubt but that they have in their own way of looking at the subject what are supposed to be sufficient precautions against these consequences. His object is accordingly to open the way for their bringing out still more fully and distinctly the entire sense of their system, in all its aspects and bearings. "This inquiry proposes to be nothing more," he says,

> than an excitement to a new revision of the christological theory in question, on the basis of the true biblical theism, and to a

solution if possible of the difficulties now presented; for which very reason it has been felt necessary to give them the most sharp and distinct expression. If they can be shown to be groundless, of course on the basis just mentioned, the writer would not wish to be among the last certainly to embrace a view, the special advantages of which for the scientific construction of Christian doctrine he can fully appreciate.[31]

J. W. N.

---

31. [Müller, "Untersuchung der Frage," 340.]

Article 6
"Jesus and the Resurrection"

(by John W. Nevin)

EDITOR'S INTRODUCTION

In this sermon, based on the text of Luke 24 dealing with the post-resurrection appearances of Christ, Nevin presents an apologia for the centrality and importance of the resurrection, and in it he underscores key christological, soteriological, and ecclesiological differences between Mercersburg and the mainstream American Protestantism of his day. The text is also significant as an example of Nevin's learned yet accessible preaching style.

Nevin insists that both the suffering and resurrection of Christ were integral to his redemptive work, but he also seeks to explain how these two elements relate to one another. While Christ's death was necessary as a satisfaction and propitiation for sin, nevertheless "[s]uffering and death abstractly considered have no force, in and of themselves, to atone for sin." Rather, the deeper answer lies in the fact that death was necessary in order to "reach the glorious consummation of his mediatorial office."

The mystery of the Incarnation means that "a life supernatural and divine" has been introduced into human history. But this life could not be fully manifested under the "conditions and limitations of our life as it holds in the order of nature," and the reasons for this are both "physical and moral." On the one hand, the world as it currently exists "could not be a sufficient theatre for the manifestation of the glory of Christ," because this "life of nature" must be "sublimated and transfigured into the life of spirit." On the other hand, in his discussion of the moral necessity Nevin underscores the depth of the problem of sin. Because of human sin creation as a whole has fallen under the dominion of the devil, who must be defeated by Christ. In addition, it was needful that Christ take on "fallen humanity" subject to the curse of death, triumph in it over death and the devil, and raise it to a new and higher level of existence. As Nevin memorably puts it, "The moral limitations of man's present state must be overcome in the way of righteousness, as well as its physical limitations in the way of power. In other words, the Redeemer must exhaust the curse by entering into it and taking the full weigh of it upon his own soul. He must suffer in order that he might be glorified." Thus, the atonement is no mere external legal transaction, and a proper understanding of it includes the resurrection as integral to Christ's redemptive work.

In his explanation of the significance of the resurrection for Christ, Nevin observes that it involves not only the recovery of the preincarnate glory of the Logos but also the elevation of Christ's incarnate humanity. Here the humiliation-exaltation schema evident in Philippians 2:5–11 is particularly emphasized, and Nevin insists that this victory and elevation of humanity must reside in Christ's person such that they are accessible to Christians through their union with Christ. Thus there is here an extraordinarily close association of Christ's person and work.

Nevin then brings his sermon to a conclusion with three "general reflections on the nature of Christianity in its relations to the present world." First, salvation involves a transcending of the present order to a "new and higher mode of existence." The old order of this present age must finally pass away in order that the kingdom of God may emerge. Here he cites both the Jewish error of a this-worldly messiah into which even the disciples fell, and the modern error of humanitarian ethical liberalism.

Second, redemption comes to completion in the resurrection of Christ. Thus the resurrection is much more than an external attestation of Christ's righteousness; it is an essential part of his redemptive work. Furthermore, the resurrection of believers is implicated in Christ's resurrection—they are saved through their union with him. In this context Nevin remarks on the "serious aberration" of "most evangelical style of religious thinking at the present time," in which the resurrection is reduced to a mere proof or witness to the gospel.

Third, Nevin closes with an apologia for the church (illustrating the close connection in Mercersburg between Christology and ecclesiology). The system and powers of the church are spiritual, and they derive their existence from the resurrection of Christ. Thus the church, with its sacraments and ministry, is, for Nevin, an "article of faith."

"Jesus and the Resurrection"[1]

"O fools, and slow of heart to believe all that the prophets have spoken," the Saviour said to his two disciples as they walked on their way to Emmaus, and were sad (Luke 24:13–33): "Ought not Christ to have suffered those things, and to enter into his glory?"

The *"ought not"* here may be referred to both clauses of the proposition, so as to mean that it was necessary for Christ to die and to enter into his glory, in order that he might by his glorification carry out in full the great purpose for which he had come into the world. Properly, however, the necessity in question is affirmed of the first part of the proposition in order to the second. Christ must pass out of the world through suffering and death as the only way in which he could enter into his glory.

[THE NECESSITY OF THE CROSS]

Why was this order necessary? Why must the Redeemer of the world die to fulfil his heavenly mission?

It may be answered that the truth of the old Testament Scriptures required it. In no other way could they be fulfilled. The disciples are charged with folly in not having understood and considered this. And so, we are told, "beginning at Moses, and all the prophets he expounded unto them in all the Scriptures the things concerning himself" (v. 27); as afterwards again in the midst of the eleven, we hear him declaring (v. 44), "These are the words which I spake unto you while I was yet with you, that all things must be fulfilled which were written in the law of Moses, and in the prophets, and in the psalms, concerning me." Whereupon it is added, "Then opened he their understanding, that they

1. [Originally printed in the *Mercersburg Review* 13:2 (April 1861): 169–91.]

might understand the Scriptures, and said unto them, Thus it is written, and thus it behooved Christ to suffer, and to rise from the dead the third day; and that repentance and remission of sins should be preached in his name among all nations."

But this answer, it is easy to see, does not carry us at all to the inward reason of the fact which it serves to authenticate as right and true. God's revelation must of course be in harmony with itself from beginning to end. The plan of salvation foreshadowed in prophecies and types must agree with the plan of salvation fulfilled finally in Christ. But this only brings back upon us with new emphasis and force the question before proposed: Why was it necessary that the Saviour should have his mission to fulfil in this way? Why were the Scriptures so framed from the beginning as to converge throughout in this strange sense, that Christ must suffer and die in order that he might enter into his glory?

The answer may be again, that in no other way could he make satisfaction for the sins of men, and thus open the way for their being restored to the favor of God. It was necessary that sin should be atoned for by the penalty of death; the whole Gospel centres in the idea of sacrifice; without the shedding of his blood Christ could not be a true Saviour for sinners. Therefore "he bare our sins in his own body on the tree, that we being dead to sins should live unto righteousness." By his death he became "the propitiation for the sins of the whole world." The *blood* of Jesus Christ the Son of God, we are told, "cleanseth us from all sin."[2]

In all this there is unutterably precious truth. But still it does not of itself at once conduct us to the last sense of our question. Suffering and death abstractly considered have no force, in and of themselves, to atone for sin. We can easily conceive of the sufferings of Christ himself being so circumstanced, that they would have been of no efficacy whatever for this end. If he had suffered, for example, in some other nature and in some other world than our own, the sacrifice must have been for us of no account. Or what is yet more to the purpose, if he had in our nature suffered and died in such way as to have continued afterwards under the power of death, it is plain that all the sorrows of Gethsemane and Calvary would have been powerless to take away a single sin. We cannot say therefore of this relation of Christ's death to the "call for blood" which is supposed to lie in the idea of God's offended justice,

---

2. [1 Pet 2:24; 1 John 2:2; 1 John 1:7.]

that it forms of itself the final cause or absolutely last reason of the law which made it necessary for him to die in order that he might be a perfect Saviour. His death made atonement for sin; just as it was an exemplification also of the highest moral truth for the saving benefit of men through all time; but neither of these purposes can be said to have exhausted its intention or bounded the full scope of its action. They were both comprehended in a necessity of religion broader and deeper than themselves; and with reference to this it is that the question still returns upon us with more solemnity than ever: *Why* did it behoove Christ—having undertaken the redemption of the world—to suffer and to pass out of the world by death, in order that he might accomplish his mediatorial office and work?

The full proper answer lies in the form of the Saviour's interrogation itself, as already explained. "Ought not Christ to have suffered these things, and to enter"—that is, so as to enter, or in order that he might enter—"into his glory." It was necessary that he should die, since only in that way could he reach the glorious consummation of his mediatorial office, and become thus qualified in full to impart life and immortality to the world.

The nature of this necessity will appear, if we reflect upon the constitution of the Redeemer's person in its relation to the present world.

[CHRISTIANITY ROOTED IN MYSTERY OF THE INCARNATION]

Christianity roots itself in the mystery of the incarnation. By the power of that great fact it started originally in the person of Christ, within the bosom of our present natural human life. To redeem man, the Word became flesh, clothing itself with our nature in the most real way. It did so because the idea of redemption required more than any merely outward foreign help. The help must incorporate itself with the life of humanity itself, so as to work by this and through this for the accomplishment of its ultimate object. Such was the meaning of Christ's person, as he stood among men in the days of his flesh. He was the wisdom and power of God unto salvation, in human form. The fulness of the Godhead dwelt in him bodily.

But the very same mystery which makes sure to us the real humanity of Christ, assures us also of the continual presence in his person of a life higher and far more powerful than that of our common manhood in its present natural form—a life supernatural and divine—in virtue of which alone it was possible for him to fulfil his mediatorial work, so as to become the author of salvation for the world. The incarnation means nothing except as it is taken to involve throughout the fact of this higher nature in Christ, and to require at the same time the full unfolding of its resources and powers in connection with his proper humanity, as the only way in which we can conceive of any such revelation as being true and complete. It lay thus in the very constitution of the Redeemer's person that its more than simply human attributes, qualities, and powers —what belonged to it as the eternal Word tabernacling in flesh—should come to suitable development and manifestation. Only so could he display the full perfection of his own being; only so could he take possession of his kingdom and glory; and only so could he be completely qualified as the prince of life, to save his people from their sins, and to bring them up finally from the power of the grave.

For all this, however, there was no room, no sufficient theatre and platform we may say, in the existing economy of the present world. The conditions and limitations of our life as it holds here in the order of nature are such that it was not possible for the full power and glory of Christ's person, and so for the full sense and purpose of his mission into the world, to come out and make themselves known under any such form. The impossibility was both physical and moral.

Regarded simply in its *natural* constitution, it was not possible that the world as it now stands could be a sufficient theatre for the manifestation of the kingdom and glory of Christ. It belongs to the very conception of nature that it should exist in the form only of continual revolution and change. The fashion of the present world, in this view, is always passing away. It subsists by a perpetual process of coming and going. To this law of vanity man himself in his present life forms no exception. As comprehended in the general constitution of nature, though including in himself at the same time the principle of a wholly different superior order of life, he is subject so far as this lower relation prevails to the same conditions of change that characterize the system everywhere else. His physical being here is in no sense commensurate with his moral or spiritual being; and nothing is more plain than that this last needs and demands for its ultimate full development some different mode of existence altogether—a mode of existence in which while the physical shall remain, it will be no longer as the physical merely holding in its own order, as in the present world, but as the life of nature sublimated and transfigured into the life of spirit. In such view the present world, the mortal condition into which men enter here by birth only to pass out of it again by death, could never as such become the seat of a truly perfect and glorified humanity; and it was not possible, therefore, that the kingdom of God as it revealed itself in Christ, for the accomplishment of man's redemption in this form, could ever actualize itself in full on any such theatre or in any such sphere. It might begin here, nay, it was necessary that it should thus come in the flesh in order to be a true redemption for men born of the flesh—but it could not keep itself throughout to such unequal bounds; it must find room for itself by going beyond them, and unfolding a new order of existence answerable to its own nature.

There is represented to be thus, in the Scriptures, a constitutional incompatibility between the present world, naturally considered, and the kingdom of God. The very idea of this kingdom involves attributes which suppose and imply the passing away of much that is essential to the notion of the world as it now stands.

But the difficulty here is not simply physical, a want of full congruity between the conception of nature and the law of life in Christ Jesus; it meets us still farther under a moral aspect, and only in that view indeed comes out at last in its whole significance and force. That man should be subject to the general vanity of nature, and need to be supernaturally redeemed from it, notwithstanding his own spiritual constitution, in virtue of which it ought to be ancillary only to the objects of his higher life, is a fact which in and of itself convicts him of having fallen from righteousness into sin. His present life, being so related to the economy of nature around him, is not normal. His subjection to such vanity is plainly a penal curse. Death with him is the wages of sin; and his whole present mortal state, accordingly, running as it does continually toward this end and having for itself no other possible issue or outlet, is comprehended in the terrible force of this law from beginning to end. How then should it be possible for him to be redeemed in full in his present mortal state? How should he be made superior to the curse of his fallen life, in the very circumstances and conditions which show the power of the fall itself, as it rests upon him in the present world from the cradle to the grave?

The case in this view is put by the Bible in the strongest light, when the present world itself, as a whole, is represented as having by reason of man's sin fallen in some way under the actual dominion of Satan, so as to be now through his bad auspices positively hostile to all righteousness and truth. He is denominated the "prince of this world," the "prince of the power of the air, the spirit that now worketh in the children of disobedience." He is the "god of this world who blinds the eyes of them that believe not"—through the objects, relations and interests of the present world of course—"lest the light of the glorious gospel of Christ, who is the image of God, should shine unto them."[3] This way of representing the subject is too general, and too explicit, to allow of its being resolved into mere metaphor. Most clearly the Scriptures see in the world, as it now stands, an organized power of sin, over which Satan presides, with the purpose of defeating if possible all God's thoughts of mercy toward our fallen race. When Christ came into the world, it was to do battle with this prince of darkness and his kingdom in the most real way. So much was signified by his personal conflict with the Devil in the wilderness, immediately after his baptism; a conflict which served to foreshadow the meaning of his whole subsequent ministry, and which came finally to its last scene only when he could say: "Now is the judgment of this world; now shall the prince of this world be cast out; and I, if I be lifted up, will draw all men unto me"[4]— signifying, we are told, what death he should die. In conformity with which, his incarnation is said in another place to have been for this purpose, "that through death he might destroy him that had the power of death, that is, the devil; and deliver them who through fear of death were all their lifetime subject to bondage."[5]

It lay thus in the very idea of man's redemption, that it could not be completed in the form, and under the conditions of his present worldly life; for that would imply that it might co-exist with the curse from which it seeks to set him free, and be in fact part of the very same constitution of things that has grown out of the curse, and which is pervaded and ruled throughout by the law of sin and death. If our human life was to be redeemed at all, it must be by its being "delivered from this present evil world" (Gal. 1:4); and such deliverance to be real must be

---

3. [John 12:31; Eph 2:2; 2 Cor 4:4.]
4. [John 12:31–32.]
5. [Heb 2:15.]

in the form of a victory, surmounting the whole order of the world as it now stands, and revealing itself as a force greater than nature, greater than sin and all the consequences of sin, under another and altogether different mode of existence.

[THE NECESSITY OF THE RESURRECTION]

While it was necessary then that the Son of God, having undertaken the work of man's redemption, should for this purpose become man, and so make himself subject to the curse of his present fallen state, it was full as much necessary that he should not continue in the sphere of the curse— the constitution of man's life as it holds in the present world—but that he should break through this sphere by exhausting and conquering the whole power of the curse, so as to make room for his kingdom and glory under a higher form. And being fully qualified for all this in the constitution of his person, through the union of the divine nature with his humanity, it was not possible that his incarnation, in its relations to the present world, could take any other course. His manifestation in the flesh here was necessarily a circumscription of his proper mediatorial life and power, an obumbration or hiding of his essential mediatorial glory, which in the nature of the case could not be permanent, but must be regarded as a temporary economy or process simply through which, in the fulness of time, the full mystery of his higher nature would break triumphantly into view. "It was not possible," we are told, "that he should be holden of the pains of death"[6]—that the grave should be able to retain him in its power. But this may be said with equal force of his whole subjection to the power of the present world—the power of nature, including in it now the curse of sin and the inevitable issue of death. That which made it impossible for him to be holden of death, made it impossible for him also to be holden of the mortal constitution through which the natural life of man in the present world is penally shut up from the beginning always to this dread conclusion. Being in himself the principle of righteousness and life, he could not stay in the region of mortal vanity, he could not remain imprisoned in the sphere of the curse; he must burst all these bars, break through all these limitations, in order that the "powers of the world to come,"[7] which were all

6. [Acts 2:24.]
7. [Heb 6:5.]

along inclosed in his person, might be able to unfold themselves in a way commensurate with their own glorious nature.

As the bearer of our fallen humanity,[8] it was necessary thus for Christ, in order that he might enter into his glory, not simply to pass out of this world, but so to pass out of it that he should at the same time bear its curse. The law of sin and death, the power of Satan which prevails in the world through this law, must be met and surmounted in its own sphere, to make room for the law of life as a superior force in another sphere. The moral limitations of man's present state must be overcome in the way of righteousness, as well as its physical limitations in the way of power. In other words the Redeemer must exhaust the curse by entering into it and taking the full weight of it upon his own soul. He must suffer in order that he might be glorified. He must die in order that he might destroy, not only death, but him that had the power of death, and so bring life and immortality to light through the gospel.

This is the idea of the atonement; an idea which centres indeed, of course, in the passion and death of the Saviour, but yet never in these apprehended under an isolated separate view—as though the death of Christ *per se*, and without reference to anything farther, were sufficient at once to take away sin in the character of a legal payment in full to God's offended justice. The power of Christ's death to take away sin, its atoning and saving efficacy, is *always* conditioned in the New Testament by the fact of his resurrection, the victorious superiority of the law of life in him as thus asserted over the law of sin and death. Without the resurrection the death could be of no account. It is his victory over the grave that gives significance to all his sufferings, and imparts to his blood the whole virtue by which it has become the propitiation for the sins of the world.

To fulfil his mission at all then as the Redeemer of our fallen race it was in every way needful that Christ should suffer and die, so as to rise again, and take possession of his kingdom in its proper, eternally glorious form. The problem of redemption itself required it; and it was made necessary also by the constitution of his own person. It would have been a grand contradiction to pretend to set up and complete his kingdom in this world. The eye of the Saviour himself, accordingly, was steadily directed through the whole course of his ministry toward what he saw to be the necessary end of it in his violent death. His disciples

---

8. [See General Introduction.]

indeed, to the very last, clung to the expectation that he would still assert his Messianic glory, agreeably to the common notion among the Jews, under an outward temporal form in the present world. But this was in the face always of their Master's own most plain and solemn words affirming just the contrary; and when their understanding was properly opened for the purpose after his resurrection, they could see easily enough that it was against the true sense also of the old Testament scriptures, as well as at war wholly with every right view of Christ's person and work. For the salvation of the world, we may say, all depended on the glorification of Christ; and this was conditioned absolutely, not simply by his coming in the flesh, but by his suffering in the flesh, and passing out of the world by death. The incarnation must complete its own necessary historical movement in the person of the blessed Redeemer himself, by his being made to suffer the contradiction of sinners, and the furious assaults of hell, out to the extremity of death itself, and by his rising again from the dead, and ascending to the right hand of God—all power being given unto him in heaven and in earth—before it could become fully available, fully prevalent rather, for the purposes of salvation in general, through the mission of the Holy Ghost as it began to take place on the day of Pentecost. "The Holy Ghost," it is said in one place, "was not yet given, because that Jesus was not yet glorified."[9] So he continually speaks of his own removal from the world as being not merely the signal, but the cause, for such a spread and triumph of his kingdom as could have place in no other way. "Except a corn of wheat fall into the ground and die," we hear him saying with reference to this very thought, "it abideth alone; but if it die, it bringeth forth much fruit." Again: "It is expedient for you that I go away; for if I go not away the comforter will not come unto you; but if I depart, I will send him unto you."[10] The entire gospel, with all its opportunities and powers of salvation, depended on Christ's glorification.

The "glory" into which Christ entered by his sufferings and death was in one view the same which he had with the Father before the world was (John 17:5). But in another view it was a new state or condition, resulting from his union with humanity and the work of redemption. It was the glory of his mediatorial life advanced to its full perfection, in the form of victory over the powers of darkness and evil in the world.

9. [John 7:39.]
10. [John 12:24; 16:7.]

It was the glorification of the man Christ Jesus, made perfect through suffering, and exalted at last to the free unobstructed use of the prerogatives and powers which belonged to him as the Son of God. This was the end and object of his humiliation from the beginning. He became a man, and made himself subject to the curse of humanity in its present fallen state, that he might roll away the curse, and in his human nature itself become head over all things to his church. Because he humbled himself, we are told, God hath highly exalted him, and given him a name which is above every name (Phil. 2:8, 9). For the joy that was set before him in this form, he endured the cross, despising the shame, and is set down at the right hand of God (Heb. 12:2). He descended first into the lower parts of the earth, that he might ascend up afterwards far above all heavens, leading captivity captive, and so have power to confer all heavenly gifts upon men (Eph. 4:8–10).

The relation of this mediatorial glory of Christ, then to his previous state of humiliation in the present world, was not one simply of local difference—the humiliation belonging to one world and the glory a waiting fact in another—making it necessary for him to pass from the first over to the second that he might possess the fact as his own; as strangers, for example, may find it necessary to cross mountains or seas in order to come to their proper homes. The relation was one at the same time of real cause and effect. The humiliation of the Redeemer, by its victorious issue, created and brought to pass his mediatorial glory—his condition of perfected humanity in virtue of which only he is the author and finisher of salvation for men; just as the seed, to use his own image, which is cast into the ground and dies there, through that very process of decomposition, is not simply metamorphosed afterwards into another form of life, but actually produces and calls into being what it thus dies to reach. Only as sin, and death, and hell were first conquered in his person; only as the principle of life which was in him became the actual presence of the resurrection, bringing the whole order of the world under his feet, and making room for his glory as a fact brought to pass in this way of victory and conquest; only as the powers of that higher life in the Spirit were first triumphantly asserted in the mediatorial glorification of Christ himself, was it possible for any such state or condition of glory, any such reign or kingdom of salvation, to have real being at all for our fallen race. Thus literally must we take his own words: "I am the resurrection and the life."[11] Because he lives, his people live. Their life is hid with him in God, so that when he appeareth they shall appear with him in glory. As he is the first-born of the natural creation, by whom all things were created that are in heaven and that are in earth, so is he also the beginning, the first-born from the dead, in whom is comprehended the whole power of the new spiritual creation, in virtue of which all his saints are to be raised up to life and immortality at the last day (Col. 1:16–18).

All this being so, well might the risen Redeemer say: "Ought not Christ to have suffered these things, and to enter into his glory?"[12] In no other way could the work of redemption become complete. In no other way could the mystery of the incarnation show itself to be true. The only order of faith here, as distinguished from all humanitarian fancies and from all Gnostic dreams, is that of the ancient Christian Creeds. Starting with the supernatural conception and birth of the Saviour, it goes on immediately to confess his passion, his death, his descent to hades; only to proclaim, however as the necessary result of this the glorious fact of his rising again from the dead, his ascension to the right hand of God, the consequent sending of the Holy Ghost, the establishment thus of the Church, and the economy of grace within its bosom, from its one baptism for the remission of sins onward and forward to the resurrection of the body and the life everlasting.

[GENERAL REFLECTIONS ON THE NATURE OF CHRISTIANITY]

The subject leads us to some general reflections on the nature of Christianity in its relations to the present world.

I. The Christian salvation, by its very conception, is a supernatural fact which must in the end transcend the constitution of the world as it now stands altogether, going out of it and beyond it, and finding room and opportunity for its full development only in a new and higher mode of existence.

This in one view seems to be so plain a truth as necessarily of itself to command universal acknowledgment; since all men do in fact

11. [John 11:25.]
12. [Luke 24:26.]

pass out of the present world by death, and if saved at all therefore can be saved in full only on the other side of death and the grave. But the proposition now before us means a great deal more than this. What it affirms is a constitutional difference between the kingdom of Christ and the present world, making it impossible for them to cohere permanently in one system, and requiring the last absolutely to pass away in order to make room for the first. This is not at once plain for the general thinking of men; and there has always been a tendency in the human mind accordingly, to reduce the difference in question to one of mere measure and degree, to make it more outward than inward, more relative than absolute, so as to invest the idea of the kingdom of God after all with something of a mundane character, carrying out more or less the order of our present natural life.

Such, we know, had come to be the reigning opinion among the Jews, when our Saviour made his appearance in the world. They looked for a Messiah who should rule as a temporal prince, restoring the throne of David, and extending his empire under a worldly form throughout the whole earth.

The same expectation was fondly cherished by the disciples of Christ, and exerted an active influence over them, even after they had come to apprehend in some measure the spiritual glory of his person, notwithstanding all the pains he himself took to eradicate every such thought from their minds. "We trusted it had been he," they say sorrowfully after his death, "which should have redeemed Israel."[13] And even when fully assured subsequently of his resurrection, they were not able at once to take in the full sense of that transcendent fact, but are heard still asking: "Lord, wilt thou at this time restore again the kingdom to Israel" (Acts 1:6). It needed the baptism of the day of Pentecost to liberate them completely from this Jewish preconception, and to reveal to them the true nature of the kingdom of heaven, as being an economy based upon the resurrection of Christ, which must therefore necessarily transcend along with this fact the entire constitution of the present world.

In different ages of the Church, the expectation of the millennium, and of Christ's personal reign upon the earth, has not unfrequently assumed a form involving virtually again the same old Jewish error.[14]

---

13. [Luke 24:21.]

14. [Nevin wrote this at a time of increased popular interest in chiliasm, or

There is however another more subtle, and more common, mode of overlooking the difference, which holds between the constitution of nature and the constitution of grace. It consists in regarding the kingdom of heaven as the continuation and carrying out in some way of the right order of the present world; so that if it may not be actualized here in full, there may be at least a near approximation to it through a proper use of the powers and possibilities of our general life this side the grave. Christianity, it is assumed, must be in harmony with the relations and needs of man's nature in his present worldly state; and what these show to be his obligation and calling here—physically, intellectually, socially, morally—that must be considered as fitting him also for his proper destination hereafter, and as forming, therefore, a direct preparation at least for the kingdom of heaven in the world to come. Such is the humanitarian evangel, which in one form or another has come to prevail so widely especially in our own time, thrusting itself into the place of the true gospel of our Lord and Saviour Jesus Christ. According to this the measure and criterion of Christianity are to be found in its supposed suitableness to the earthly interests of men in their present earthly state; and the prosperous furtherance of these interests, accordingly, is held to be the onward march of the gospel itself, advancing steadily to its millennial glory, and anticipating the full idea of the kingdom of heaven. The order of nature is regarded thus as a system or process, which completes itself by its own movement, in the order of grace. "From nature up to nature's God," is made to be the watchword of religion in place of that grand announcement: "No man hath seen God at any time; the only begotten Son, which is in the bosom of the Father, he hath declared him."[15] To bring matter into subjection to mind through science and art—to verify the sense of the eighth psalm, as far as possible, in a merely natural way, instead of reaching after its verification in the way signified in the second chapter of the

---

premillennial eschatology (Millerism, Adventism). Nevin's own reflections on eschatology were restrained, though he insisted that the orders of the present creation and the future kingdom of God not be conflated. The future state of the redeemed, he insisted, will be a "different mode of existence." Erb, *Dr. Nevin's Theology* (1913), 352.]

15. [John 1:18. The phrase "from nature up to nature's God" comes from the English poet Alexander Pope's (1688–1744), who wrote in his "Essay on Man" (Epistle IV, line 330): "Slave to no sect, who takes no private road, But looks through Nature up to Nature's God." It became an oft-quoted watchword of natural religion in the nineteenth century.]

Epistle to the Hebrews—is held to be for man the great problem of his life, the first law of his ethical being, in fulfilling which he cannot fail to be true at the same time to the claims and behests of religion. Material interests readily transmute themselves thus into spiritual interests. Gain becomes godliness. The triumphs of political economy, the successes of agriculture and trade, pass themselves off for the triumphs and successes of Christianity. Knowledge affects to be, not only power, but piety also and faith. The idea of freedom and the rights of man puts itself forward as synonymous with the idea of redemption. The civilization of the world challenges acknowledgment and regard, as being in truth the evangelical salvation of the world.

But how different now from all these terrestial schemes and conceptions is the representation of Christianity and the kingdom of heaven with which we are met when we look into the New Testament? My kingdom, Christ says, is not of this world. The way to it for himself lay through the world, and out of it, into another order of existence altogether; and how could it be for his people then any new disposition simply of the mortal *seculum* ["age"] in which they have their being this side the grave, or any continuation merely of its laws and forces over into the world beyond. There can be but one law here for Christ and his followers; the disciple must be as his Master. If it was necessary for Christ to conquer and transcend the whole constitution of the world as it now stands, in the way of death, that he might enter into his glory, it must be no less necessary for Christians, if they are to have part in this glory, to pass out of the world in the same way. So much indeed is comprehended in the fundamental rule of Christianity: "Deny thyself, take up thy cross, and *follow me*"; as well as in the pregnant aphorism: "He that loveth his life shall lose it; and he that hateth his life in this world shall keep it unto life eternal."[16] The kingdom of heaven is no mere continuation or carrying forward of the order of this life, whether physical or ethical; it is constitutionally different from this; and is to be reached and possessed only as the whole system of things seen and temporal is superseded at last, through death and the resurrection, by things unseen and eternal.

II. Hence the true significance of the doctrine of the resurrection, and its momentous importance in the Christian system.

---

16. [Matt 16:24; John 12:25.]

The gospel begins in the birth of Christ only to complete itself in his resurrection. Without Easter, Christmas can never be more than an Ebionitic lie or a Gnostic dream. The higher life which joined itself with our dying humanity in the person of Christ, to authenticate itself as real and true, must return again with this humanity to its original sphere. He that descended must also ascend—far above all heavens—up where he was before (Eph. 4:10. John 6:62). "I came forth from the Father," we hear him saying, "and am come into the world; again I leave the world, and go to the Father" (John 16:28). Being what he was from the beginning, the Word incarnate, the only begotten of the Father tabernacling in flesh, it was not possible that his life could hold itself to the bounds of our present earthly state—still less that it could remain shut up under the natural conclusion of that state in the grave and in the dark world of Sheol or Hades; it must rise from the dead, and in doing so burst the cerements at the same time of this whole mortal economy, showing death and sin to be conquered forces, and asserting its own original superiority in a new order of existence altogether. This is what we mean by the resurrection of Jesus Christ from the dead; and it is easy to see how in this view it forms the grand argument or proof of his mission, and becomes for all genuine faith the keystone which binds together the universal arch of Christian doctrine. It is no outward seal simply—the attestation of a stupendous miracle—ratifying and confirming the Messiahship of the Saviour; it is the necessary end and completion of the idea itself which entered into the constitution of his person, without which this must be at once convicted of fantastic unreality. Without it he would have been an impostor, even if he had not pledged his truth previously on the fact. It was the only way in which he could be demonstrated effectually to be the Son of God (Rom. 1:4). Being put to death in the flesh, he must be quickened in the spirit (1 Peter 3:18). Manifested in the flesh, he must be justified in the spirit, that is, vindicated and shown to be divine through the power of the higher life which was in him, surmounting the law of death, and advancing him to heavenly glory, through the resurrection (1 Tim. 3:16).

The resurrection of Christ, being thus the natural result and necessary issue of his heavenly life in its union with the mortal life of men in this world, it could not be a return simply to the condition in which he was previously to his death, the mere recovery of what had been transiently lost by that change. The restoration of Lazarus from the grave was nothing more than this; it served merely to re-instate him in his old life. But it was not for Christ to be brought back from the dead in any such way as that. With the view that is sometimes taken of his death, indeed, as including in itself the whole power of the gospel in the light of a purely outward price paid for sin, and complete for this purpose by itself alone, a resurrection of this mundane sort, bringing after it the setting up of Christ's kingdom in the present world, might seem to involve no fatal contradiction; and it is easy to see also that it would fall in happily enough with much of the humanitarian thinking of the present day, if only we were allowed to conceive of the Saviour's victory over the grave in this way. But every such conception turns the mystery of the incarnation into a figment at last, just as really as if it were pretended that his death was followed by no resurrection whatever. He rose from the dead in virtue of what he was *more* than all that belonged to humanity beyond his own person; and his resurrection, therefore, was not only a return to what he was as a man before, but a free unfolding at the same time of the living power which was previously veiled under his earthly state—but which made itself known now in the way of victory over the universal order of the natural world, abolishing death, and bringing life and immortality to light.

And what the resurrection of Christ is for the doctrine of his person, that in the view of the New Testament the resurrection of believers is also for the doctrine of their future salvation. They are saved through the power of a new heavenly birth—the birth of the Spirit in contradistinction to the birth of the flesh—a birth from above, made possible by the coming down of the Divine Logos into the sphere of our present fallen life—in virtue of which, they are made through union with him to be partakers of the Divine nature, to be the children of God, so as to have in them even here the principle of an indestructible life, which shall be found to triumph hereafter over death itself, in bringing up their bodies from the grave and causing them to be fashioned into the likeness of the glorious body of Christ himself. The idea of the Christian redemption is never that of a salvation which consists in the mere perfecting of the order of man's present life (Ebionitic humanitarianism); nor yet that of a salvation which has to do with his soul only, magically transferred to some other state (Gnostic spiritualism); it looks always to a deliverance that shall make him as a part of the present world superior to its constitutional curse, carrying him victoriously through it, and crowning him at last with immortality in his whole person, body as well as soul. The doctrine of the future state for the righteous becomes thus the doctrine of the resurrection. How full the New Testament is of this thought everywhere, it is not necessary to say.

No one can attentively consider, however, the stress which is laid by the sacred writers on this whole topic, the resurrection of Christ and as flowing from that the resurrection of believers, without being made painfully sensible of a serious aberration from this evangelical peculiarity in much of what claims to be the most evangelical style of religious thinking at the present time.

In the Acts of the Apostles, it is remarkable how the whole idea of preaching with St. Peter first and afterwards with St. Paul seems to revolve continually around the same theme. On all occasions it is the great fact of Christ's resurrection from the dead which is insisted upon, not as a proof merely that the Gospel in some other form is entitled to credit, but as being in reality the sum and substance of the Gospel itself—the whole power of which stands in the consequent glorification of Christ, and the mission of the Holy Ghost making it effectual for the salvation of men through the Church.—Not only at Athens, but in all places, it might be said of Paul emphatically, that he "preached Jesus and the resurrection." So in all the New Testament Epistles. The burden of their teaching throughout is Christ crucified and raised again from the dead, the hope and power of a like resurrection in due course of time for all his people. Let it suffice for the present to quote that trumpet toned passage, Eph. 1:17–23, as an epitome of the universal gospel in *their* sense.

> The God of our Lord Jesus Christ, the Father of glory, give unto you the spirit of wisdom and revelation in the knowledge of him. The eyes of your understanding being enlightened; that ye may know what is the hope of his calling, and what the riches of the glory of his inheritance in the saints, and what the exceeding greatness of his power to us-ward who believe; according to the working of his mighty power, which he wrought in Christ when he raised him from the dead, and set him at his own right hand in the heavenly places—far above all principality, and power, and might, and dominion, and every name that is named, not only in this world but also in that which is to come: and hath put all things under his feet and gave him to be the head over

all things to the Church—which is his body, the fulness of him that filleth all in all.

Who will say that either the resurrection of Christ, or the resurrection of believers, is made to be of the same central interest in the Protestant Christian teaching generally of the present time? With a large part of our pulpits the theme rarely comes into full view at all; and when it does receive attention it is too often in such a way as virtually to kill it by making no account of its proper relations and connections. The truth is, the evangelical theory which rules very much of what is now regarded as Christian teaching would seem to be essentially complete in its own way, both christologically and soteriologically, without either the resurrection of Christ or the resurrection of believers.

III. The system of agencies and powers by which the kingdom of heaven is upheld and carried forward in the present world, in its course of preparation for the world to come, is supernatural, and can be properly apprehended only by the power of faith.

It is not magical—an economy of unearthly forces playing over into the world in a ghost-like visionary way. As the manifestation of Christ himself in the flesh was real, and not simply apparitional as pretended by the Gnostics, so is the constitution of grace also proceeding from his person and work, in its relations to those who are still in the flesh, an earthly constitution. It belongs to the present world, and reveals itself historically under worldly forms and relations. With all this, however, it is a constitution which derives its whole being and force from the resurrection and glorification of Christ. It is brought to pass, and made to be of effect, not through any power that is comprehended in the natural organization of the world, but only through that higher power in Christ's person, in virtue of which he transcended at last the entire constitution of nature, and became head over all things to the church in another order of existence. The very conception of the church, in this view, is that of a spiritual organization in the world, proceeding from the resurrection life of Christ, which while it is in the world is yet not of the world, but the result and presence always of powers and forces which in relation to it are supernatural.

The kingdom of Christ among men is something widely different thus from any other moral or spiritual dominion. Take for example, the authority of Aristotle, which ruled the world of mind through so many centuries. It stands forth as a grand fact in human history, worthy of more admiration than the outward empire of Alexander. But who thinks of ascribing to it, for this reason, any superhuman character. The kingdom of Aristotle was after all part and parcel only of the world's natural life, as it culminates in human intelligence—a true and genuine product, historically, of the powers of humanity in its present mundane state, just as much as the victories of Alexander or the wars of Julius Cesar. But we have no right to conceive of the kingdom of Jesus Christ, under its earthly character, in the same way. It is *not* the product of any forces that are comprehended in the natural constitution of the world; and by no such powers can it be maintained or carried forward, in the exercise of its legitimate functions, to its heaven appointed end. It starts from the glorification of Christ; it is the form and manner in which the glorified Christ reveals his presence, and puts forth his power in the world for purposes and ends that lie beyond the world altogether in his own state and condition of glory. How is it possible then to conceive of it all, if it be not considered a supernatural constitution, carrying in itself supernatural resources, fulfilling supernatural offices, and bringing to pass supernatural results?

Thus it is that the Church is made to be an article of *faith*—one of the primary fundamental articles—in the Creed. Faith in the Church, however, cannot stop with its abstract conception. It must extend to its agencies and powers, its modes and means of grace generally. These may not be estimated by any merely natural standard. We are bound to own in them a supernatural efficacy and force. The word of God is quick and powerful, in a way that transcends all human rhetoric or logic. The sense of the sacraments is not to be plumbed and sounded by any mere natural reason; baptism is supernaturally more than the washing of water, and the Lord's Supper is supernaturally more than the eating of bread and the drinking of wine. The ministry of reconciliation, as it comes by commission from the risen Saviour, and forms part of his ascension gift, includes in it also some portion of his resurrection authority and ascension power. Ecclesiastical acts are not of one order simply with civil acts—they bind and loose, we are told, in heaven. These are hard "sayings," we know, for the common thinking of the world; but it is not easy to see how they can be successfully gainsaid, if we are to admit at all the idea of a constitution of grace on earth, differing from the constitution of nature, and flowing from the glorification of the Saviour regarded as an abiding fact. To make the Church of one order after all with the powers and possibilities of the present world, is to turn the resurrection of Jesus Christ into a Gnostic myth.

J. W. N.

Article 7
"The Moral Character of Jesus Christ"

by Philip Schaff

EDITOR'S INTRODUCTION

This is the one article by John W. Nevin's colleague Philip Schaff included in this volume. Born in Switzerland in 1819, Schaff was exposed to German pietism as a young student in Stuttgart before entering the University of Tübingen, where he sat under F. C. Baur and the mediating theologian I. A. Dorner. Then Schaff matriculated at Halle, where he became friends with the pietist F. A. G. Tholuck, before moving on to Berlin, where he studied under the great church historian August Neander and E. W. Hengstenberg. Clearly Schaff had received as a good a theological education as was to be had in Germany, or anywhere in the world for that matter.

After earning his doctorate at Berlin in 1841, Schaff became a *Privatdocent* (a teacher recognized and appointed by a German university, whose income came from student fees rather than from a university salary) in Berlin. While there he received an invitation to teach at the German Reformed seminary at Mercersburg in Pennsylvania, which he accepted, arriving in America in 1844. Upon his arrival he discovered in his new colleague Nevin a kindred spirit whose theological interests and inclinations matched his own.

This article is a fine example of the broader mid-nineteenth century tendency to approach the Christological problem "from below" (i.e., from the standpoint of Christ's incarnate humanity). This impulse owed much to Schleiermacher, who had sought to understand the significance and distinctiveness of Christ in terms of his archetypal humanity, and who placed particular emphasis on his "unclouded blessedness" (i.e., sinlessness). But, as Schaff notes in this article, such an approach also meshed well with the concerns of a "humanitarian, philanthropic, and yet skeptical age."

Schaff begins the article in a devotional key: "the life and character of Jesus is truly the holy of holies in the history of the world." But such devotion to Christ must not replace careful thought, for faith and knowledge are interrelated, and the goal is an "intelligent faith." After affirming the centrality of Christology for theology, Schaff explains the method utilized—a Christology "from below" which focuses on Christ's "personal character" as pointing to his divinity.

Citing Irenaeus (though rejecting Irenaeus's odd suggestion that Jesus died an old man) Schaff suggests that "Christ passed through all the stages of human life from infancy to manhood . . . that he might redeem and sanctify them all and be a perpetual model for imitation." Furthermore, Jesus' humble and unlettered background cannot explain the learning and sublimity of his teachings, and yet he accomplished so much in such a brief span of time. Through it all he remained "singularly unostentatious, modest and quiet."

In his description of Jesus' sinlessness, Schaff rejects impeccability (the notion that Jesus was immune to temptation and sin), for this would make Jesus' moral life on earth "an unreal show." Rather, his sinlessness initially was the "relative sinlessness of Adam before the fall," and here Schaff cites the Augustinian language of *posse non peccare* ("able not to sin") and *non posse peccare* ("not able to sin"). Through continued obedience Christ gradually attained to the "absolute sinlessness" of *non posse peccare*. This sinlessness of Christ, so inexplicable on merely human terms, implies that "Christ differed from all other men not in degree only, but in kind."

This sinlessness was also accompanied by "absolute moral and religious perfection," in which all virtues were exercised in perfect harmony, and Christ's religious perfection is described in terms reminiscent of Schleiermacher as a "self-consciousness . . . at every moment conditioned, animated and impregnated by the consciousness of God." Schaff goes on to speak of "the completeness or pleromatic fullness of the moral and religious character of Christ." While other great men speak to the needs and aspirations of their own ages, Christ is of universal significance and relevant to all times in human history. Informing this, of course, is the Mercersburg conception of Christ as possessing a generic human nature and as the one who has taken humanity comprehensively considered into union with God.

Given that the sinlessness and moral perfection of Christ are completely unprecedented in human history, the only explanation is to be found in "his superhuman and divine origin." In designating himself the "Son of Man," Christ proclaims his genuine humanity, but he is no mere man; he is "the ideal, the universal, the absolute man, the second Adam descended from heaven, the head of a new and superior order of the race." Likewise, he is the "Son of God" who is "eternally begotten of the substance of the Father." In this context Schaff notes the express claims to deity by Christ recorded in the Gospels, and he observes that such claims would be completely inappropriate for a mere human being to make.

Finally, Schaff examines other attempts to account for the sinlessness of Christ but without recognizing the deity of Christ. Socinian and Unitarian efforts to explain the moral character of Christ are inconsistent and avoid inconvenient teachings of Scripture. Some outright "enemies of Christianity" resort to the "hypothesis of imposture," maintaining that Jesus was a deceitful fraud, but this theory is singularly incompatible with the picture of Jesus in the New Testament. Others suggest the "hypothesis of enthusiasm," arguing that Jesus was delusional, but this too is inconsistent with the presentation of Jesus' calmness and humility in the Gospels. Still others attribute mistaken delusions, not to Jesus himself, but to his disciples, and here he cites the rationalistic criticism of H. E. G. Paulus, who proposed far-fetched "rational" explanations for the miracle stories in the Gospels. Finally, Schaff mentions the "hypothesis of a poetical fiction" which he associates with D. F. Strauss's view of the Gospels as permeated with myth. This Schaff regards as unable to explain either the narratives or the composition of the Gospels. Furthermore, if consistently applied to other narratives from the past, the method would dissolve Socrates and Charlemagne into myth as well.

"The Moral Character of Jesus Christ, or The Perfection of Christ's Humanity a Proof of His Divinity"[1]

When the Angel of the Lord appeared to Moses in the burning bush, he was commanded to put off his shoes from his feet: for the place whereon he stood was holy ground. With what reverence and awe then should we approach the contemplation of the great reality—God manifest in the flesh—of which the vision of Moses was but a significant type and shadow!

The life and character of Jesus Christ is truly the holy of holies in the history of the world. Eighteen hundred years have passed away, since He appeared in the fulness of time on this earth to redeem a fallen race from sin and death, and to open a never ceasing fountain of righteousness and life. The ages before him anxiously awaited his coming, as the desire of all nations; the ages after him proclaim his glory and ever extend his dominion. The noblest and best of men under every clime hold him in the purest affection and the profoundest gratitude, not only, but in divine adoration and worship. His name is above every name that may be named in heaven or on earth, and the only one whereby the sinner can be saved. He is Immanuel, God with us, the Eternal Word become flesh, very God and very man in one undivided person, the Author of the new creation, the Way, the Truth, and the Life, the Prophet, Priest and King of regenerate humanity, the Saviour of the world. Thus He stands out to the faith of the entire Christian Church, Greek, Latin, and Evangelical, in every civilized country on the globe. His power is now greater, his kingdom larger than ever, and will

---

1. [Originally printed in the *Mercersburg Review* 13:3 (July 1861): 321–73.]

continue to spread, until all nations shall bow before him and kiss his sceptre of righteousness and peace.

Blessed is he who from the heart can believe that Jesus is the Son of God and the fountain of salvation. True faith is indeed no work of nature, but an act of God wrought in the soul by the Holy Ghost, who reveals Christ to us in his true character, as Christ revealed the Father. Faith with its justifying, sanctifying and saving power is independent of science and learning, and may be kindled even in the heart of a little child and an illiterate slave. It is the peculiar glory of the Redeemer and his religion to be coextensive with humanity itself without distinction of sex, age, nation and race. His saving grace flows and overflows to all and for all, on the simple condition of repentance and faith.

This fact, however, does not supersede the necessity of thought and argument. Revelation, although above nature and above reason, is not against nature and against reason. On the contrary, nature and the supernatural as has been well said by a distinguished New England divine, "constitute together the one system of God."[2] Christianity satisfies the deepest intellectual as well as moral and religious wants of man who is created in the image and for the glory of God. It is the revelation of truth as well as of life. Faith and knowledge, *pistis* and *gnosis*, are not antagonistic but complementary forces, not enemies but inseparable twin sisters. Faith precedes knowledge, but it just as necessarily leads to knowledge; while true knowledge on the other hand is always rooted and grounded in faith and tends to confirm and to strengthen it. Thus we find the two combined in the famous confession of Peter when he says in the name of all the other apostles: "We believe and we

---

2. By Horace Bushnell in his recent work on the subject. [Horace Bushnell: *Nature and the Supernatural, as together constituting the one System of God* (New York: Charles Scribner, 1858). Bushnell (1802–76) was a Congregational minister and theologian who, like the Mercersburg theologians, rejected the older Scottish Common Sense empiricism in favor of a more intuitive, idealistic mode of thought. Nevin reviewed *Nature and the Supernatural* in the 1860 issue of the *Mercersburg Review*, in an article entitled "Natural and Supernatural," pp. 176–211. This essay is slated to appear in vol. 13 of the present series.] The same idea Dr. John W. Nevin, in his able work *The Mystical Presence*, Philad., 1846, p. 199, expresses in these words: "Nature and Revelation, the world and Christianity, as springing from the same divine Mind, are not two different systems joined together in a merely outward way. They form a single whole, harmonious with itself in all its parts. The sense of the one then is necessarily included and comprehended in the sense of the other. The mystery of the new creation must involve in the end the mystery of the old; and the key that serves to unlock the meaning of the first, must serve to unlock the inmost secret of the last."

know that Thou art the Christ."³ But so intimately are both connected that we may also reverse the famous maxim of Augustine, Anselm and Schleiermacher: *Fides praecedit intellectum*,⁴ and say: *Intellectus praecedit fidem*. For how can we believe in any object without at least some general historical knowledge of its existence and character? Faith even in its first form, as a submission to the authority of God and an assent to the truth of his revelation, is an exercise of the mind and reason as well as of the heart and the will. An idiot or a madman cannot believe. Our religion demands not a blind, but a rational, intelligent faith, and this just in proportion to its strength and fervor aims at an ever deepening insight into its own sacred contents and object.

As living faith in Christ is the soul and centre of all sound practical Christianity and piety, so the true doctrine of Christ is the soul and centre of all sound Christian theology. St. John makes the denial of the incarnation of the Son of God the criterion of antichrist, and consequently the belief in this central truth the test of Christianity. The incarnation and the divine glory shining through the veil of Christ's humanity is the grand theme of his Gospel, which he wrote with the pen of an angel from the very heart of Christ, as his favorite disciple and bosom-friend. The Apostles' Creed, starting as it does from the confession of Peter, makes the article on Christ most prominent and assigns to it the central position between the preceding article on God the Father and the succeeding article on the Holy Ghost. The development of ancient Catholic theology commenced and culminated with the triumphant defense of the true divinity and true humanity of Christ, against the opposite heresies of Judaizing Ebionism which denied the former, and paganizing Gnosticism which resolved the latter into a shadowy phantom. The evangelical Protestant theology is essentially christological or controlled throughout by the proper idea of Christ as the God-man and Saviour. This is emphatically the article of the standing or falling Church. In this the two most prominent ideas of the Reformation, the doctrine of the supremacy of the Scriptures, and the doctrine of justification by grace through faith, meet and are

---

3. John 6:69: ἡμεῖς πεπιστεύκαμεν καὶ ἐγνώκαμεν, *credidimus et cognovimus*. [Trans. "we have believed, and have come to know" (RSV).] The reverse order we have in John 10:38: "that ye may know and believe that the Father is in me, and I in him."

4. [Trans. "faith precedes understanding." This principle, that faith in the general truths of revelation precedes understanding of the particulars of creation, was a hallmark of the Augustinian and Anselmian tradition of Christian Platonism.]

vitally united. Christ's word—the only unerring and efficient guide of truth, Christ's work—the only unfailing and sufficient source of peace, Christ—all in all, this is the principle of genuine Protestantism.[5]

[A CHRISTOLOGY FROM BELOW]

In the construction of the true doctrine of Christ's person we may, with St. John in the prologue to his Gospel, begin from above with his eternal Godhead and proceed through the creation and the preparatory revelation of the Old Testament dispensation till we reach the incarnation and his truly human life for the redemption of the race. Or, with the other evangelists, we may begin from below with his birth from the Virgin Mary and rise up through the successive stages of his earthly life, his discourses and miracles to his assumption into that divine glory which he had before the foundation of the world. The result reached in both cases is the same, that Christ unites in his person the whole fulness of the Godhead and the whole fulness of sinless manhood.

The older theologians, both Catholic and Evangelical, proved the divinity of the Saviour in a direct way from the miracles performed by him, and the prophecies fulfilled in him, from the divine names which he bears, from the divine attributes which are predicated of him, from the divine works which he performed, and from the divine honors which he claimed, and which were fully accorded to him by his apostles and the whole Christian Church to this day.

But it may also be proved by the opposite process, the contemplation of the singular perfection of his humanity, which rises, by almost universal consent even of unbelievers, so far above every human greatness known before or since, that it can only be rationally explained on the ground of such an essential union with the Godhead as he claimed himself and as his inspired apostles ascribed to him. The more deeply we penetrate through the veil of his flesh, the more clearly we behold the glory of the Only Begotten of the Father shining through the same, full of grace and of truth.[6]

---

5. [See Philip Schaff, *The Principle of Protestantism* (Chambersburg, PA: German Reformed Church, 1845), included in volume 3 of the present series, where this theme is developed.]

6. Ullmann, *Suendlosigkeit Jesu*, 6th ed. p. 215: "*So führt schon das Vollendet-Menschliche in Jesu, wenn wir es mit allem Uebrigen, was die Menschheit darbietet, vergleichen, zur Anerkennung des Göttlichen in ihm.*" [Trans. "Thus the perfect humanity in

166   The Incarnate Word

Modern evangelical theology owes this new homage to the Saviour. The powerful attacks of the latest phase of infidelity upon the credibility of the Gospel History call for it and have already led, by way of reaction, to new triumphs of the old faith of the Church in her divine head. Our humanitarian, philanthropic and yet skeptical age is more susceptible for this argument than for the old dogmatic method of demonstration. With Thomas, the representative of honest and earnest skepticism among the apostles, it refuses to believe in the divinity of the Lord unless supported by the testimony of its senses; it desires to lay the finger into the print of his nails and to thrust the hand into his side, before it exclaim in humble adoration: " My Lord and my God."[7]

Jesus, when we compare it with all the rest of humanity, already leads us to a recognition of the divine in him." Karl (or Carl) Christian Ullmann (1796–1865), German mediating theologian of considerable importance to the Mercersburg movement. His 1845 article ("Ueber den unterschiedenen Charakter des Christenthums, mit Beziehung auf neuere Auffassungsweisen," *Theologische Studien und Kritiken* 18/1 (1845): 7–61 (trans. "On the Distinctive Character of Christianity, with Reference to Newer Thinking") was translated and published as a "Preliminary Essay" in John W. Nevin's *The Mystical Presence*. His *Ueber die Sündlosigkeit Jesu. Eine apologetische Betrachtung* (trans. *On the Sinlessness of Jesus. An Apologetic Examination*) went though seven German editions, and was twice translated into English.] Dorner, *Entwicklungsgeschichte der Lehre von der Person Christi*, 2nd ed. vol. II. p. 1211: "*Jesu Heiligkeit und Weisheit, durch die er unter den sündigen, viel-irrenden Menschen einzig dasteht, weiset . . . auf einen übernatürlichen Ursprung seiner Person. Diese muss, um inmitten der Sünderwelt begreiflich zu sein, aus einer eigenthümlichen und wunderbar schöpferischen That Gottes abgeleitet, ja es muss in Christus . . . von Gott aus betrachtet, eine Incarnation göttlicher Liebe, also göttlichen Wesens gesehen werden, was ihn als den Punkt erscheinen lässt, wo Gott und die Menschheit einzig und innigst geeiniget sind.*" [Trans. "The holiness and wisdom of Jesus, which give Him an unique position amongst sinful, much-erring men . . . do therefore point to a supernatural origin of His person. If we are to understand its appearance in the midst of a world of sinners, we must trace it back to a peculiar and miraculously creative deed of God; . . . Christ, looked at in connection with God must be deemed an incarnation of divine love, in other words, to be of divine essence; and this makes Him appear to be the point in which deity and humanity are uniquely and most intimately united." J. A. Dorner, *History of the Development of the Doctrine of the Person of Christ* (Edinburgh: T. & T. Clark, 1872), II/3: 223.] Compare also Ebrard, *Christliche Dogmatik*, 1852, vol. II. p. 24–31. [Johann Heinrich August Ebrard (1818–1888), German Reformed theologian who taught at Zurich and Erlangen. His *Das Dogma vom heiligen Abendmahl und seiner Geschichte* (trans. *The Doctrine of the Lord's Supper and Its History*), 2 vols. (Frankfurt: Heinrich Zimmer, 1845–46) was influential on John W. Nevin.]

7. A Life of Christ written from this stand-point and rising from the humanity to the divinity of the Saviour, is yet a desideratum in our theological literature. But we have important contributions towards it, especially by three modem divines, a German, an English, and an American, which shows that this view of Christ forces itself upon

It is from this point of view that we will endeavor, in as popular and concise a manner as the difficulty of the subject and the dignity of the occasion permit, to analyze and exhibit the human character of Christ. We propose to take up the man Jesus of Nazareth as he appears on the simple, unsophisticated record of the plain and honest fishermen of Galilee, and as he lives in the faith of Christendom, and we shall find him in all the stages of his life both as a private individual and as a public character so far elevated above the reach of successful rivalry and so singularly perfect that this very perfection in midst of an imperfect and sinful world constitutes an irresistible proof of his divinity.

A full discussion of the subject would require us to consider Christ in his official as well as personal character, and to describe him as a teacher, a reformer, a worker of miracles, and the founder of a spiritual kingdom universal in extent and perpetual in time. From every point of view we would be irresistibly driven to the same result. But our present purpose confines us to the consideration of his personal character, and this alone, we think, is sufficient for the conclusion.

[THE STAGES OF CHRIST'S HUMAN LIFE]

Christ passed through all the stages of human life from infancy to manhood, and represented each in its ideal form, that he might redeem and

---

the thinking minds of the three nations which now take the lead in Protestant theological science and literature. We refer to Dr. C. Ullmann: *Die Suendlosigkeit Jesu. Eine apologetische Betrachtung* (first published in the "Studien und Kritiken," 1828, Heft 1), 6th ed. Heidelberg, 1853 (translated into English by Lundin Brown: *The Sinlessness of Jesus: an Evidence of Christianity.* Edinburgh, 1858); John Young: *The Christ of History; an Argument grounded in the facts of his Life on earth,* republ. New York, 1856; and Horace Bushnell: *Nature and the Supernatural, as together constituting the one System of God,* New York, 1858; Chapter X and XI. p. 276–366. Compare also the beautiful Essay of the late Dr. James W. Alexander of New York, on the *Character of Jesus, an Argument for the Divine Origin of Christianity* (published in the "Lectures on the Evidences of Christianity delivered at the University of Virginia," New York, 1852, p. 193–211), and my *History of the Apostolic Church,* New York, 1853 (first in German at Mercersburg, 1851), p. 433 ff., and my *History of the Christian Church in the first three Centuries,* p. 53–59. It should be stated that the apologetic anti-Strauss literature on the Life of Jesus, especially Neander, Lange, Olshausen, Ebrard, Tholuck, Hoffmann, Schmid and Dorner, have brought out the ethical element and human perfection of Christ more fully than had been done before. The French works of E. Dandiran: *Essai sur la divinite du caractere moral de Jesus-Christ,* Genève, 1850, and of Edm. de Pressensé: *Le Redempteur,* Par., 1854, which seem to follow the same train of thought, we know only by name.

sanctify them all and be a perpetual model for imitation, He was the model infant, the model boy, the model youth, and the model man.[8] But the weakness, decline and decrepitude of old age would be incompatible with his character and mission. He died and rose in the full bloom of early manhood, and lives in the hearts of his people in unfading freshness and unbroken vigor for ever.

Let us first glance at the infancy and boyhood of the Saviour. The history of the race commences with the beauty of innocent youth in the garden of Eden, "when the morning stars sang together and all the sons of God shouted for joy," in beholding Adam and Eve created in the image of their Maker, the crowning glory of all his wonderful works. So the second Adam, the Redeemer of the fallen race, The Restorer and Perfecter of man, comes first before us in the accounts of the Gospels as a child born, not in paradise, it is true, but among the dreary ruins of sin and death, from an humble virgin, in a lowly manger—yet pure and innocent, the subject of the praise of angels and the adoration of men. Heaven and earth, the Shepherds of Bethlehem in the name of Israel longing after salvation, and the Wise Men from the East as the representatives of heathenism in its dark groping after the "Unknown God," unite in the worship of the new born King and Saviour. Here we meet at the very threshold of the earthly history of Christ that singular

---

8. This idea is almost as old as the Christian Church and was already pretty clearly taught by Irenaeus, who, through the single link of his teacher Polycarp, stood connected with the age of St. John the apostle. He says, *Adv. haereses*, lib. II. cap. 22. § 4: "*Omnes enim venit (Christus) per semetipsum salvare, omnes, inquam, qui per eum renascuntur in Deum, infantes et parvulos et pueros et seniores. Ideo per omnom venit aetatem et infantibus infans factus, sanctificans infantes; in parvulis parvulus, sanctificans hanc ipsam habentes aetatem, simul et exemplum illis pietatis effectus et justitiae et subjectionis; in juvenibus juvenis, exemplum juvenibus fiens et sanctificans Domino. Sic et senior in senioribus (?), ut sit perfectus magister in omnibus,*" etc. [Trans. "For He came to save all though means of Himself—all, I say, who through Him are born again to God—infants, and children, and boys, and youths, and old men. He therefore passed through every age, becoming an infant for infants, thus sanctifying infants; a child for children, thus sanctifying those who are of this age, being at the same time made to them an example of piety, righteousness, and submission; a youth for youths, becoming an example to youths, and thus sanctifying them for the Lord. So likewise He was an old man for old men, that He might be a perfect master for all . . ." Irenaeus, *Against Heresies*, in *The Ante-Nicene Fathers*, ed. Alexander Roberts and James Donaldson (Grand Rapids: Eerdmans, 1981 [reprint.]), I:391.] But Irenaeus erred in carrying the idea too far and assuming Christ to have lived over fifty years, on the ground of the indefinite estimate of the Jews, John 8:57. Hippolytus, in his recently discovered *Philosophumena*, expresses the same view.

combination of humility and grandeur, of simplicity and sublimity, of the human and divine which characterizes it throughout, and distinguishes it from every other history. He is not represented as an unnatural prodigy, anticipating the maturity of a later age, but as a truly human child, silently lying and smiling on the bosom of his Virgin mother, "growing" and "waxing strong in spirit,"[9] and therefore subject to the law of regular development; yet differing from all other children by his supernatural conception and perfect freedom from hereditary sin and guilt. He appears in the celestial beauty of unspotted innocence, a veritable flower of paradise. He was "that Holy Thing," according to the announcement of the angel Gabriel,[10] admired and loved by all who approached him in childlike spirit, but exciting the dark suspicion of the tyrant king who represented his future enemies and persecutors. Who can measure the ennobling, purifying and cheering influence which proceeds from the contemplation of the Christ-child at each returning Christmas season upon the hearts of young and old in every land and nation! The loss of the first estate is richly compensated by the undying innocence of paradise regained.

Of the boyhood of Jesus we know only one fact, recorded by Luke, but it is in perfect keeping with the peculiar charm of his childhood and forshadows at the same time the glory of his public life, as one uninterrupted service of his heavenly Father.[11] When twelve years old we find him in the temple in the midst of the Jewish doctors, not teaching and offending them, as in the apocryphal Gospels, by any immodesty or forwardness, but hearing and asking questions, thus actually learning

---

9. Luke 2:40. Comp. 2:52, Heb. 2:10–18 and 5:8 and 9, where it is said, that he *learned* obedience, and being made perfect he *became* the author of eternal salvation.

10. Luke 1:35.

11. Dr. J. P. Lange, in his Leben Jesu nach den Evangelien, Heidelberg, 1844, sqq,. vol. II. p. 127, says; "*Die Geschichte des zwölfjährigen Jesu repräsentirt seine ganze Entwicklung. Sie ist seine charakterische Knabenthat, die Offenbarung seines jugendlichen Lebens; ein Wiederglanz der Herrlichkeit seiner Geburt, ein Vorzeichen seines zukünftigen Heldenlaufes. Sie stellt die Kinderheit seiner Idealität dar; desswegen auch die Idealität der Kindheit überhaupt.*" [Trans. "The history of Jesus in his twelfth year represents his whole development. It is the characteristic deed of his youth, the revelation of his youthful life, a reflection of his birth, a sign and anticipation of his future heroic career. It represents the childhood of his ideality, therefore also the ideality of childhood in general." In Philip Schaff, *The Person of Christ: The Perfection of His Humanity Viewed as a Proof of His Divinity* (London: James Nisbet, 1880), 150.] Compare also the suggestive remarks of Olshausen to that passage, *Commentar* (3rd Germ. ed.), vol I. p. 145 ff.

from them; and yet filling them with astonishment at his understanding and answers. There is nothing premature, forced or unbecoming his age, and yet a degree of wisdom and an intensity of interest in religion which rises far above a purely human youth. "He increased," we are told, "in wisdom and stature and in favor with God and man"[12]; he was subject to his parents and practised all the virtues of an obedient son; and yet he filled them with a sacred awe as they saw him absorbed in "the things of his Father,"[13] and heard him utter words, which they were unable to understand at the time, but which Mary treasured up in her heart as a holy secret, convinced that they must have some deep meaning answering to the mystery of his supernatural conception and birth.

Such an idea of a harmless and faultless heavenly childhood, of a growing, learning, and yet surprisingly wise boyhood, as it meets us in living reality at the portal of the Gospel history, never entered the imagination of biographer, poet, or philosopher before. On the contrary, as has been justly observed by an able American divine,[14]

> in all the higher ranges of character, the excellence portrayed is never the simple unfolding of a harmonious and perfect beauty contained in the germ of childhood, but it is a character formed by a process of rectification in which many follies are mended and distempers removed, in which confidence is checked by defeat, passion moderated by reason, smartness sobered by experience. Commonly a certain pleasure is taken in showing how the many wayward sallies of the boy are, at length, reduced by discipline to the character of wisdom, justice, and public heroism so much admired. Besides, if any writer, of almost any age, will undertake to describe, not merely a spotless, but a superhuman or celestial childhood, not having the reality before him, he

---

12. Luke 2:52.

13. Luke 2:49: ἐν τοῖς τοῦ πατρός μου δεῖ (the δεῖ indicates a *moral* necessity which is identical with true freedom) εἶναι με. ["I must be about my Father's business," KJV.] The fathers and most of the modern commentators refer the τοῖς to the *house* of God, or the temple. This is grammatically allowable, but restricts the sense and deprives it of its deeper meaning. For he could only occasionally be in the temple of Jerusalem. Nearly all the English versions, Tyndal, Cranmer, Geneva, and James, translate more correctly "about my father's business." But we object to the *business* in this connection, and prefer the more literal translation "*in* (not *about*) the *things* (or affairs) of my Father." The *in* signifies the life element in which Christ moved during his whole life, whether in the temple or out of it.

14. Horace Bushnell, in his genial work already quoted, on *Nature and the Supernatural*, p. 280.

must be somewhat more than human himself, if he does not pile together a mass of clumsy exaggerations, and draw and overdraw, till neither heaven nor earth can find any verisimilitude in the picture.

This unnatural exaggeration, into which the mythical fancy of man, in its endeavor to produce a superhuman childhood and boyhood, will inevitably fall, is strikingly exhibited in the apocryphal Gospels, which are related to the canonical Gospels as the counterfeit to the genuine coin, or as a revolting caricature to the inimitable original, but which by the very contrast tend, negatively, to corroborate the truth of the evangelical history. While the evangelists expressly reserve the performance of miracles to the age of maturity and public life, and observe a significant silence concerning the parents of Jesus, the pseudo-evangelists fill the infancy and early years of the Saviour and his mother with the strangest prodigies, and make the active intercession of Mary very prominent throughout. According to their representation, even dumb idols, irrational beasts, and senseless trees, bow in adoration before the infant Jesus on his journey to Egypt, and after his return, when yet a boy of five or seven years, he changes balls of clay into flying birds for the idle amusement of his playmates, strikes terror round about him, dries up a stream of water by a mere word, transforms his companions into goats, raises the dead to life, and performs all sorts of miraculous cures through a magical influence which proceeds from the very water in which he was washed, the towels which he used, and the bed on which he slept.[15] Here we have the falsehood and absurdity of unnatural fiction, while the New Testament presents us the truth and beauty of a supernatural, yet most real history which shines out only in brighter colors by the contrast of the mythical shadow.

With the exception of these few but significant hints, the youth of Jesus and the preparation for his public ministry are enshrined in mysterious silence. But we know the outward condition and circumstances under which he grew up; and these must be admitted to furnish no explanation for the astounding results without the admission of the supernatural and divine element in his life.

---

15. See the particulars with ample quotations from the sources in Rud. Hofmann's *Leben Jesu nach den Apokryphen im Zusammenhang aus den Quellen erzaehlt und wissenschaftlich untersucht.* Leipzig, 1851. p. 140–263 [trans. "The Life of Jesus according to the Apocrypha, recounted and scientifically investigated from the sources."].

He grew up among a people seldom and only contemptuously named by the ancient classics, and subjected at the time to the yoke of a foreign oppressor; in a remote and conquered province of the Roman empire; in the darkest district of Palestine; in a little country town of proverbial insignificance; in poverty and manual labor, in the obscurity of a carpenter's shop; far away from universities, academies, libraries, and literary or polished society; without any help, as far as we know, except the parental care, the book of nature, the Old Testament Scriptures, and the secret intercourse of his soul with God the heavenly Father. Hence the question of Nathanael: "What good can come out of Nazareth?"[16] Hence the natural surprise of the Jews, who knew all his human relations and antecedents. "How knoweth this man letters," they asked, when they heard Jesus teach, "having never learned?"[17] And on another occasion, when he taught in the synagogue: "Whence hath this man this wisdom and these mighty works? Is not this the carpenter's son? is not his mother called Mary? and his brethren, James and Joses and Simon and Judas? And his sisters, are they not all with us? Whence then hath this man all these things?"[18] These questions are unavoidable and unanswerable if Christ be regarded a mere man. For each effect presupposes a corresponding cause.

The difficulty here presented can by no means be solved by a reference to the fact that many, perhaps the majority of great men, especially in the Church, have risen by their own industry and perseverance from the lower walks of life and from a severe contest with poverty and obstacles of every kind. The fact itself is readily conceded; but in every one of these cases schools, or books, or patrons and friends, or peculiar events and influences, can be pointed out, as auxiliary aids in the development of intellectual or moral greatness. There is always some human or natural cause, or combination of causes, which accounts for the final result.

Luther, for instance, was, indeed, the son of poor peasants and had a very hard youth, but yet he went to the schools of Mansfeld, Magdeburg and Eisenach, to the University of Erfurt, passed through

---

16. [John 1:46.]

17. John 7:15.

18. Matth. 13:54–56. Comp. also Mark 6:3. "Is not this the carpenter, the son of Mary," etc., from which it would appear that Jesus himself engaged in the trade of Joseph.

the ascetic discipline of convent life, lived in a university surrounded by professors, students and libraries, and was innocently as it were made a reformer by extraordinary events and the irresistible current of his age.

Shakspeare is generally and justly regarded as the most remarkable and almost wonderful example of a self-taught man, who without the regular routine of school education became the greatest dramatic poet of all times. But the absurd idea that the son of the Warwickshire yeoman, or butcher, or glover—we hardly know which—was essentially an unlearned man, and jumped with one bound from the supposed but poorly authenticated youthful folly of deer-stealing to the highest position in literature, has long since been abandoned. It is certain that he spent several years in the free grammar school of Stratford upon-Avon, where he probably acquired the "small Latin and less Greek" which, however small in the eyes of so profound a scholar as Ben Johnson, was certainly large enough to make the fortune of any enterprising young Yankee. And whatever were the defects of his training, he must have made them up by intense private study of books and the closest observation of man and things. For his dramas—the occasional chronological, historical and geographical mistakes notwithstanding, which are small matters at all events, and in most cases, as in "Pericles" and in "Midsummer Night's Dream," intentional or mere freaks of fancy—abound in the most accurate and comprehensive knowledge of human nature under all its types and conditions, in the cold north and the sunny south, in the fifteenth century and at the time of Caesar, under the influence of Christianity and of Judaism, together with a great variety of historical and other information which cannot be acquired without immense industry and the help of oral or written instruction.[19] Moreover he lived in the city of London, united the offices of actor, manager and writer, in the classic age of Elizabeth, during the closing scenes of the greatest upheaving of the human mind which ever took place since the introduction of Christianity, in the company of genial and gifted friends, and with free access to the highest ranks of blood, wealth and wit.

19. Comp. G. G. Gervinus: *Shakspeare*, Leipzig, 1850, vol. i. p. 38–41. This masterly critic and expounder of the British poet pronounces him one of the best and most extensively informed men of his age: "*Es ist heute kein Wagniss mehr, zu sagen, dass Shakspeare in jener Zeit an Umfang vielfachen Wissens sehr wenige seines Gleichen gehabt habe.*" [Trans. "There is today no more risk in saying that Shakespeare in that time possessed a scope of knowledge had by very few of his contemporaries."]

In the case of Christ no such natural explanation can be given. All the attempts to bring him into contact with Egyptian wisdom, or the Essenic theosophy, or other sources of learning, are without a shadow of proof, and explain nothing after all. For, unlike all other great men, even the prophets and the apostles, he was absolutely original and independent. He taught the world as one who had learned nothing from it and was under no obligation to it. "His character and life were originated and sustained in spite of circumstances with which no earthly force could have contended, and therefore must have had their real foundation in a force which was preternatural and divine."[20] At the same time it in easy to see, from the admission of Christ's divinity, that by this condescension he has raised humble origin, poverty, manual labor, and the lower orders of society, to a dignity and sacredness never known before, and has revolutionized the false standard of judging the value of men and things from their outward appearance, and of associating moral worth with social elevation, and moral degradation with low rank.

[THE PUBLIC MINISTRY OF JESUS]

We now approach the public life of Jesus. In his thirtieth year, after the Messianic inauguration through the baptism by John as his immediate forerunner and personal representative of the Old Testament, both in its legal, and prophetic or evangelical aspect, and after the Messianic probation by the temptation in the wilderness—the counterpart of the temptation of the first Adam in paradise—he entered upon his great work.

His public life lasted only three years, and before he had reached the age of ordinary maturity, he died, in the full beauty and vigor of early manhood, without tasting the infirmities of declining years, which would inevitably mar the picture of the Regenerator of the race and the Prince of life. And yet, unlike all other men of his years, he combined with the freshness, energy and originating power of youth that wisdom, moderation and experience, which belong only to mature age. The short triennium of his public ministry contains more, even from a purely historical point of observation, than the longest life of the greatest and best of men. It is pregnant with the deepest meaning of the counsel of God and the destiny of the race. It is the ripe fruit of all preceding ages, the

---

20. John Young, *The Christ of History*, p. 35.

fulfilment of the hopes and desires of the Jewish and heathen mind, and the fruitful germ of succeeding generations, containing the impulse to the purest thoughts and noblest actions down to the end of time. It is, "the end of a boundless past, the centre of a boundless present, and the beginning of a boundless future."[21]

How remarkable, how wonderful this contrast between the short duration, and the immeasurable significance of Christ's ministry! The Saviour of the world a youth!

Other men require a long succession of years to mature their minds and character and to make a lasting impression upon the world. There are exceptions, we admit. Alexander the Great, the last and most brilliant efflorescence of the ancient Greek nationality, died a young man of thirty three after having conquered the East to the borders of the Indus. But who would think of comparing an ambitious warrior, conquered by his own lust and dying a victim of his passion, with the spotless friend of sinners; a few bloody victories of the one with the peaceful triumphs of the other; and a huge military empire of force which crumbled to pieces as soon as it was erected, with the spiritual kingdom of truth and love which stands to this day and will last for ever? Nor should it be forgotten that the true significance and only value of Alexander's conquest lay beyond the horizon of his ambition and intention, and that by carrying the language and civilization of Greece to Asia and bringing together the Oriental and Occidental world, it prepared the way for the introduction of the universal religion of Christ.

There is another striking distinction of a general character between Christ and the heroes of history, which we must notice here. We should naturally suppose that such an uncommon personage, setting up the most astounding claims and proposing the most extraordinary work, would surround himself with extraordinary circumstances and maintain a position far above the vulgar and degraded multitude around him. We should expect something uncommon and striking in his look, his dress, his manner, his mode of speech, his outward life, and the train of his attendants. But the very reverse is the case. His greatness is singularly unostentatious, modest and quiet, and far from repelling

---

21. Heinrich Steffens, a follower of Schelling, says this of man, and bases upon this thought his System of Anthropology. But it may be applied in its fullest and absolute sense to Christ, as the ideal man, in whom and through whom alone the race can become complete. [Heinrich (or Henrik) Steffens (1773–1845), Danish philosopher and scientist who taught at Halle, Breslau, and Berlin.]

the beholder, it attracts and invites him to familiar approach. His public life never moved on the imposing arena of secular heroism, but within the humble circle of every day life, and the simple relations of a son, a brother, a citizen, a teacher and a friend. He had no army to command, no kingdom to rule, no prominent station to fill, no worldly favors and rewards to dispense. He was an humble individual, without friends and patrons in the Sanhedrim or at the court of Herod. He never mingled in familiar intercourse with the religious or social leaders of the nation, whom he had startled in his twelfth year by his questions and answers. He selected his disciples from among the illiterate fishermen of Galilee and promised them no reward in this world but a part in the bitter cup of his sufferings. He dined with publicans and sinners and mingled with the common people, without ever condescending to their low manners and habits. He was so poor that he had no place on which to rest his head. He depended for the supply of his modest wants on voluntary contributions of a few pious females, and the purse was in the hands of a thief and a traitor. Nor had he learning, art, or eloquence, in the usual sense of the term, nor any other kind of power, by which great men arrest the attention and secure the admiration of the world. The writers of Greece and Rome were ignorant even of his existence until, several years after the crucifixion, the effects of his mission in the steady growth of the sect of his followers forced from them some contemptuous notice and then roused them to opposition.

And yet this Jesus of Nazareth without money and arms conquered more millions than Alexander, Caesar, Mahomet, and Napoleon; without science and learning he shed more light on things human and divine than all philosophers and scholars combined; without the eloquence of schools he spoke words of life as were never spoken before or since, and produced effects which lie beyond the reach of orator or poet; without writing a single line he has set more pens in motion and furnished themes for more sermons, orations, discussions, learned volumes, works of art and sweet songs of praise than the whole army of great men of ancient and modern times. Born in a manger, and crucified as a malefactor, he now controls the destinies of the civilized world, and rules a spiritual empire which embraces one third of the inhabitants of the globe. There never was in this world a life so unpretending, modest and lowly in its outward form and condition, and yet producing such extraordinary effects upon all ages, nations and classes of men.

The annals of history produce no other example of such complete and astounding success in spite of the absence of those material, social, literary and artistic powers and influences which are indispensable to success for a mere man. Christ stands also in this respect solitary and alone among all the heroes of history, and presents to us an insolvable problem, unless we admit him to be the eternal Son of God.

We will now attempt to describe his personal or moral and religious character, as it appears in the record of his public life, and then examine his own testimony of himself, as giving us the only rational solution of this mighty problem.

The first impression which we receive from the life of Jesus is that of its perfect innocency and sinlessness in midst of a sinful world. He and He alone carried the spotless purity of childhood untarnished through his youth and manhood. Hence the lamb and the dove are his appropriate symbols.

He was, indeed, tempted as we are, but he never yielded to temptation.[22] His sinlessness was at first only the *relative* sinlessness of Adam before the fall, which implies the necessity of trial and temptation and the peccability, or the possibility of the fall. Had he been endowed with absolute impeccability from the start, he could not be a true man, nor our model for imitation, his holiness instead of being his own self-acquired act and merit would be a mechanical gift, and his temptation an unreal show. But here is the great fundamental difference between the first and the second Adam: the first Adam lost his innocence by the abuse of his freedom and fell by his own act of disobedience into the dire necessity of sin, while the second Adam was innocent in the midst of sinners and maintained his innocence against all and every temptation. Christ's relative sinlessness or the *posse non peccare* became more and more *absolute* sinlessness or a *non posse peccare*,[23] by his own moral

---

22. Comp. with the history of the temptation in the wilderness, Matth. 4 and Luke 4, the significant passages in the epistle to the Hebrews, 4:15: πεπειραμένον [δὲ] κατὰ πάντα καθ' ὁμοιότητα, χωρὶς ἁμαρτίας, and 5:8: καίπερ ὢν υἱός, ἔμαθεν ἀφ' ὧν ἔπαθεν τὴν ὑπακοήν. [Trans. "but one who in every respect has been tempted as we are, yet without sin." . . . "Although he was a Son, he learned obedience through what he suffered." (RSV)]

23. [These terms, *posse non peccare* ("able not to sin") and *non posse peccare* ("not able to sin"), come from Augustine. According to Bishop of Hippo, human beings as created were able not to sin. After the fall, however, they were unable not to sin (*non posse non peccare*). By God's grace Christians are now able not to sin, and at the eschaton they will be in the blessed state of inability to sin. See Augustine, "On Rebuke and

act or the right use of his freedom in the absolute active and passive obedience to God.

In vain we look through the entire biography of Christ for a single stain or the slightest shadow on his moral character. There never lived a more harmless being on earth. He injured nobody, he took advantage of nobody. He never spoke an improper word, he never committed a wrong action. He never repented, never asked God for pardon and forgiveness.[24] He stood in no need of regeneration and conversion, nor even of reform, but simply of the regular harmonious unfolding of his moral powers. He exhibited a uniform elevation above the objects, opinions, pleasures and passions of this world, and disregard to riches, displays, fame and favor of men. The apparent outbreak of passion in the expulsion of the profane traffickers from the temple is the only instance on the record of his history which might be quoted against his freedom from the faults of humanity. But the very effect which it produced, shows that far from being the outburst of passion, the expulsion was a judicial act of a religious reformer, vindicating in just and holy zeal the honor of the Lord of the temple, and that with a dignity and majesty which at once silenced the offenders, though superior in number and physical strength, and made them submit to their well deserved punishment without a murmur and in awe of the presence of a superhuman power. The cursing of the unfruitful fig tree can still less be urged, as it evidently was a significant symbolical act foreshadowing the fearful doom of the impenitent Jews in the destruction of Jerusalem.

The perfect innocence of Jesus, however, is based not only negatively on the absence of any recorded word or act to the contrary and his absolute exemption from every trace of selfishness and worldliness, but, positively also on the unanimous testimony of John the Baptist and the apostles who bowed before the majesty of his character in unbounded veneration and declare him "just," "holy," and " without sin."[25] It is admitted, moreover, by his enemies: the heathen judge Pilate,

---

Grace," (*De Correptione et Gratia*), chaps. 28–35, in *Nicene and Post-Nicene Fathers*, 1st series, ed. Philip Schaff (Grand Rapids: Eerdmans, 1971 [reprint]), V:483-486.]

24. The petition for forgiveness in the Lord's Prayer, Matth. 6:12, is no exception, as it was no expression of individual need on his part, but was intended as a model for his disciples.

25. Acts 3:14. 1 Peter 1:19; 2:22; 3:18. 2 Cor. 5:21; 1 John 2:29; 3:6, 7. Heb. 4:15; 7:26. Considering the infinite superiority of the ethics of the apostles to the ethics of the ancient Greeks it is absurd to weaken the force of this unanimous testimony (as is done

and his wife, representing as it were the Roman law and justice when they shuddered with apprehension and washed the hands to be clear of innocent blood; by the rude Roman centurion confessing under the cross in the name of the disinterested spectators, "Truly this was the Son of God," and by Judas himself, the immediate witness of his whole public and private life, exclaiming in despair: "I have betrayed innocent blood."[26] Even dumb nature responded in mysterious sympathy, and the beclouded heavens above and the shaking earth beneath united in paying their unconscious tribute to the divine purity of their dying Lord. It is finally placed beyond all possibility of doubt by his own freedom from any sense of guilt or unworthiness, and by his open and fearless challenge to his bitter enemies: "Which of you convinceth me of sin ?"[27] In this question he clearly exempts himself from the common fault and guilt of the race. In the mouth of any other man this question would at once betray either the hight of hypocrisy, or a degree of self-deception bordering on madness itself, and would overthrow the very foundation of all human goodness; while from the mouth of Jesus we instinctively receive it as the triumphant self-vindication of one, who stood far above the possibility of successful impeachment or founded suspicion.[28]

[CHRIST'S SINLESSNESS A PROOF OF HIS UNIQUENESS]

Admit once this fact of the perfect sinlessness of Christ, as is done even by divines who are by no means regarded orthodox,[29] and you admit

---

by D. F. Strauss, *Die christliche Glaubenslehre*, Vol. II. p. 102, and to some extent even by Hase, *Leben Jesu*, p. 61), by a reference to Xenophon's estimate of Socrates: Οὐδεὶς [δὲ] πώποτε Σωκράτους οὐδὲν ἀσεβὲς οὐδὲ ἀνόσιον οὔτε πράττοντες εἶδεν, οὔτε λέγοντες ἤκουσιν. Memorab. I. 11. [Trans.: "Yet none ever knew him to offend against piety and religion in deed or word." *Xenophon IV: Memorabilia and Oeconomicus*, trans. E. C. Marchant, Loeb Classical Library (Cambridge, Mass.: Harvard, 1968), pp. 7, 9.] Comp. the just remarks of Ullmann, *Suendlosigkeit Jesu*, p. 83 ff.

26. Matth. 27:19, 24–64. Luke 23:22–47. Matth. 27:4.

27. John 8:46. Comp. the Commentators, and the reflections of Ullmann, 1. c. p. 92 ff.

28. Compare the striking remarks of H. Bushnell, p. 325: "If Jesus was a sinner, he was conscious of sin as all sinners are, and therefore was a hypocrite in the whole fabric of his character; realizing so much of divine beauty in it, maintaining the how of such unfaltering harmony and celestial grace, and doing all this with a mind confused and fouled by the affectations acted for true virtues! Such an example of successful hypocrisy would be itself the greatest miracle ever heard of in the world."

29. As Schleiermacher, *Der Christliche Glaube*, 3d ed. (1836) vol. ii. p. 78: "*Christus*

that Christ differed from all other men not in degree only, but in kind. For although we must repudiate the pantheistic notion of the necessity of sin, and must maintain that human nature in itself considered is capable of sinlessness, that it was sinless in fact before the fall, and that it will ultimately become sinless again by the redemption of Christ: yet it is equally certain that human nature in its *present* condition is not and never was sinless since the fall, except in the single case of Christ, and that for this very reason Christ's sinlessness can only be explained on the ground of such an extraordinary indwelling of God in him as never took place in any other human being before or after. The entire Christian world, Greek, Latin, and Protestant, agree in the scriptural doctrine of the universal depravity of human nature since the apostacy of the first Adam. Even the modern and unscriptural Romish dogma of the freedom of the Virgin Mary from hereditary as well as actual sin, can hardly be quoted as an exception: for her sinlessness is explained in the papal decision by the assumption of a miraculous interposition of divine favor and the reflex influence of the merit of her Son. There is not a single mortal who must not charge himself with some defect or folly, and man's consciousness of sin and unworthiness deepens just in proportion to his self-knowledge and progress in virtue and goodness. There is not a single saint who has not experienced a new birth from above and an actual conversion from sin to holiness, and who does not feel daily the need of repentance and divine forgiveness. The

---

war von allen andern Menschen unterschieden durch seine wesentliche Unsündlichkeit und seine schlechthinige Vollkommenheit." [Trans. "Christ was distinguished from all other men by His essential sinlessness and His absolute perfection." Schleiermacher, *The Christian Faith*, 413.] Karl Hase, *Leben Jesu*, 4th ed. 1854, p. 60 f. (Clarke's Eng. translation, Boston, 1860, p. 54) likewise admits it. D. F. Strauss denies it in his two destructive works, the *Life of Jesus*, and the *Dogmatics in conflict with Modern Science*, [David Friedrich Strauss, *Die christliche Glaubenslehre in ihrer geschichtliche Entwicklung und im Kampf mit der modernen Wissenschaft*, 2 vols. (Tübingen: Osiander, 1840–41)] but he does so from the a priori philosophical argument of the impossibility of sinlessness, or the pantheistic notion of the inseparableness of sin from all finite existence. The only exegetical proof he urges (Dogmat. ii. 192), is Christ's word, Matth. 19:17: "There is none good but one, that is God." But Christ answers here to the preceding question and the implied misconception of goodness. He does not decline the epithet *good* as such, but only in the superficial sense of the rich youth who regarded him simply as a distinguished rabbi and a good *man*, not as one with God. In no case can he be supposed to have contradicted his own testimony concerning his innocence. See the commentators *ad locum*, especially Olshausen, Meyer and Lange.

very greatest and best of them, as St. Paul and St. Augustin, have passed through a violent struggle and a radical revolution, and their whole theological system and religious experience rested on the felt antithesis of sin and grace.

But in Christ we have the one solitary and absolute exception to this universal rule, an individual thinking like a man, feeling like a man, speaking, acting, suffering and dying like a man, surrounded by sinners in every direction, with the keenest sense of sin and the deepest sympathy with sinners, commencing his public ministry with the call: "Repent, for the kingdom of heaven is at hand,"[30]—yet never touched in the least by the contamination of the world, never putting himself in the attitude of a sinner before God, never shedding a tear of repentance, never regretting a single thought, word or deed, never needing or asking divine pardon, and boldly facing all his present and future enemies in the absolute certainty of his spotless purity before God and man!

A sinless Saviour in midst of a sinful world is an astounding fact indeed, and a miracle in history. But this freedom from the common sin and guilt of the race is after all only the negative side of his character, which rises in magnitude as we contemplate the positive side, namely, absolute moral and religious perfection. It is universally admitted, even by Deists and Rationalists, that Christ taught the purest and sublimest system of ethics, which throws all the moral precepts and maxims of the wisest men of antiquity far into the shade. The Sermon on the Mount alone is worth infinitely more than all that Confucius, Socrates, and Seneca ever said or wrote on duty and virtue. But the difference is still greater if we come to the more difficult task of practice. While the wisest and best of men never live up even to their own imperfect standard of excellency, Christ fully carried out his perfect doctrine in his life and conduct. He is the living incarnation of the ideal standard of virtue and holiness, and universally acknowledged to be the highest model for all that is pure and good and noble in the sight of God and man.

We find Christ moving in all the ordinary and essential relations of life,[31] as a son, a friend, a citizen, a teacher, at home and in public; we

---

30. Matth. 4:17.

31. The relation of husband and father must be excepted on account of his elevation above all equal partnership and the universalness of his character and mission, which requires the entire community of the redeemed as his bride instead of any individual daughter of Eve.

find him among all classes of society, with sinners and saints, with the poor and the wealthy, with the sick and the healthy, with little children, grown men and women, with plain fishermen and learned scribes, with despised publicans and honored members of the Sanhedrim, with friends and foes, with admiring disciples and bitter persecutors, now with an individual as Nicodemus, or the woman of Samaria, now in the familiar circle of the twelve, now in the crowds of the people; we find him in all situations, in the synagogue and the temple, at home and on journeys, in villages and the city of Jerusalem, in the desert and on the mountain, along the banks of Jordan and the shores of the Galilean sea, at the wedding feast and the grave, in Gethsemane, in the judgment hall and on Calvary. In all these various relations, conditions and situations, as they are crowded within the few years of his public ministry, he sustains the same consistent character throughout, without ever exposing himself to censure. He fulfils every duty to God, to man, and to himself, without a single violation of duty, and exhibits an entire conformity to the law, in the spirit as well as the letter. His life is one unbroken service of God in active and passive obedience to his holy will, one grand act of absolute love to God and love to man, of personal self-consecration to the glory of the heavenly Father and the salvation of a fallen race. In the language of the people who were "beyond measure astonished at his works," we must say, the more we study his life: "He did all things well."[32] In a solemn appeal to his heavenly Father in the parting hour, he could proclaim to the world that he had glorified him in the earth and finished the work he gave him to do.[33]

The first feature in this singular perfection of Christ's character which strikes our attention is the perfect harmony of virtue and piety, of morality and religion, or of love to God and love to man. Every moral action in him proceeded from supreme love to God, and looked to the temporal and eternal welfare of man. The groundwork of his character was the most intimate and uninterrupted union and communion with his heavenly Father, from whom he derived, to whom he referred every thing. Already in his twelfth year he found his life element and

---

32. Mark 7:37: Καλῶς πάντα πεποίηκα, *bene omnia fecit* [trans. "He has done all things well" (RSV)]—is to be taken as a general judgment, inferred not only from the concrete case related before, but from all they had heard and seen of Christ.

33. John 17; 8:22.

delight in the things of his Father.[34] It was his daily food to do the will of Him that sent him and to finish his work.[35] To him he looked in prayer before every important act, and taught his disciples that model prayer which, for simplicity, brevity, comprehensiveness and suitableness, can never be surpassed. He often retired to a mountain or solitary place for prayer, and spent days and nights in this blessed privilege. But so constant and uniform was his habit of communion with the great Jehovah, that he kept it up amid the multitude, and converted the crowded city into a religious retreat. His self-consciousness was at every moment conditioned, animated and impregnated by the consciousness of God. Even when he exclaimed in indescribable anguish of body and soul, and in vicarious sympathy with the misery of the whole race: "My God, my God, why hast thou forsaken me!"[36] the bond of union was not broken or even loosened, but simply obscured for a moment, as the sun by a passing cloud, and the enjoyment, not the possession of it, was withdrawn from his feelings; for immediately afterwards he commended his soul into the hands of his Father and triumphantly exclaimed: "It it finished!" So strong and complete was this moral union of Christ with God at every moment of his life, that he fully realized for the first time the idea of religion whose object is to bring about such a union, and that he is the personal representative and living embodiment of Christianity as the true and absolute religion. But the piety of Christ was no inactive contemplation, or retiring mysticism, and selfish enjoyment, but thoroughly practical, ever active in works of charity, and tending to regenerate and transform the world into the kingdom of God. "He went about doing good." His life is an unbroken series of good words and virtues in active exercise, all proceeding from the same union with God, animated by the same love, and tending to the same end, the glory of God and the happiness of man.

The next feature, we would notice, is the completeness or pleromatic fulness of the moral and religious character of Christ. While all other men represent at best but broken fragments of the idea of

---

34. Luke 2:49.

35. John 4:34, comp. 5:30.

36. Matth. 27:46. It should be remembered, that Jesus speaks here in the prophetical and typical words of David, Ps. 22:2; while, when speaking in his own language, he uniformly addresses God as his *Father*.

goodness and holiness, he exhausts the list of virtues and graces, which may be named.

History exhibits to us many examples of commanding and comprehensive geniuses, who stand at the head of their age and nation and furnish material for the intellectual activity of whole generations and periods, until they are succeeded by other heroes at a new epoch of development. As rivers generally spring from high mountains, so knowledge and moral power rises and is continually nourished from the heights of humanity. Abraham, the father of the faithful; Moses, the lawgiver of the Jewish theocracy; Elijah among the prophets; Peter, Paul and John among the apostles; Athanasius and Chrysostom among the Greek, Augustin and Jerome among the Latin fathers; Thomas Aquinas and Duns Scotus among the schoolmen; Leo and Gregory among the popes; Luther and Calvin in the line of protestant reformers and divines; Socrates, the patriarch of the ancient schools of philosophy; Homer, Dante, Shakspeare and Milton, Goethe and Schiller in the history of poetry among the various nations to which they belong; Raphael among painters; Charlemagne, the first and greatest in the long succession of German emperors; Napoleon, towering high above all the generals of his training: Washington, the wisest and best as well as the first of American Presidents and the purest and noblest type of the American character, may be mentioned as examples of such representative heroes in history who anticipate and concentrate the powers of whole generations. But they never represent universal, but only sectional humanity; they are identified with a particular people or age and partake of its errors, superstitions and failings almost in the same proportion in which they exhibit their virtues. Moses, though revered by the followers of three religions, was a Jew in views, feelings, habits and position as well as by parentage; Socrates never rose above the Greek type of character; Luther was a German to the back-bone and can only be properly understood as a German; Calvin, though an exile from his native land, remained a Frenchman; and Washington can be to no nation on earth what he is to the American. Their influence may and does extend far beyond their respective national horizon, yet they can never furnish a universal model for imitation. We regard them as extraordinary but fallible and imperfect men, whom it would be very unsafe to follow in every view and line of conduct. Very frequently the failings and vices of great men are in proportion to their virtues and powers, as the tallest bodies cast the longest shadow. Even the three leading apostles are models of piety and virtue only as far as they reflect the image of their heavenly Master, and it is only with this qualification that Paul exhorts his spiritual children: "Be ye followers of me even as I am also of Christ."[37]

What these representative men are to particular ages or nations, or sects, or particular schools of science and art, Christ was to the human family at large in its relation to God. He and he alone is the universal type for universal imitation. Hence he could, without the least impropriety or suspicion of vanity, call upon all men to forsake all things and to follow him.[38] He stands above the limitations of age, school, sect, nation, and race. Although a Jew according to the flesh, there is nothing Jewish about him which is not at the same time of general significance. The particular and national in him is always duly subordinated to the general and human. Still less was he ever identified with a party or sect. He was equally removed from the stiff formalism of the Pharisees, the loose liberalism of the Sadducees, and the inactive mysticism of the Essenes. He rose above all the prejudices, bigotries and superstitions of his age and people, which exert their power even upon the strongest and otherwise most liberal minds. Witness his freedom in the observance of the sabbath, by which he offended the scrupulous literalists, while he fulfilled, as the Lord of the sabbath, the true spirit of the law in its universal and abiding significance;[39] his reply to the disciples, when they traced the misfortune of the blind man to a particular sin of the subject or his parents;[40] his liberal conduct towards the Samaritans as contrasted with the inveterate hatred and prejudice of the Jews including his own disciples at the time;[41] and his charitable judgment of the slaughtered Galileans whose blood Pilate had mingled with their sacrifices, and the eighteen upon whom the tower in Siloam fell and slew them.[42] "Think ye," he addressed the children of superstition, "that these

37. 1 Cor. 11:1. Comp. 1 Thess. 1:6: "Ye became followers of us and of the Lord."

38. Matth. 4:19; 8:22; 9:9; Mark 2:14; 8:34; 10:21; Luke 5:27; 9:23, 59; 18:22; John 1:43; 10:27; 12:26.

39. Matth. 12:1–8.; Mark 2:23–28; Luke 5:1–9; John 5:16–18.

40. John 9:3: "Neither hath this man sinned, nor his parents, (but he was born blind) that the works of God should be made manifest in him."

41. See the dialogue with the woman of Samaria, John 4:5 ff., and the parable of the merciful Samaritan, Luke 10:30–37.

42. Luke 13:1–4.

men were sinners above all the Galileans, and above all men that dwelt in Jerusalem, because they suffered such things? I tell you, Nay: but except ye repent, ye shall all likewise perish." All the words and all the actions of Christ, while they were fully adapted to the occasions which called them forth, retain their force and applicability undiminished to all ages and nations. He is the same unsurpassed and unsurpassable model of every virtue to the Christians of every generation, every clime, every sect, every nation, and every race.

It must not be supposed, however, that a complete catalogue of virtues would do justice to the character under consideration. It is not only the completeness, but still more the even proportion and perfect harmony of virtues and graces apparently opposite and contradictory, which distinguishes him specifically from all other men. This feature has struck with singular force all the more eminent writers on the subject."[43] It gives the finish to that beauty of holiness which is the sublimest picture presented to our contemplation.

He was free from all one sidedness which constitutes the weakness as well as the strength of the most eminent men. He was not a man of one idea nor of one virtue towering above all the rest. The moral forces were so well tempered and moderated by each other that none was unduly prominent, none carried to excess, none alloyed by the kindred failing. Each was checked and completed by the opposite grace. His character never lost its even balance and happy equilibrium, never needed modification or readjustment. It was thoroughly sound and uniformly consistent from the beginning to the end. We cannot properly attribute to him any one temperament. He was neither sanguine,

---

43. Comp Ullmann, *Suendlosigkeit* p. 67, J. P. Lange, *Leben Jesu* I. 27–34, Ebrard, *Dogmatik* II. 23 and 24. [Johannes Heinrich August Ebrard, *Christliche Dogmatik* (Königsburg: A. W. Unzer, 1851–52)] Also Hase, in his *Leben Jesu* p. 63 (4th ed.) places the ideal beauty of Christ's character in *"das schöne Ebenmaass aller Kräfte"* and in *"vollendete Gottesliebe dargestellt in reinster Humanität"* ("the beautiful symmetry of all powers, and perfect love exhibited in purest humanity"). [Karl Hase, *Das Leben Jesu*, 4th ed. (Leipzig: Breitkopf und Härtel, 1854)]

Bishop D. Wilson, in his *Evidences of Christianity*, vol. II. 116 (Boston ed. of 1830) remarks: "The opposite, and to us apparently contradictory graces were found in him in equal proportion." Dr. W. E. Channing, the Unitarian, in his sermon on the *Character of Christ* (*Works* ["Discourse on the Character of Christ," in *The Works of William Ellery Channing*, 6 vols. (Boston: American Unitarian Assoc., 1903)], vol. IV. p. 23) says: "This combination of the spirit of humanity, in its lowliest, tenderest form, with the consciousness of unrivaled and divine glories, is the most wonderful distinction of this wonderful character."

like Peter, nor choleric, like Paul, nor melancholic like John, nor phlegmatic as James is sometimes, though incorrectly, represented to have been, but he combined the vivacity without the levity of the sanguine, the vigor without the violence of the choleric, the seriousness without the austerity of the melancholic, the calmness without the apathy of the phlegmatic temperaments. He was equally far removed from the excesses of the legalist, the pietist, the ascetic, and the enthusiast. With the strictest obedience to the law he moved in the element of freedom; with all the fervor of the enthusiast he was always calm, sober and self-possessed; notwithstanding his complete and uniform elevation above the affairs of this world, he freely mingled with society, male and female, dined with publicans and sinners, sat at the wedding feast, shed tears at the sepulchre, delighted in God's nature, admired the beauties of the lilies, and used the occupations of the husbandman for the illustration of the sublimest truths of the kingdom of heaven. His zeal never degenerated into passion or rashness, nor his constancy into obstinacy, nor his benevolence into weakness, nor his tenderness into sentimentality. His unworldliness was free from indifference and unsociability, his dignity from pride and presumption, his affability from undue familiarity, his self-denial from moroseness, his temperance from austerity. He combined child-like innocence with manly strength, all-absorbing devotion to God with untiring interest in the welfare of man, tender love to the sinner with uncompromising severity against sin, commanding dignity with winning humility, fearless courage with wise caution, unyielding firmness with sweet gentleness. He is justly compared with the lion in strength and with the lamb in meekness. He equally possessed the wisdom of the serpent and the simplicity of the dove. He brought both the sword against every form of wickedness, and the peace which the world cannot give. He was the most effective, and yet the least noisy, the most radical, and yet the most conservative, calm and patient of all reformers. He came to fulfil every letter of the law, and yet he made all things new. The same hand which drove the profane traffickers from the temple, blessed little children, healed the lepers, and rescued the sinking disciple; the same ear which heard the voice of approbation from heaven, was open to the cries of the woman in travail; the same mouth which pronounced the terrible woe on the hypocrites and condemned the impure desire and unkind feeling as well as the open crime, blessed the poor in spirit, announced pardon to the adulteress, and prayed for his murderers; the same eye which beheld the mysteries of God and penetrated the heart of man shed tears of compassion over ungrateful Jerusalem, and tears of friendship at the grave of Lazarus. These are indeed opposite, yet not contradictory traits of character as little as the different manifestations of God's power and goodness in the tempest and the sunshine, in the towering alps and the lily of the valley, in the boundless ocean and dew-drop of the morning. They are separated in imperfect men indeed, but united in Christ, the universal model for all.

Finally as all the active virtues meet in him, so he unites the active or heroic virtues with the passive and gentle. He is equally the highest standard of all true martyrdom.

No character can become complete without trial and suffering, and a noble death is the crowning act of a noble life. Edmund Burke said to Fox in the English Parliament: "Obloquy is a necessary ingredient of all true glory. Calumny and abuse are essential parts of triumph." The ancient Greeks and Romans admired a good man struggling with misfortune as a sight worthy of the gods. Plato describes the righteous man as one who without doing any injustice, yet has the appearance of the greatest injustice and proves his own justice by perseverance against all calumny unto death; yea he predicts that if such a righteous man should ever appear, he would be "scourged, tortured, bound, deprived of his sight, and after having suffered all possible injury nailed on a post."[44] No wonder that the ancient fathers saw in this remarkable passage an unconscious prophecy of Christ. But how far is this ideal of the great philosopher from the actual reality as it appeared three hundred years afterwards. The great men of this world, who rise even above themselves on inspiring occasions and boldly face a superior army, are often thrown off their equilibrium in ordinary life and grow impatient at trifling obstacles. Only think of Napoleon at the head of his conquering legions and at the helm of an empire, and the same Napoleon after the defeat at Waterloo and on the island of St. Helena. The highest form of passive virtue attained by ancient heathenism or modern secular heroism is that stoicism which meets and overcomes the trials and misfortunes of life in the spirit of haughty contempt and unfeeling

---

44. Politia p. 74 sqq. ed. Ast (Plat. Opera vol. IV.) p. 361 E. ed. Bip. [For a recent translation, see Plato, *The Republic II*, in *The Collected Dialogues of Plato* (Princeton: Princeton University Press, 1961), 609.]

indifference, which destroys the sensibilities and is but another exhibition of selfishness and pride.

Christ has set up a far higher standard by his teaching and example, never known before or since, except in imperfect imitation of him. He has revolutionized moral philosophy and convinced the world that forgiving love to the enemy, holiness and humility, gentle patience in suffering and cheerful submission to the holy will of God is the crowning excellency of moral greatness. "If thy brother," he says, "trespass against thee seven times in a day, and seven times in a day turn again to thee, saying, I repent; thou shalt forgive him."[45] "Love your enemies, bless them that curse you, do good to them that hate you, and pray for them that despitefully use you and persecute you."[46] This is a sublime maxim truly, but still more sublime is its actual exhibition in his life.

Christ's passive virtue is not confined to the closing scenes of his ministry. As human life is beset at every step by trials, vexations, and hindrances, which should serve the educational purpose of developing its resources and proving its strength, so was Christ's. During the whole state of his humiliation he was "a man of sorrows and acquainted with grief,"[47] and had to endure " the contradiction of sinners."[48] He was poor, and suffered hunger and fatigue. He was tempted by the devil. His path was obstructed with apparently unsurmountable difficulties from the outset. His words and miracles called forth the bitter hatred of the world, which resulted at last in the bloody counsel of death. The Pharisees and Sadducees forgot their jealousies and quarrels in opposing him. They rejected and perverted his testimony; they laid snares to him by insiduous questions; they called him a glutton and a winebibber for eating and drinking like other men, a friend of publicans and sinners for his condescending love and mercy, a sabbath-breaker for doing good on the sabbath day; they charged him with madness and blasphemy for asserting his unity with the Father, and derived his miracles from Beelzebub, the prince of devils. The common people, though astonished at his wisdom and mighty works, pointed sneeringly at his origin; his own country and native town refused him the honor of a prophet. Even his brothers, we are told, did not believe in him,

---

45. Luke 17:4.
46. Matth. 5:44.
47. Isai. 50:3. [The reference is actually to Isaiah 53:3.]
48. Heb. 12:3.

and in their impatient zeal for a temporal kingdom they found fault with his unostentatious proceeding.[49] His apostles and disciples, with all their profound reverence for his character and faith in his divine origin and mission as the Messiah of God, yet by their ignorance, their carnal Jewish notions and their almost habitual misunderstanding of his spiritual discourses, must have constituted a severe trial of patience to a teacher of far less superiority to his pupils.

But how shall we describe his passion more properly so called with which no other suffering can be compared for a moment! Never did any man suffer more innocently, more unjustly, more intensely, than Jesus of Nazareth. Within the narrow limits of a few hours we have here a tragedy of universal significance, exhibiting every form of human weakness and infernal wickedness, of ingratitude, desertion, injury and insult, of bodily and mental pain and anguish, culminating in the most ignominious death then known among the Jews and Gentiles. The government and the people combined against him who came to save them. His own disciples forsook him; Peter denied him; Judas, under the inspiration of the devil betrayed him. The rulers of the nation condemned him, the furious mob cried: "Crucify him!" rude soldiers mocked him. He was seized in the night, hurried from tribunal to tribunal, arrayed in a crown of thorns, insulted, smitten, scourged, spit upon and hung like a criminal and a slave between two robbers and murderers!

How did Christ bear all these little and great trials of life, and the death on the Cross? Let us remember first, that unlike the icy Stoics, in their unnatural and repulsive pseudo-virtue, he had the keenest sensibilities and the deepest sympathies with all human grief, that made him even shed tears at the grave of a friend and in the agony of the garden, and provide a refuge for his mother in the last dying hour. But with this truly human tenderness and delicacy of feeling, he ever combined an unutterable dignity and majesty, a sublime self-control and imperturbable calmness of mind. There is a grandeur in his deepest sufferings, which forbids a feeling of pity and compassion on our side as incompatible with the admiration and reverence for his character. We feel the force of his words to the women of Jerusalem, when they bewailed him on the way to Calvary: "Weep not for me, but weep for yourselves and

---

49. John 7:3–5. It is immaterial for our purpose whether we understand by his brothers (not "brethren" as the Common Version has it) younger sons of Joseph and Mary, or older sons of Joseph from a former marriage, or cousins.

your children,"⁵⁰ &c. We never hear him break out in angry passion and violence, although he was at war with the whole ungodly world. He never murmured, never uttered discontent, displeasure or resentment. He was never disheartened, discouraged, ruffled or fretted, but full of unbounded confidence that all was well ordered in the providence of his heavenly Father. He moved serenely like the sun above the clouds as they sailed under him. He was ever surrounded by the element of peace, and said in his parting hour: "Peace I leave with you, my peace I give unto you: not as the world giveth, give I unto you. Let not your heart be troubled, neither let it be afraid."⁵¹ He was never what we call unhappy, but full of inward joy which he bequeathed to his disciples in that sublimest of all prayers, "that they might have his joy fulfilled in themselves."⁵² With all his severe rebuke to the Pharisees, he never indulged in personalities. He ever returned good for evil. He forgave Peter for his denial, and would have forgiven Judas, if in the exercise of sincere repentance he had sought his pardon. Even while hanging on the cross, he had only the language of pity for the wretches who were driving the nails into his hands and feet, and prayed in their behalf: "Father forgive them, for they know not what they do."⁵³ He did not seek or hasten his martyrdom, like many of the early martyrs of the Ignatian type in their morbid enthusiasm and ambitious humility,⁵⁴ but quietly and patiently waited for the hour appointed by the will of his heavenly Father. But when it came, with what self-possession and calmness, with what strength and meekness, with what majesty and gentleness did he pass through its dark and trying scenes! Here every word and act are unutterably significant, from the agony in Gethsemane, when overwhelmed with the sympathetic sense of the entire guilt of mankind, and in full view of the terrible scenes before him—the only guiltless being in the world—he prayed that the cup might pass from him, but immediately added: "Not my, but thy will be done," to the triumphant

---

50. [Luke 23:28.]
51. John 14:27.
52. John 17:13, comp. 16:33.
53. [Luke 23:34.]
54. [The reference is to Ignatius, bishop of Antioch (died c. 107), who eagerly sought martyrdom and urged his fellow Christians not to seek his release. See his "Epistle to the Romans," 1–3.]

exclamation on the cross: "It is finished!"[55] Even his dignified silence before the tribunal of his enemies and the furious mob, when "as a lamb dumb before his shearers he opened not his mouth,"[56] is more eloquent than any apology, and made Pilate tremble. Who will venture to bring a parallel from the annals of ancient or modern sages, when even a Rousseau confessed: "If Socrates suffered and died like a philosopher, Christ suffered and died like a God!"[57] The passion and crucifixion of Jesus, like his whole character, stands without a parallel, solitary and alone in its glory, and will ever continue to be what it has been for these eighteen hundred years, the most sacred theme of meditation, the highest exemplar of suffering virtue, the strongest weapon against sin and Satan, the deepest source of comfort to the noblest and best of men.

Such was Jesus of Nazareth—a true man in body, soul and spirit, yet differing from all men, a character absolutely unique and original from tender childhood to ripe manhood, moving in unbroken union with God, overflowing with the purest love to man, free from every sin and error, innocent and holy, teaching and practising all virtues in perfect harmony, devoted solely and uniformly to the noblest ends, sealing the purest life with the sublimest death, and ever acknowledged since as the one and only perfect model of goodness and holiness! All human greatness loses on closer inspection; but Christ's character grows more and more pure, sacred and lovely, the better we know him. No biographer, moralist, or artist can be satisfied with any attempt of his to set it forth. It is felt to be infinitely greater than any conception or representation of it by the mind, the tongue and the pencil of man or angel. We might as well attempt to empty the waters of the boundless sea into a narrow well, or to portray the splendor of the risen sun and the starry heavens with ink. No picture of the Saviour, though drawn by the master-hand of a Raphael, or Dürer, or Rubens; no epic, though conceived by the genius of a Dante, or Milton, or Klopstock, can improve on the artless narrative of the gospel, whose only but all-powerful charm is truth. In this case certainly truth is stranger and stronger than fiction, and speaks best for itself without comment, explanation and eulogy. Here and here alone the highest perfection of art falls short of

---

55. [John 19:30.]

56. [Isaiah 53:7.]

57. [Jean-Jacques Rousseau, *Emile, or On Education*, trans. Allan Bloom (New York: Basic Books, 1979), 308.]

the historical fact, and fancy finds no room for idealizing the real. For here we have the absolute ideal itself in living reality. It seems to me that this consideration alone should satisfy the reflecting mind that Christ's character, though truly natural and human, must be at the same time truly supernatural and divine.

The whole range of history and fiction furnishes no parallel to such a character. There never was any thing even approaching to it before or since, except in faint imitation of his example. It cannot be explained on purely human principles, nor derived from any intellectual and moral forces of the age in which he lived. On the contrary it stands in marked contrast to the whole surrounding world of Judaism and heathenism, which present to us the dreary picture of internal decay, and which actually crumbled into ruin before the new moral creation of the crucified Jesus of Nazareth. He is the one absolute and unaccountable exception to the universal experience of mankind. He is the great central miracle of the whole gospel history, and all his miracles are but the natural and necessary manifestations of his miraculous person performed with the same ease with which we perform our ordinary daily works.

[CHRIST'S OWN TESTIMONY TO HIS DIVINE ORIGIN]

There is but one rational explanation of this sublime mystery, and this is found in Christ's own testimony concerning his superhuman and divine origin.[58] This testimony challenges at once our highest regard and belief from the absolute veracity which no one ever denied him or could deny without destroying at once the very foundation of his universally conceded moral purity and greatness.

Christ strongly asserts his humanity, and calls himself, in innumerable passages, the Son of man.[59] This expression, while it places him

---

58. For a very full exposition of this testimony, we refer to the instructive and able work of W. Fr. Gess: *Die Lehre von der Person Christi entwickelt aus dem Selbstbewusstsein Christi und aus dem Zeugnisse der Apostel.* Basel, 1856. [Trans. *The Doctrine of the Person of Christ, Developed from the Self-understanding of Christ and the Witness of the Apostles.* Wolfgang Friedrich Gess (1819–1891) was a Lutheran theologian who taught at Göttingen and Breslau; he was particularly known for his radical form of the kenosis Christology, in which the Logos completely "emptied himself" of the divine attributes and effectively ceased to be divine.]

59. Comp. the Dictionaries, and especially Schmid's and Bagster's Greek Concordances of the N. T. (the latter republished by the Harpers, N. York, 1855) sub. v. υἱὸς τοῦ ἀνθρώπου [trans. "son of man."].

in one view on common ground with us as flesh of our flesh and bone of our bone, already indicates at the same time that he is more than an ordinary individual, not merely *a* son of man like all other descendants of Adam, but *the* Son of man, the man in the highest sense, the ideal, the universal, the absolute man, the second Adam descended from heaven, the head of a new and superior order of the race, the King of Israel, the Messiah. The same is the case with the cognate term, "the Son of David," which is frequently given to Christ, by the two blind men, the Syrophenician woman, and the people at large.[60] The appellation does not express then, as many suppose, the humiliation and condescension of Christ simply, but his elevation rather above the ordinary level and the actualization in him and through him of the ideal standard of human nature under its moral and religious aspect or in its relation to God. This interpretation is suggested grammatically by the use of the definite article, and historically by the origin of the term in Daniel 7:13, where it signifies the Messiah as the head of a universal and eternal kingdom. It commends itself moreover at once as the most natural and significant in such passages as: "Ye shall see the heaven open, and the angels of God ascending and descending upon the Son of man"[61]; "He that came down from heaven, even the Son of man which is in heaven"[62]; "The Son of man hath power on earth to forgive sins"[63]; "The Son of man is Lord even of the sabbath day"[64]; "Except ye eat the flesh of the Son of man, and drink his blood, ye have no life in you"[65]; "The Son of man shall come in the glory of his Father"[66]; "The Son of man is come to save"[67]; "The Father hath given him authority to execute judgment also, because he is the Son of man."[68] Even those passages which are quoted for the opposite view, receive, in our interpretation, a greater force and beauty from the sublime contrast which places the voluntary condescension and humiliation of Christ in the most striking light, as

60. Matth. 9:27; 15:22; 12:23; 21:9; 22:41ff., etc.
61. John 1:51 (or v. 52 in the Greek text and the German version).
62. John 3:13.
63. Matth. 9:6; Mark 2:10.
64. Matth. 12:8; Mark 2:28.
65. John 6:53.
66. Matth. 16:17, comp. 19:28; 24:30; 25:31; 26:64; Luke 21:27, 36.
67. Matth. 18:11, comp. Luke 19:10.
68. John 5:27.

when he says: "Foxes have holes, and birds of the air have nests; but the Son of man hath not where to lay his head"[69]; or, "Whosoever will be chief among you, let him be your servant: even as the Son of man came not to be ministered unto, but to minister and to give his life a ransom for many."[70] Thus the manhood of Christ, rising far above all ordinary manhood, though freely coming down to its lowest ranks with the view to their elevation and redemption, is already the portal of his godhood.

But he calls himself at the same time, as he is most frequently called by his disciples, "the Son of God" in an equally emphatic sense. He is not merely *a* Son of God among others, angels, archangels, princes and judges, and redeemed men, but *the* Son of God as no other being ever was, is, or can be, all others being sons or children of God only by derivation or adoption after a new spiritual birth, and in dependance on his absolute and eternal Sonship.[71] He is, as his favorite disciple calls him, the "Only begotten Son," or, as the old Catholic theology expresses it, eternally begotten of the substance of the Father. In this high sense the title is freely given to him by his disciples,[72] without a remonstrance on his part, and by God the Father himself at his baptism and at the transfiguration.[73] Christ represents himself moreover as being not of this world, but sent from God, as having come from God, and as being in heaven while living on earth.[74] He not only announces and proclaims the truth as other messengers of God, but declares himself to be the Light of the World;[75] the Way, the Truth, and the Life;[76] the Resurrection and the Life.[77] "All things," he says, "are delivered unto me of my Father, and no man knoweth the Son but the Father; neither knoweth any man the Father save the Son, and he to whomsoever the Son will reveal

---

69. Luke 9:58.

70. Matth. 20:27, 28.

71. Matth. 11:27; 21:37; 22:42; 26:63f.; 27:43; Mark 12:6; 13:32; 14:62; Luke 10:22; John 5:19–26; 9:35–38; 10:36; 11:4; 14:13; 17:1; 19:7.

72. Matth. 16:16; Mark 3:11; John 1:18, 34, 49; 11:27; 20:31,—besides the many passages in the Acts and Epistles, where the term υἱὸς τοῦ θεοῦ [trans. "son of God."] is as frequent as the term υἱὸς τοῦ ἀνθρώπου [trans. "son of man."] in the Gospels.

73. Matth. 3:17; Luke 3:22; Matth. 17:5; Luke 9:35.

74. John 3:13.

75. John 8:12.

76. John 14:6.

77. John 11:25.

him."[78] He invites the weary and heavy laden to come to him for rest and peace.[79] He promises life in the highest and deepest sense, even eternal life to every one who believes in him.[80] He claims and admits to be the Christ or the Messiah of whom Moses and the prophets of old testify, and the King of Israel.[81] He is the Lawgiver of the new and last dispensation,[82] the Founder of a spiritual kingdom coextensive with the race, and everlasting as eternity itself,[83] the appointed Judge of the quick and the dead,[84] the only Mediator between God and man, the Saviour of the world.[85] He parts from his disciples with those sublime words which alone certify his divinity: "All power is given to me in heaven and in earth. Go ye, therefore, and teach all nations, baptizing them in the name of the Father, and of the Son, and of the Holy Ghost: teaching them to observe all things whatsoever I have commanded you: and, lo, I am with you alway, even to the end of the world."[86]

Finally he claims such a relation to the Father, which implies both the equality of substance and the distinction of person, and which in connection with his declarations concerning the Holy Spirit leads with logical necessity, as it were, to the doctrine of the Holy Trinity. For this doctrine saves the Divinity of Christ and of the Holy Spirit without affecting the fundamental truth of the Unity of the Godhead, and keeps the proper medium between an abstract and lifeless monotheism and a polytheistic tritheism.

He always distinguishes himself from God the Father, who sent him, whose work he came to fulfil, whose will he obeys, by whose power he performs his miracles, to whom he prays, and with whom he communes as a self-conscious personal being. And so he distinguishes himself with equal clearness from the Holy Spirit, whom he received at

78. Matth. 11:27. This passage is a striking parallel to the sublimest sayings in the fourth gospel, and proves the essential identity of the Synoptic and the Johannean picture of Christ.

79. Matth. 11:28.

80. John 3:36; 5:24; 6:40, 47, 50–58; 11:25.

81. John 4:26; 5:39, 46; Matth. 14:33; 16:16f., 26, 63f., etc.

82. Matth. 5:22–44; 28:19, 20.

83. Matth. 16:19; 27:11; Luke 22:30; John 18:36; Comp. Dan. 7:13. Luke 1:33.

84. John 5:22, 25–27. Matth. 25:31 ff., etc.

85. Matth. 18:11; Luke 9:56; 19:10; John 3:17; 5:34; 10:9; 12:47.—Comp. Luke 1:47; 2:11; John 4:42, etc.

86. Matth. 28:18—20.

his baptism, whom he breathed into his disciples and whom he promised to send and did send on them as the other paraclete, as the Spirit of truth and holiness with the whole fulness of the accomplished salvation. But he never makes a similar distinction between himself and the Son of God; on the contrary he identifies himself with the Son of God, and uses this term, as already remarked, in a sense which implies much more than the Jewish conception of the Messiah and nothing short of the equality of essence or substance. For he claims as the Son a real self-conscious preexistence before man and even before the world, consequently also before time—for time was created with the world. "Before Abraham was," he says, "I am"[87]—significantly using the past in the one, and the present in the other case to mark the difference between man's temporal and his own eternal mode of existence—and in the sacerdotal prayer he asks to be clothed again with the glory which he had with the Father before the foundation of the world.[88] He assumes divine names and attributes as far as consistent with his state of humiliation, he demands and receives divine honors.[89] He freely and repeatedly exercises the prerogative of pardoning sin in his own name, which the unbelieving Scribes and Pharisees with a logic whose force is irresistible on their premises, looked upon as blasphemous presumption.[90] He familiarly classes himself with the infinite majesty of Jehovah in one common plural, and boldly declares: "He that hath seen me hath seen the Father;"[91] "I and the Father are one."[92] He coordinates himself, in the baptismal formula, with the Divine Father, and the Divine Spirit,[93] and

---

87. John 8:58.

88. John 17:5. Comp. the testimony of the apostles on the preexistence, John 1:1–14; Col. 1:16. Heb. 1:2. 3.

89. John 5:23.

90. Matth. 9:6; Luke 5:20–24; 7:47, 48.

91. John 14:9.

92. John 10:30. The passage teaches certainly more than the ethical unity of will, it asserts according to the context the unity of power which is based on the unity of essence or the homousia. The ἕν [trans. "one."] excludes Arianism, the plural ἐσμεν [trans. "are."] Sabellianism and Patripassianism. [Sabellianism or modalism was the ancient heresy which held that there is but one divine person who assumes different roles; Patripassianism was associated with the modalistic heresy and affirmed that the Father suffered on the cross.]

93. Matth. 28:19.

allows himself to be called by Thomas in the name of all the apostles: "My Lord and my God!"[94]

These are the most astounding and transcendant pretensions ever set up by any being. He, the humblest and lowliest of man, makes them repeatedly and uniformly to the last in the face of the whole world, even in the darkest hour of suffering. He makes them not in swelling, pompous, ostentatious language, which almost necessarily springs from false pretensions, but in a natural, spontaneous style, with perfect ease, freedom and composure, as a native prince would speak of the attributes and scenes of royalty at his father's court. He never falters or doubts, never apologizes for them, never enters into an explanation. He sets them forth as self-evident truths which need only be stated to challenge the belief and submission of mankind.

Now suppose for a moment a purely human teacher, however great and good, suppose a Moses or Elijah, a John the Baptist, an apostle Paul or John—not to speak of any father, schoolman, or reformer—to say: "I am the Light of the world," "I am the Way, the Truth, and the Life," "I and the Father are one," and call upon all men: "Come unto me," "Follow me," that you may find "life" and "peace" which you cannot find elsewhere: would it not create a universal feeling of pity or indignation? No human being on earth could set up the least of these pretensions without being set down at once as a madman or a blasphemer.

But from the mouth of Christ these colossal pretensions excite neither pity nor indignation, nor even the least feeling of incongruity or impropriety. We read and hear them over and over again without surprise.[95] They seem perfectly natural and well sustained by a most extraordinary life and the most extraordinary works. There is no room here for the least suspicion of vanity, pride, or self-deception. For these eighteen hundred years these claims have been acknowledged by millions of people of all nations and tongues, of all classes and conditions, of the most learned and mighty as well as the most ignorant and humble with an instinctive sense of the perfect agreement of what Christ claimed to be with what he really was. Is not this fact most remarkable?

94. John 20:28.

95. "Of all the readers of the Gospel," says Bushnell [*Natural and the Supernatural*], p. 290, "it probably never even occurs to one in a hundred thousand, to blame his conceit, or the egregious vanity of his pretensions." Even the better class of Unitarians instinctively bow before these claims. See the remarkable passage of Dr. Channing quoted below.

Is it not a triumphant vindication of Christ's character and an irresistible proof of the truth of his pretensions?

[REPLY TO UNITARIAN, SOCINIAN, AND SKEPTICAL OBJECTIONS]

There is no other solution of the mighty problem within the reach of human learning and ingenuity. Let us briefly review in conclusion the various attempts of Unitarians and unbelievers to account for the character of Christ without admitting his divinity.

The semi-infidelity of Socinians and Unitarians is singularly inconsistent. Admitting the faultless perfection of Christ's character and the truthfulness of the Gospel-history, and yet denying his divinity, they must either charge him with such egregious exaggerations and conceit as would overthrow at once the concession of his moral perfection, or they must so weaken and pervert his testimony concerning his relation to God as to violate all the laws of grammar and sound interpretation. Dr. W. E. Channing, the ablest and noblest representative of American Unitarianism,[96] prefers to avoid the difficulty which he was unable to solve. In his admirable discourse on the Character of Christ he goes as far almost as any orthodox divine in vindicating to him the highest possible purity and excellency as a man, but he stops halfway and passes by in silence those extraordinary claims, which are inexplicable on merely human principles. He approaches, however, the very threshold of the true faith in the following remarkable passage which we have a right to quote against his own system. "I confess," he says,

> when I can escape the deadening power of habit, and can receive the full import of such passages as the following,—'Come unto me, all ye that labor and are heavy laden, and I will give you rest,'—'I am come to seek and to save that which was lost,'—'He that confesseth me before men, him will I confess before my Father in heaven,'—'Whosoever shall be ashamed of me before men, of him shall the Son of Man be ashamed when he cometh in the glory of the Father with the holy angels,'—'In my Father's house are many mansions; I go to prepare a place for you:'—I

---

96. [William Ellery Channing (1780–1842), American Unitarian minister and theologian. Schaff collected quite a number of "impartial testimonies" to the dignity and character of Christ from Channing (whom Schaff regarded as "the great leader of American Unitarianism, and one of the brightest ornaments of American literature"); see Schaff, *The Person of Christ*, 257–265.]

say, when I can succeed in realizing the import of such passages, I feel myself listening to a being, such as never before and never since spoke in human language. I am awed by the consciousness of greatness which these simple words express; and when I connect this greatness with the proofs of Christ's miracles which I gave you in a former discourse, I am compelled to exclaim with the centurion, 'Truly, this was the Son of God.'[97]

But this is not all. We have seen that Christ goes much further than in the passages here quoted, that he forgives sins in his own name, that he asserts pre-existence before Abraham and before the world—not only ideally in the mind of God, for this would not distinguish him from Abraham or any other creature, but in the real sense of self-conscious personal existence—that he claims and receives divine honors and attributes, and calls himself equal with the great Jehovah. How can a being so pure and holy, and withal so humble and lowly, so perfectly free from every trace of enthusiasm and conceit, as Dr. Channing freely and emphatically asserts Christ to have been, lay claim to any thing which he was not in fact?[98] Why then not also go beyond the exclamation of the heathen centurion, and unite with the confession of Peter and the adoration of the skeptical St. Thomas: "My Lord and my God!" Unitarianism admits altogether too much for its own conclusions and is therefore driven to the logical alternative of falling back upon an infidel, or of advancing to the orthodox christology. Such a man as Channing, who was certainly under the influence of the holy example of Christ, would not hesitate for the choice, as we may infer from his general spirit and from his last address delivered at Lenox, Massachusetts in 1842, shortly before his death, where he said: "The doctrine of the Word made flesh shows us God uniting himself intimately with our nature, manifesting himself in a human form, for the very end of making us partakers of his own perfection."[99]

The infidelity of the enemies of Christianity is logically more consistent, though absolutely untenable in the premises. It resorts either to imposture, or enthusiasm, or poetical fiction.

The hypothesis of *imposture* is so revolting to moral as well as common sense that its mere statement is its condemnation. It has

---

97. [Channing, "Character of Christ," *Works*, IV:20.]
98. Discourse on the *Character of Christ*, in Channing's *Works*, vol. IV. p. 20.
99. [Channing, *Works*, VI: 408.]

never been seriously carried out, and no scholar of any decency and self-respect would now dare to profess it.[100] How, in the name of logic and experience, could an imposter, that is a deceitful, selfish, depraved man, have invented and consistently maintained from beginning to end the purest and noblest character known in history, with the most perfect air of truth and reality? How could he have conceived and successfully carried through, in the face of the strongest prejudices of his people and age, a plan of unparalleled beneficence, moral magnitude and sublimity, and sacrificed his own life for it? The difficulty is not lessened by shifting the charge of fraud from Christ upon the apostles and evangelists, who were any thing but designing hypocrites and deceivers, and leave upon every unsophisticated reader the impression of an artless simplicity and honesty rarely equalled and never surpassed by any writers learned or unlearned, of ancient or modern times. What imaginable motive could have induced them to engage in such a wicked scheme, when they knew that the whole world would persecute them even to death? How could they have formed and successfully sustained a conspiracy for such a purpose without ever falling out or betraying themselves by some inconsistent word or act? And who can believe that the Christian Church for these eighteen hundred years, now embracing nearly the whole civilized world, should have been duped and fooled by a Galilean carpenter or a dozen illiterate fishermen? Verily this lowest form of infidelity is the grossest insult to reason and sense and to the dignity of human nature.

The hypothesis of *enthusiasm* or self-deception, though less disreputable, is equally unreasonable in view of the uniform clearness, calmness, self-possession, humility, dignity and patience of Christ—qualities the very opposite to those which characterize an enthusiast. We might imagine a Jew of that age to have fancied himself the Messiah

---

100. It was first suggested by the heathen assailants of Christianity, Celsus and Julian the Apostate, then insinuated by French deists of the Voltairean school, but never raised to the dignity of scientific argument. The only attempt to carry it out, and that a mere fragmentary one, was made by the anonymous "*Wolfenbuettel Fragmentist*," since known as Hermann Samuel Reimarus, professor of oriental literature in the College at Hamburg, who died in 1786. His *Fragments* were never intended for publication, but only for a few friends. Lessing found them in the library at Wolfenbüttel and commenced to publish them, without the author's knowledge, in 1774, not, as he said, because he agreed with them, but because he wished to arouse the spirit of investigation. This mode of procedure Semler, the father of German neology, wittingly compared to the act of setting a city on fire for the purpose of trying the engines.

and the Son of God, but instead of opposing all the popular notions, and discouraging all the temporal hopes of his countrymen, he would, like Barcochba of a later period,[101] have headed a rebellion against the hated tyranny of the Romans and endeavored to establish a temporal kingdom. Enthusiasm, which in this case must have bordered on madness itself, instead of calmly and patiently bearing the malignant opposition of the leaders of the nation, would have broken out in violent passion and precipitate action. "The charge," says Dr. Channing,

> of an extravagant, self-deluding enthusiasm is the last to be fastened on Jesus. Where can we find the traces of it in his history? Do we detect them in the calm authority of his precepts; in the mild, practical, and beneficent spirit of his religion; in the unlabored simplicity of the language with which he unfolds his high powers, and the sublime truths of religion; or in the good sense, the knowledge of human nature, which he always discovers in his estimate and treatment of the different classes of men with whom he acted? Do we discover this enthusiasm in the singular fact, that whilst he claimed power in the future world, and always turned men's minds to Heaven, he never indulged his own imagination, or stimulated that of his disciples, by giving vivid pictures, or any minute description, of that unseen state? The truth is, that, remarkable as was the character of Jesus, it was distinguished by something more than by calmness and self-possession. This trait pervades his other excellences. How calm was his piety! Point me, if you can, to one vehement, passionate expression of his religious feelings. Does the Lord's Prayer breath a feverish enthusiasm? . . . His benevolence, too, though singularly earnest and deep, was composed and serene. He never lost the possession of himself in his sympathy with others; was never hurried into the impatient and rash enterprises of an enthusiastic philanthrophy; but did good with the tranquility and constancy which mark the providence of God.[102]

But the champions of this theory may admit all this, and yet fasten the delusion upon the disciples of Christ who were so dazzled by his character, words and works that they mistook an extraordinary man for a divine being, and extraordinary cures for supernatural miracles. This is the view of the older German rationalism (the so called *rationalismus*

---

101. [Simon Bar-Kokhba, a messianic pretender who led the second Jewish revolt against Rome (AD 132–135).]

102. *Discourse on the Character of Christ, Works*, vol. IV., 17 and 18.

communis, or *vulgaris*[103]), and forms a parallel to the heathen rationalism of Euhemerus, of the Cyrenaic school, who explained the gods of the Greek mythology as human sages, heroes, kings and tyrants, whose superior knowledge or great deeds secured them divine honors or the hero-worship of posterity.[104] It was fully developed, with a considerable degree of patient learning and acumen, by the late professor H. E. G. Paulus of Heidelberg.[105] He takes the gospel history as actual history, but by a critical separation of what he calls *fact* from what he calls *judgement* of the actor or narrator, he explains it exclusively from natural causes and thus brings it down to the level of every day events. This "natural" interpretation, however, turns out to be most unnatural and commits innumerable sins against the laws of hermeneutics and against common sense itself. To prove this it is only necessary to give some specimens from the exegesis of Paulus and his school. The glory of the Lord which, in the night of his birth, shone around the shepherds of Jerusalem, was simply an *ignis fatuus,*[106] or a meteor; the miracle at Christ's baptism may be easily reduced to thunder and lightening and a sudden disappearance of the clouds; the tempter in the wilderness was a cunning Pharisee, and was only mistaken by the evangelists for the devil who does not exist except in the imagination of the superstitious; the supposed miraculous cures of the Saviour turn out on closer examination to be simply deeds either of philanthrophy, or medical skill, or good luck: the changing of water into wine was an innocent

103. Or the rationalism of common sense, as distinct from the rationalism of uncommon sense or speculative reason. The sense of both systems, however, ends is nonsense. Dr. Marheineke defined a Rationalist or, as Paulus called him, a *Denkglaeubige,* as a man, *der zu denken glaubt und zu glauben denkt; es ist aber mit beiden gleich null.* [trans. "who believes to think and thinks to believe; but both end in nothing"]. The Hegelian school has successfully ridiculed common rationalism and made every scholar of philosophical pretensions ashamed of it. But the infidel wing of that school has at last relapsed into the same or still greater absurdities.

104. Comp. Diodorus Siculus, *Bibli. Fragm.* I. vii [a reference to the famed *Library of History*, a compendium by the first-century BC Greek historian Diodorus Siculus, some of which is preserved only in fragments.]; Cicero, *De natura deor.* I. 42 [Cicero, *De Natura Deorum* ("On the Nature of the Gods")]; Sextus Empir., *Adv. math.* ix. 17 [Sextus Empiricus, *Adversus Mathematicos* ("Against the Mathematicians")].

105. Born in the kingdom of Würtemberg 1761, then successively professor in different universities, at last in Heidelberg, where he died in 1847, after having long outlived himself. His rationalistic exegesis is laid down in his *Commentary on the Gospels,* published since 1800, and his *Life of Jesus,* 1828.

106. [Trans. "foolish fire," a term used for will-o'-the-wisp.]

and benevolent wedding joke, and the delusion of the company must be charged on the twilight, not upon Christ; the daughter of Jairus, the youth of Nain, Lazarus, and Jesus himself, were raised not from real death, but simply from a trance or swoon; and the ascension of the Lord is nothing more than his sudden disappearance behind a cloud that accidentally intervened between him and his disciples! And yet these very evangelists, who must have been destitute of the most ordinary talent of observation and even of common sense, have contrived to paint a character and to write a story which in sublimity, grandeur and interest throws the productions of the proudest historians into the shade, and has exerted an irresistible charm upon Christendom for these eighteen hundred years! No wonder that those absurdities of a misguided learning and ingenuity hardly survived their author. It is a decided merit of Strauss that he has thoroughly refuted the work of his predecessor, and given it the death blow. But his own theory has shared no better fate.

The last hypothesis of a *poetical fiction* was matured and carried out with a high degree of ability and ingenuity by the speculative or pantheistic rationalism of David Frederick Strauss, the author of the famous *Life of Jesus*.[107] This writer sinks the Gospel history, as to the mode of its origin and realness, substantially on a par with the ancient mythologies of Greece and Rome. Without denying altogether the historical existence of Jesus, and even admitting him to have been a religious genius of the first magnitude, he yet, from pantheistic premises and by a cold process of hypercritical dissection of the apparently contradictory accounts of the witnesses, resolves all the supernatural and miraculous elements of his person and history into myths, or imaginative representations of religious ideas in the form of facts which were honestly believed by the authors to have actually occurred. The ideas symbolized in these facts are declared to be true in the abstract or as applied to humanity as a whole, but denied as false in the concrete or in their application to an individual. The authorship of the evangelical myths is ascribed to the primitive Christian society pregnant with Jewish Messianic hopes and kindled to hero worship by the appear-

---

107. The *Leben Jesu* by Strauss, Dr. phil., who was born in 1806 and is still living, was first published 1835 at Tübingen in 2 volumes, and for the fourth, in all probability also for the last time in 1840. It was also translated into. English by a Miss Evans. [David Friedrich Strauss, *The Life of Jesus Critically Examined*, ed. Peter C. Hodgson, trans. George Eliot (Philadelphia: Fortress Press, 1972). The translator, novelist Mary Anne Evans, wrote under the pen-name "George Eliot."]

ance of the extraordinary person of Jesus of Nazareth whom they took to be the promised Messiah. But this theory is likewise surrounded by insurmountable difficulties. Who ever heard of a poem unconsciously produced by a mixed multitude and honestly mistaken by them all for actual history? How could the five hundred persons, to whom the risen Saviour is said to have appeared, dream the same dream at the same time, and then believe it as a veritable fact at the risk of their lives? How could a man like St. Paul submit his strong and clear mind and devote all the energies of his noble life to a poetical fiction of the very sect whom he once persecuted unto death? How could such an illusion stand the combined hostility of the Jewish and heathen world, and the searching criticism of an age of high civilization, and even of incredulity and skepticism? How strange that unlettered and unskilled fishermen, and not the philosophers and poets of classic Greece and Rome, should have composed such a grand poem and painted a character to whom Strauss himself is forced to assign the very first rank among all the religious geniuses and founders of religion!

The poets must in this case have been superior to the hero, and yet the hero is admitted to be the purest and greatest man that ever lived! Where are the traces of a fervid imagination and poetic art in the Gospel history? Is it not, on the contrary, remarkably free from all rhetorical and poetical ornament, from every admixture of subjective notions and feelings, even from the expression of sympathy, admiration and praise? The writers evidently felt that the story speaks best for itself and could not be improved by the art and skill of man. Their discrepancies, which at best do not affect the picture of Christ's character in the least but only the subordinate details of his history, prove the absence of conspiracy, attest the honesty of their intention and confirm the general credibility of their account. Verily, the Gospel history, related with such unmistakable honesty and simplicity by immediate witnesses and their pupils, proclaimed in open daylight from Jerusalem to Rome, believed by thousands of Jews, Greeks and Romans, sealed with the blood of apostles, evangelists and saints of every grade of society and culture, is better attested by external and internal evidence than any other history. The same negative criticism, which Strauss applied to the Gospels, would with equal plausibility destroy the strongest chain of evidence before a court of justice, and resolve the life of Socrates, or Charlemagne, or Luther, or, Napoleon into a mythical dream. The secret of the mythical hypothesis is the pantheistic denial of a personal living God and the a priori assumption of the impossibility of a miracle. In its details it is so complicated and artificial that it can not be made generally intelligible, and in proportion as it is popularized, it reverts to the vulgar hypothesis of intentional fraud from which it professed at the start to shrink back in horror and contempt.

With this last and ablest effort, infidelity seems to have exhausted its scientific resources. It could only repeat itself hereafter. Its different theories have all been tried and found wanting. One has in turn transplanted and refuted the other, even during the lifetime of their champions. They explain nothing in the end; on the contrary, they only substitute an unnatural for a supernatural miracle, an inextricable enigma for a revealed mystery. They equally tend to undermine all faith in God's Providence, in history, and ultimately in every principle of truth and virtue, and they deprive a poor and fallen humanity, in a world of sin, temptation and sorrow, of its only hope and comfort in life and in death.

Dr. Strauss, by far the clearest and strongest of all assailants of the Gospel-history, seems to have had a passing feeling of the disastrous tendency of his work of destruction and the awful responsibility he assumed. "The results of our inquiry," he says in the closing chapter of his *Life of Jesus*,

> have apparently annihilated the greatest and most important part of that which the Christian has been wont to believe concerning his Jesus, have uprooted all the encouragements which he has derived from his faith, and deprived him of all his consolations. The boundless store of truth and life which for eighteen hundred years have been the aliment of humanity, seems irretrievably devastated, the most sublime levelled with the dust, God divested of his grace, man of his dignity, and the tie between heaven and earth broken. Piety turns away with horror from so fearful an act of desecration, and strong in the impregnable self-evidence of its faith, boldly pronounces that—let an audacious criticism attempt what it will—all which the Scriptures declare and the Church believes of Christ, will still subsist as eternal truth, nor needs one iota of it to be renounced.[108]

---

108. *Leben Jesu, Schlussabhandlung*, vol. ii., p. 663 (4th ed. of 1840).

Strauss makes then an attempt, it is true, at a philosophical reconstruction of what he vainly imagines to have annihilated as a historical fact by his sophistical criticism. He professes to admit the abstract truth of the orthodox christology, or the union of the divine and human, but perverts it into a purely intellectual and pantheistic meaning. He refuses divine attributes and honors to the glorious head of the race, but applies them to a decapitated humanity. He thus substitutes, from pantheistic prejudice, a metaphysical abstraction for a living reality, a mere notion for a historical fact, a progress in philosophy and mechanical arts for the moral victory over sin and death, a pantheistic hero worship, or self-adoration of a fallen race, for the worship of the only true and living God, the gift of a stone for the bread of eternal life![109]

Humanity scorns such a miserable substitute, which has yet to give the first proof of any power for good, and which will probably never convert or improve a single individual. It must have a living head, a real Lord and Saviour from sin and death. With renewed faith and confidence it returns from the dreary desolations of a heartless infidelity and the vain conceits of a philosophy falsely so called, to the historical Christ, and exclaims with Peter: "Lord, where shall we go but to Thee,

---

109. "In an individual," says Strauss, *Leben Jesu,* vol. ii. p. 710, "in one Godman the properties and functions which the church doctrine ascribes to Christ, contradict themselves; in the idea of the race they agree. *Humanity* is the union of the two natures—the incarnate God, the infinite externalizing itself in the finite, and the finite spirit remembering its infinitude; it is the child of the visible mother and the invisible father, Nature and Spirit; it is the worker of miracles, in so far as in the course of human history the spirit more and more completely subjugates nature, both within and around man, until it lies before him as an inert matter of his activity; it is the sinless existence, for the coarse of its development is a blameless one; pollution cleaves to the individual only, and does not touch the race or its history. It is Humanity that dies, rises, and ascends to heaven; for from the negation of its natural life there ever proceeds a higher spiritual life; from the suppression of its limitation as a personal, national, and terrestial spirit, arises its union with the infinite spirit of the heavens. By faith in this Christ, especially in his death and resurrection, man is justified before God: that is, by the kindling within him of the idea of Humanity, especially by the negation of its natural and sensual aspects, the individual man partakes of the divinely human life of the species."—But the idea of the human and divine is no more contradictory in an individual than in the race. What is true in idea or principle, must also actualize itself or be capable of actualization in a concrete living fact. History teaches moreover that every age, every great movement, and every nation have their representative heads, who comprehend and act out the life of the respective whole. This analogy points us to a general representative head of the entire race, Adam in the natural, and Christ in the spiritual order. The divine humanity of Strauss is like a stream without a fountain, or like a body without a head.

Thou alone hast words of eternal life, and we believe and are sure that Thou art the Son of God!"[110]

Yes! There He lives, the Divine man and incarnate God, on the ever fresh and self-authenticating record of the Gospels, in the unbroken history of eighteen centuries, and in the hearts and lives of the wisest and best of our race. Jesus Christ is the most certain, the most sacred, and the most glorious of all facts, arrayed in a beauty and majesty which throws the "starry heavens above us and the moral law within us"[111] into obscurity, and fills us truly with over growing reverence and awe. He shines forth with the self-evidencing light of the noon-day sun. He is too great, too pure, too perfect to have been invented by any sinful and erring man. His character and claims are confirmed by the sublimest doctrine, the purest ethics, the mightiest miracles, the grandest spiritual kingdom, and are daily and hourly exhibited in the virtues and graces of all who yield to the regenerating and sanctifying power of his spirit and example. The historical Christ meets and satisfies our deepest intellectual and moral wants. Our souls, if left to their noblest impulses and aspirations, instinctively turn to him as the needle to the magnet, as the flower to the sun, as the panting hart to the fresh fountain. We are made for him, and "our heart is without rest until it rests in him."[112] He commands our assent, he wins our admiration, he overwhelms us to humble adoration and worship. We cannot look upon him without spiritual benefit. We cannot think of him without being elevated above all that is low and mean, and encouraged to all that is good and noble. The very hem of his garment is healing to the touch; one hour spent in his communion outweighs all the pleasures of sin. He is the most precious and indispensable gift of a merciful God to a fallen world. In him are the treasures of true wisdom, in him the fountain of pardon and peace, in him the only substantial hope and comfort in this world and that which is to come. Without him history is a dreary waste, an inextricable enigma; with him it is the unfolding of a plan of infinite wisdom and love. He is the glory of the past, the life of the present, the hope of the future. Mankind could better afford to lose the whole literature of Greece and Rome, of Germany and France, of England and America,

---

110. [John 6:68.]

111. [An oft-quoted phrase from Immanuel Kant, *Critique of Practical Reason*, trans. Lewis White Beck (Indianapolis: Bobbs-Merrill, 1956), 166.]

112. [A well-known quote from Augustine's *Confessions*, I.1.]

than the story of Jesus of Nazareth. Not for all the wealth and wisdom of this world would I weaken the faith of the humblest Christian in his Divine Lord and Saviour; but if, by the grace of God, I could convert a single skeptic to a childlike faith in him, who lived and died for me and for all, I would feel that I had not lived in vain.

P. S.

ARTICLE 8
"The Person of Christ"

(by Daniel Gans)

EDITOR'S INTRODUCTION

This is the one selection in this volume not written by one of the principal Mercersburg figures, but rather by one of their students. Daniel Gans graduated from the Seminary at Mercersburg in 1849 (the same year that the *Mercersburg Review* commenced publication). His published work demonstrates a keen concern for the objectivity of the church, its ministry and sacraments, and it is perhaps not entirely surprising that he finally entered the Roman Catholic Church in 1878, after a lengthy period of ministry in the German Reformed Church. In this article (really a sermon on the Johannine discourse on the bread of life), Gans explores the implications of the Mercersburg approach to the Incarnation for soteriology and ecclesiology.

Gans insists that Jesus' words about eating the flesh and drinking the blood of the Son of man speak of a real participation in the humanity of Christ. But what about the explanation by Jesus after the Jews took offense in which he declared that "the Spirit . . . quickeneth; the flesh profiteth nothing"? This, Gans contends, must be regarded as an explanation of the previous statement, not a rejection of it. The explanation pertains first of all to the person of Christ as lifegiving, and second to the ordinances whereby that life-giving humanity is made accessible to Christians.

In his discussion of the person of Christ, Gans emphasizes the unity of the two natures—divine and human—in a single person. He deplores the popular focus, characteristic of much American Protestantism at the time, on the deity of Christ at the expense of the humanity, noting that the Incarnation was undertaken not merely for the atonement, but also for the ongoing application of salvation to Christians, and he laments the fact that the resurrection and ascension imply to many that Christ as to his humanity is no longer accessible to Christians.

In explaining this accessibility, Gans first argues that Christ as to his deity and humanity is now available "under the form of Spirit," a "deeper and more vital form" than during Christ's earthly ministry. In short, the human nature of Christ has been "taken up into the divine by the power of the Holy Ghost, and penetrated and spiritualized." This humanity that is available through the Holy Spirit is also identified as a "generic" humanity, an "inward power comprehending all that is real and necessary as to the germ of an actual humanity."

The humanity of Christ is also available under the "form of life." The term *life* here accompanies *Spirit*, Gans argues, in order to underscore the importance of the humanity and demonstrate that this is no spiritualistic "Gnostic show." Here he decries the popular dualism that pits the "spiritual" against what is physically human, for salvation involves the redemption of the body as well as the soul. Thus this source of divine life must be brought within the Christian and become real nourishment, and here Gans inveighs against an "outward, legal scheme, which mechanically sets the merits of the second Adam over against the demerits of the first." Here Gans doubtless has in mind the later Reformed federal orthodoxy, with its notion of immediate imputation (as taught by Charles Hodge of Princeton, who had recently done battle with John W. Nevin over these issues). Not only must the outward reconciliation between God and sinners take place, but also their depravity and corruption of nature must be healed, and this sets up the discussion of the church and its ministry that follows.

In the second section Gans discusses the sacraments as the means whereby the divine-human life of Christ is carried over into the Christian. Baptism, he says, is the "primary sacrament," the sacrament of initiation and incorporation into the body of Christ. In this context Gans discusses the responsibilities of parents for the Christian nurture of their baptized children. In a section reminiscent of Nevin's

The Anxious Bench he discusses the role of family, church life, and catechesis, all of which should lead the child to confirmation.

Gans describes the Lord's Supper as "an eating of the flesh and a drinking of the blood of Christ, under the form of spirit and life." He takes pains to distinguish the "spiritual real presence" of Calvin from the "real actual presence" of Rome, and (ironically in light of his later Roman Catholicism) he declares transubstantiation to be "an absurdity, contradicting reason, and destructive to faith." Echoing Nevin's *The Mystical Presence*, he points to Calvin's doctrine of the Supper as the proper middle ground between Zwinglian memorialism and Lutheran consubstantiation.

Finally, Gans argues that faith in the person of Christ should lead to faith in God's plan for applying salvation through the church. Again echoing Nevin's *The Anxious Bench*, with its condemnation of the individualism and psychological manipulation of revivalism, he notes that lack of faith in this plan has led to the "adoption of other systems of human origin." Thus a proper understanding of the person of Christ should lead to a new appreciation of the Church, and to the recognition that "Christian character" flowers only in the bosom of the Church.

Daniel Gans,[1] "The Person of Christ: An Exposition of John 6:63"[2]

"The words that I speak unto you, they are Spirit, and they are life."

Thus spake the Saviour. They are words which will be regarded as truly precious by all who are qualified, by an earnest habit of thought and piety, to penetrate and understand them. In reading over the inspired pages of divine revelation, which contain the same infinite variety as we behold in nature, it is not unfrequent that we meet with passages of a peculiarly emphatic character, like the present. Whenever we do so, we ought to pause, and give ourselves time for serious reflection and meditation. These are words that fell directly from the Saviour's lips, trembling with his divinity. What passage can be said to carry with it a more solemn emphasis: "The words that I speak unto you, they are Spirit, and they are life." What, at the same time, could be more perfect in its connection, and complete in itself.

Christ had been teaching the people the nature of eternal life under the figure of bread: that this life, so strongly demanded by our fallen nature, was contained in, and inseparably connected with, his person; that the prophecy contained in the manna which was given to the children of Israel, in a miraculous way, in the wilderness, constituting a

---

1. [Daniel Gans (1822–1903), German Reformed minister, later attorney and judge. Gans graduated from Marshall College in 1847 and the Theological Seminary of the German Reformed Church at Mercersburg in 1849. Closely associated with the Mercersburg Theology movement for many years, he pastored German Reformed congregations in Pennsylvania and Maryland until his reception into the Roman Catholic Church in 1878. After demitting the ministry he studied law, worked as a judge, and practiced law with his son. See *Franklin and Marshall College Obituary Record* 8, Vol. 2/4 (1904): 108–10.]

2. [Originally printed in the *Mercersburg Review* 6:4 (October 1854): 505–31.]

marked evidence of God's merciful concern, in sustaining their natural lives, was completely met and fulfilled in the person of Christ, as the bread of life. He says himself definitely, "I am the bread of life." And more emphatic still, "I am *that* bread of life;"[3] namely, "everlasting life," which is received by faith in his person. After making, in this way, his own person the fountain of spiritual and everlasting life, he then proceeds to insist upon the necessity, on the part of men, to eat that bread in order to participate really in that life. "Except ye eat the flesh of the Son of man, and drink his blood, ye have no life in you. Whoso eateth my flesh and drinketh my blood, hath everlasting life; and I will raise him up at the last day. For my flesh is meat indeed, and my blood is drink indeed,"[4] &c. No language certainly could be employed which would implicate in a more real way the humanity of Christ, and none make its participation on our part, under some real form, more essential to everlasting life. But the people losing sight, for the time being, of the divinity and consequent almighty power of Him who uttered these words, were disposed to murmur at him, and say, "Is not this Jesus the son of Joseph, whose father and mother we know? how is it then that he saith, I came down from heaven? and how can this *man* give us his flesh to eat?"[5] In this view, they regarded the whole representation as *an hard saying*, and asked, *who can hear it?*

From this it is plain that their unbelief in regard to the doctrine of Christ, as to the possibility and necessity of their participating in his real humanity, as an essential condition of everlasting life, originated in an unbelief of the divinity of his person. It was this latter that created the former. If they had seen and felt the presence of divinity as vitally connected with the human side of his person, they would, doubtless, have been prepared, depending upon his unerring wisdom to teach, and infinite power to condition the human nature of which he spake, to have believed implicitly all that he had said, however high it might have towered above their finite comprehension. Nay, more: the very circumstance that the thing taught, lay beyond the grasp of their reason, would have served as an additional confirmation of their faith, in the very thing in regard to which they disbelieved because of their infidelity as to his divinity. They seemed to be in possession of no deeply

---

3. [John 6:35, 48 (KJV).]
4. [John 6:53–55.]
5. [John 6:42.]

penetrating consciousness that *Christ* had actually come in the *flesh,* and that in his person, as the *incarnate* Son of God, a divine-human fountain was now opened, competent in all respects to meet and remedy the diseased condition of our nature. They regarded him rather in the light of a mere man, like one of their own number, and hence could not receive a doctrine in reference to his nature as human which could not hold in reference to their own nature under the same form.

It is worthy, therefore, of definite remark here, that, whilst the people to whom Christ was addressing himself upon this occasion, understood him as teaching the necessity of a participation in his humanity, their own belief in its possibility did not refer to the subject *per se,* but as it stood connected with a mere man.

When Jesus perceived the exercises of their minds in regard to this matter, he said to them, "Doth this offend you?" He refers again to his divinity as the ground of his representation: "What and if ye shall see the Son of man ascend up where he was before;" and then condescends to aid their weak faith by the explanation: "It is the Spirit that quickeneth; the flesh profiteth nothing; *The words that I speak unto you, they are Spirit, and they are life.*"[6]

We are not, of course, at liberty to suppose for one moment, that any of the constituent parts of the representation made previous to the announcement of these last words, may be excluded from them altogether. As an *explanation,* their design is not to *take out* of the previous representation any of its prominent points, but to render them intelligible, to bring them, if possible, more fully within the range of the understanding, assisted by faith. If the effect of the explanation should be to ignore any prominent position taken in the representation, it would indicate a vacillating uncertainty in the teachings of Christ that could not fail to induce doubt as to his divinity. We know of no such changing of position in him who was a Teacher sent from God, and who spake as man never spake.

The absence of capacity on the part of the people, arising from their wicked unbelief as to the divinity of his person, to receive the representation he had made, could not certainly constitute a sufficient inducement for him to accommodate himself to them in the explanation in such a way as to change substantially any position formerly assumed. To accommodate does not mean to obliterate or destroy; and

---

6. [John 6:62–63.]

we fail to read of any instance in which any want of moral ability on the part of the people has ever induced Christ so to modify any scheme or doctrine, as to destroy any of its primary and essential features; especially when, in his own person which was now at hand, and in the very doctrine in relation to this person which he was now preaching, all that grace was to be found, the absence of which constituted the negative cause of their incapacity. Rather are we constrained to believe that the words last quoted—constituting the basis of discussion—although different in some respects from those used before, which, as explanatory, it is necessary they should be, still embody in a real and vital way, every point and aspect of the subject as presented before, in the use of a different phraseology. If this be true in regard to points in the representation that might be regarded as minor, or less essential, then it must certainly be true in relation to the *humanity* of Christ, which is, in fact, the great burthen of the whole chapter.

Regarding then all the prominent points in the representation as contained really in the explanation, the only question for human investigation that remains is, the precise meaning which the explanation gives to these points. This, definitely, is the question.

We regard these words of explanation as referring, in the first place, to the *Person* of Christ, as the bread of life; and, in the second place, as referring, indirectly it may be, to his *ordinances*, in which that person, in substance the same as when upon the earth, but spiritualized and glorified, is always at hand, to meet and satisfy, in a real way, the demand for spiritual life in our nature.

It might seem that these propositions would, in themselves, carry such a degree of self-evidencing power as to their truthfulness, that would induce all, who have come to any degree of inward sympathy with divine things, to embrace and rest upon them at once. But, unfortunately for the precious interests of true faith, this may not be expected. Although the Christian mind at the present is generally satisfied in regard to the divinity of Christ, the primary difficulty in the Jewish mind, yet, such is the degree to which it is tainted, in every direction, with the various systems of rationalism, closing the door upon the whole region of Christianity which is seen and occupied only by faith, as utterly to disqualify us, as it would seem, for any such calm letting of ourselves down into the embrace of a life which lies beyond the discernment of reason as such, however strongly its own divine nature might draw, and our own deeper instincts urge. Discarding the ground on which the Jewish mind rested and sought to justify its unbelief as to the doctrine of a real participation in Christ's humanity (i.e. their infidelity as touching his divinity), do we not, for the most part, with them practically regard the same thing as monstrous and absurd!

[CHRIST'S DIVINE-HUMAN PERSON THE SOURCE OF THEANTHROPIC LIFE]

I. We have said that these words of explanation refer to the doctrine of Christ's person, as the principle of eternal life. "I am that bread of life." What, now, do we understand by the person of Christ, under this form? It is not too much to say here that the merit of the whole subject lies definitely in this inquiry. Our views of every other subject within the range of the Christian faith will take their character or complexion from the view we take of the person of Christ; for that person is evidently the conscious centre of the entire system of Christianity—imparting to it all the force and vitality which it is found to carry with it.

The point is readily conceded by all orthodox Churches that Christ possessed, definitely, two natures—divine and human—that the "Word"—which was the divine—"became flesh," which was the human; that these two natures, in the incarnation, became so united as to form but *one* personality, or "I." Not, indeed, that the two natures, thus flowing together, amalgamated in the form of confused blending of the properties that were peculiar to each, but in such a form as to produce a most complete unity of personality, while the peculiar properties of each are allowed to carry with them relatively their own distinct force. The person or personality of Christ, then, is the flowing together, in a real way, of the divine and human natures which he possessed, so as to constitute a unity, the elements in which are neither wholly divine, nor yet entirely human, but both. The pronoun "I" is the exponent of this unity, and must hence always imply the real presence of both natures. This is the force of the term "I" in this connection—"*I* am that bread of life." If it were possible to divide the person of Christ into two distinct and separate parts (which can hardly be allowed even in thought), the question would be, which of these parts thus separated does he designate by the pronoun *I*—his human or his divine nature? Could he be a Saviour of men in either character, separated wholly from all connection with the other? Evidently he could not. Hence being divine he became human, that, in this double character, he might be "Immanuel"—God with us. On this account we have always disliked the terms which some, in their unenlightened zeal to compliment Christ, are in the habit of applying to him—such as "divine Saviour," &c. Such a habit of mind indicates the utter absence of all practical sense of the only form in which he is the Saviour in deed and in truth. No form of speech is to be regarded as complimentary to Christ, as a Saviour, but rather as degrading, which virtually ignores the human side of his nature, which, in conjunction with the divine, is essential to constitute him such. If he thought it not beneath the dignity of his nature as divine to take upon himself the human, and incorporate it into vital union with the divine, for the very purpose of becoming a Saviour, it should certainly not be the effort of those who are saved by him, to rend those two asunder, and thus destroy his saving power.

But, although this be, in fact, the form of vital union of the human and divine natures in the person of Christ, which constitutes him the Saviour of men, it is, nevertheless, contended by many that a separate office, under certain circumstances, is given to these natures respectively in the Scriptures. For the basis of this distinction, we are directed to those passages of the word of God, where Christ is spoken of as the "Son of God," on the one hand, and as the "Son of man," on the other. It may be a sufficient answer to this to say, that in all cases where such phraseology is made use of, the distinction is more formal than real; and that the general reason why even the appearance of such a distinction is made at all, lay in the necessity, on the part of the inspired writers, to accommodate themselves as far as possible to the capacities of the human mind. In those cases, however, where Christ is spoken of in his official capacity, as the Saviour, such a distinction is never even intimated in the most distant form. He is always regarded in the integrity of his person, as uniting the two in one, in a real and vital way: the "Son of God" and the "Son of man" become one Saviour—Immanuel, God with us.

This union of the two natures, constituting the person of Christ, holds in the form of the Theanthropic Life, i.e., a life resulting from the union of the divine and human natures in his person, which contains the legitimate elements of both under the most real and vital form. "I am that bread of life." Now this life, although it contains the real elements of his humanity as well as his divinity, is not by any means, on that account, an object for the senses, but for the faith, of men. It exists in the person of Christ now just as really as in the days of his flesh; for his union with our human nature, in the sense already explained, was not effected merely for the purpose of enabling him to accomplish a saving act upon the cross, but of carrying forward the redemption in a real way within us, by a continued impartation of himself to us, until, being filled with his nature, we shall be borne, by its own innate and heavenward tendency, to himself at the right hand of God.

It is to be deeply lamented that the resurrection and ascension of Christ should seem to make it necessary in the faith of many, that his humanity, as such, can in no real way be looked upon as present in the world. In the generic form of that humanity, as now explained, his resurrection and ascension imply no such necessity; but rather, in the clearest way conceivable, constitute the condition only of its presence under a deeper and more vital form.

Being then, by the nature of his person, a real Divine-Human Saviour now, as much so as he was in the days of his flesh, the question is, under what form is this true?

[Christ's Divine-Human Person Accessible Under the Form of Spirit]

1. We answer, in the first place, and say under the form of *Spirit*. "The words that I speak unto you, *they are Spirit*." We have already said that the Jews understood the Saviour in his discourse, as referring to his humanity. In this they certainly understood him correctly. Their only fault, in this respect, was that they regarded him as referring to his human nature under too coarse and gross a form—as literal flesh, blood, &c. This understanding, or rather, misunderstanding, he designed to correct by the use of the term "Spirit." We certainly may discover a polemic opposition in this term, to the *carnal* apprehension of his person. While the humanity which is assumed in the incarnation is ever most vitally connected with it so as to be part and parcel of its true nature, yet it is never to be regarded in a gross, materialistic sense. In the case of a mere man, as they regarded him, this perhaps was the highest form in which "flesh," as such, could be viewed, at least by them. But now, connecting with the power of the godhead which resided permanently in his person, and which stood in vital union with his humanity, rendering the whole divinely transparent, it was not to be apprehended in that

low, coarse sense, but as elevated and spiritualized. The flesh of Christ, as begotten by the Holy Ghost, and as rising generically into, and uniting with, his divine life, becomes itself a πνευματικόν ["spiritual"]; so that whilst all its attributes, holding only in time and space, are left behind, its inward power comprehending all that is real and necessary as the germ of an actual humanity remains permanently and forever linked with his person. Were the human nature of Christ not thus taken up into the divine by the power of the Holy Ghost, and penetrated and spiritualized, it would indeed profit nothing, as, in that case, we should lack the evidence of a proper and necessary union of it with the divine; for the most satisfactory proof of the vital union of the two lies in the fact, which we here discover, that the one is *conditioned* by the other, and yet not in such a way as to destroy any essential and necessary quality that may attach to either. "It is the Spirit that quickeneth" the human—raises it into its proper sphere as human; it does not destroy or ignore it, but infuses it with its own proper vitality as human, and not as spirit.

There is then a deeper sense to be attached to the discourse of Christ, in its reference to his humanity, than that caught up by his hearers upon this occasion: and this undercurrent of thought and doctrine is not confined to his teaching in this instance merely, but underlies, as we have reason to believe, all the discourses that fell from his lips. Whilst this fact is generally conceded, the tendency seems to be equally general to seize hold of the inward sense as purely spiritual, or visionary (for it amounts to just that in the end), and array it against the outward as carnal. Why may not the inward, by the power of the Holy Ghost, contain all the reality of the outward? This view admits of no contrariety or contradiction, and prepares the way for a complete reconciliation—the inward is the outward really in all respects in which this last appeals to the senses, only under a deeper and more powerful form. It is in this way that our faith is assisted in the higher and mysterious realities of our holy religion. "The letter" (that is, the literal or gross sense) "killeth, but the Spirit" (i.e., the higher or more spiritual sense) "maketh alive."[7] The humanity in the person of Christ, then, holds in the form of the Spirit, as opposed to the carnal or gross view of flesh.

---

7. [2 Cor 3:6.]

[Christ's Divine-Human Person Accessible Under the Form of Life]

2. This human nature is said still further to exist in the person of Christ under the form of *life*. We may not regard this term as containing the same thought, and nothing more, that was contained in the other. There is a shade of difference. It is an advance upon the former. The term "Spirit" or "Spiritual," which the Saviour applied to the doctrine which the Jews had understood in its "carnal" sense, seemed to be the very utmost limits of two extremes, capable of no real connection. We have not explained it thus, because this is not the true sense in fact; but would it not appear so to the mind he was now addressing? Occupying, as they did, the carnal side of the extreme, how natural would it be for them to seize the Saviour's intimation and fly to the opposite; and, under the form of "Spirit," exclude the idea of humanity altogether? Hence the propriety of introducing a middle term which may fix and hold the human nature in its proper place, and make it real, notwithstanding it is taken up into the sphere of the spiritual. For this purpose the term "life" is used as explanatory of the term Spirit; and the term is well selected. "The words that I speak unto you, they are life." The Spirit is conditioned by the Life.

This term is applicable, properly, only to the union of the two natures in the person of Christ. It is the word definitely in which they come to their proper union, and become suffused with active power respectively to accomplish in a joint way the great work of human salvation. By the term *life*, he would have them to understand that in the constitution of his person, as the Saviour of man, his humanity forms a necessary factor, not merely under the form of Spirit, that is, of Spirit in such a sense as to exclude its reality, and thus leave a mere Gnostic show or an unsubstantial picture, but as a *real life,* or *life-fact*; as if he had said, "Because I say that the humanity, forming part of my person, does not exist in the gross form of flesh, as you understand me to mean, do not, therefore, say that it does not exist there at all, save as a picture, a fancy, an abstraction. By avoiding one extreme, do not run into another; for both are equally dangerous."

The fact that we have an everliving Divine-Human Saviour is every where taught in the New Testament. "We have not an high priest who is passed into the heavens that cannot be touched with the feeling of our infirmities; for he was in all points tempted like as we are, yet without sin."[8]

There is a universal tendency in the human mind to look upon that which is spiritual as *opposed* radically to that which is human. It seems to see no relation between them—no inward and real adaptation for each other—no common ground on which they can meet and unite in a vital and free way. This is Gnosticism—Rationalism. It leaves no room for a real, vital union of the human to the person of Christ—it exists only in appearance; or if the union was real, it was constrained, and continued only through the short period of his earthly life, and was then glorified into an abstraction.

The tendency thus to think and feel is the result of the divorce of these two factors of existence in our own persons by the power of sin. "It was not so from the beginning."[9] This divorce in our persons constituted the very destruction in which we lay as helpless sinners, and from which we were calling to be delivered. In Christ was our help, because it was in him that the human and the divine again met inwardly and vitally; and thus the way became opened really for their meeting again in our persons. Thus the *body*, as well as the soul, is made the subject of his salvation. How, we may ask, were this possible in any real way if there were no capacity in the body for the spiritual and divine? But now we see that the very body, by the power of Christ's divine-human life, is made thus to possess a germ of spiritual life which will finally raise it from the grave of decay, and bring it forth in the glory of the resurrection body, without the destruction of any one constituent element of its nature as human. "Because I live, ye shall live also."[10]

The conclusion then of the whole matter, as touching the person of Christ, is that it comprehends the divine and human natures in the form of the most real though spiritual life—the only life competent to raise the world from the death of sin to the life of holiness; that He, constituting as he does, by his incarnation, the real centre of the world under all its forms, has most fully opened the way for a real communication between heaven and earth; so that in his person—world embracing as it is, the power is comprehended by which the whole creation, groaning and travailing in pain from centre to circumference, as well as

---

8. [Heb 4:15.]
9. [Matt 19:8.]
10. [John 14:19.]

the human which groans within itself, waiting for the adoption, to wit, the redemption of its whole being, body and soul, may be raised from the dreadful death of sin, and brought back to the life of God. This, and nothing short of this, is the significance of the person of Christ as the principle of real, spiritual and eternal life.

But, heavenly and delightful as all this is, were we compelled to stop here, our highest hopes would still be disappointed. Something more is needed than merely to *behold* by the *mind* all fulness treasured up in the person of Christ, in all respects adapted to our spiritual necessities. A royal feast, bountiful in all its provisions, may indeed greatly gratify the eye, but this would not satisfy our hunger. It must be brought near to us in a more real way. The provisions must be taken *into us,* not in the way of thought or fancy, but really. Then they become nourishment—impart strength and animation, and enable us to accomplish the purposes of life. Why should we regard the provisions in the person of Christ in a less real light, and why should the necessity of a real appropriation of them to our persons be looked upon as less essential and important? Is not our Christian life as real as our natural? And who will say that its demand for a real participation in the merits of Christ, under a divine-human form, is not equally imperative? "Except ye eat the flesh of the son of man, and drink his blood, ye have no life in you."[11] Is all this a mere picture? Does it imply nothing more than the mere outward contemplation of the merits of Christ? This were indeed turning the whole sublime scheme of redemption into a figment or fancy. The outward, legal scheme, which mechanically sets the merits of the second Adam over against the demerits of the first, thus freeing us in the eye of the law, might indeed be satisfied with such a view. But it certainly is not easy to see why the system of Universalism should not occupy the same ground? Surely it has a right to the same hope. If the merits, divine and human, contained in the person of the Redeemer, in a form wholly separated and distinct from the human subject, can avail to the salvation of one individual, then it can, and by necessity will, avail in like manner for all. Here the doctrine of universal salvation is consistent; for there is no room for distraction, but on the ground of an arbitrary decree, and much less for limitation, seeing that the merits of Christ are infinite.[12]

11. [John 6:53.]

12. [By an "outward, legal scheme, which mechanically sets the merits of the

These systems might answer if our disease as sinners lay wholly in a thought or law out of, and beyond us. But this is not the condition of our nature. Whilst it is true that the divine law, as a power standing beyond and over us, has been violated and broken, and must be rendered honorable in this outward way by the merits of the Redeemer, we feel that our own nature demands an *application* of the same merits. We are sick at heart. We are corrupt and depraved in the very constitution of our being. We are diseased in *nature* as well as in the eye of the law; and how can the satisfaction of the law, as something beyond us, and having no vital connection with us, remedy the disease which has become constitutional, affecting our whole being? Will the mere contemplation of the merits of Christ remedy this constitutional disorder? Then would contemplation be the Saviour, and not Christ. Can the Holy Spirit do it, while the merits of Christ's person remain out of and beyond us?[13] Then the Holy Spirit, as a divine power separate from Christ, would be the Saviour, and not Christ, in and by the Spirit. Can the First Person in the Blessed Trinity accomplish it in the same outward way? Who but feels the folly of all such questions! Christ *alone* is the incarnate Saviour, neither is there salvation in *any* other. And if the salvation is to be real in our case and not a mere fancy, it is plain that we must participate, in a real way, in those elements definitely which constitute him the Saviour. These we have seen to be his *Life*, embodying in a true way the divine and human natures. "This is the record, that God hath given to us eternal life; and this life is in his Son. He that hath the Son, hath life; and he that hath not the Son of God, hath not life." 1 John 5:11, 12. "He that eateth my flesh, and drinketh my blood, dwelleth *in me, and I in*

---

second Adam over against the demerits of the first," Gans doubtless has in mind the later, bi-covenantal federal Calvinism, which spoke of the "immediate imputation" (a completely extrinsic legal act) of the original sin of Adam to his posterity, and of the active obedience of Christ to the believer. Gans would have been particularly aware of the position of Charles Hodge of Princeton on this issue because of Hodge's extended controversy with John W. Nevin over the doctrine of the Lord's Supper. Interestingly, the connection drawn with universalism has some basis in fact in that early New England Universalism emerged out of federal Calvinism. See Evans, *Imputation and Impartation*, 120–21.]

13. [Here we sense an echo of Calvin's famous statement in *Inst.* III.1.1 (McNeill ed.): "First, we must understand that as long as Christ remains outside of us, and we are separated from him, all that he has suffered and done for the salvation of the human race remains useless and of no value for us."]

him."[14] It is needless, as it would indeed be an endless task, to multiply passages of Scripture upon the real participation of the Saviour's life, in order to accomplish, in a personal and practical way, the end of his incarnation—human salvation.

The only question is how, or by what means, can this participation be secured? Can it be done by faith in his person abstractly considered? The Scriptures, in individual instances, might perhaps create and nourish a conviction of this kind. But when we come to an apprehension of the grand scheme which God has devised—a scheme which starts in the person of Christ—comes to an actual, tangible existence in the world, and is ever vitally connected with his person, and which reaches in an actual way the persons of his people, we at once feel that faith in Christ, as the Saviour, involves confidence to the same degree in the scheme itself. The one is the proper measure of the other. Now this general scheme is the Church, starting in his person, and declared to be "his Body—the fulness of him that filleth all in all."[15] This Church contains ordinances or sacraments, divinely instituted for the purpose of bringing this *Theanthropic* Life of the Redeemer into real contact with our nature.

[THE SACRAMENTS AS MEANS WHEREBY CHRIST'S DIVINE-HUMAN LIFE IS COMMUNICATED]

II. This brings us to the second general thought of our subject, viz: That the words under discussion refer to the sacraments, in which the person of Christ, as now described, is always at hand to meet and satisfy, in a real way, the demand for spiritual life in our nature. These sacraments are Holy Baptism and the Lord's Supper.

It is a matter of controversy with some, we arc aware, as to whether the sacraments are at all referred to in this chapter. We have very little disposition, and still less ability, to enter largely into the debate; especially have we no thought of pleading for any formal basis for baptism. We may state, however, that the ground which is generally taken against its reference to the Supper is the *improbability* that our Lord would speak of it *before* its institution. This is the main, and indeed, the only ground. This was the view particularly of Origen, who held it,

---

14. [John 6:56.]
15. [Eph 1:23.]

doubtless, because of his belief that the benefits of the death of Christ, received *directly* by faith in his name, were the primary things referred to; although, strange to discover, Christ had not spoken one word of his death. After Origen, Basil the Great maintained the same view, and for the same reason.[16] But the great majority of the early Christians seem to have been of one mind in the firm belief that this 6th chapter of John did clearly refer to the sacrament of the Supper. Chrysostom, who was followed by Cyril, Theophylact,[17] and others, and afterwards by the scholastics generally, all, to a man, stand firmly in the conviction that it refers primarily to the Eucharist, and that the mention of it before its institution was to be regarded as a prediction on the part of Christ, designed to prepare the way for the full benefits it involved. The universal belief of the early Church, as we may say, being therefore decidedly in favor of its reference to the Supper, we have no hesitation whatever, in the absence of all Scripture prohibition, to fall in fully with the same. We do this the more readily as we know the general design of the gospel of St. John was to illustrate the prominent doctrines which he perceived to be the characteristic features of the Christian faith. These doctrines were chiefly three; first, the doctrine of the Blessed Trinity; second, the doctrine of the Church; and third, the doctrine of the Holy Sacraments. To this free sympathy with the early Church in this particular, we are led in the second place, because of our belief that the divine-human merits of Christ's life are not received immediately and directly from his person by faith in an abstract way, but mediately, through the Church, and especially by the sacraments, which were instituted definitely for this purpose.

We regard this chapter rather as containing the idea of *Sacrament*, and as embodying for our faith the true *power* and *significance* of Sacrament, than as furnishing a formal ground for it. In this view, although the 3d chapter and 5th verse is the place where Holy Baptism is formally and with evident design referred to, the potential force and

---

16. [Basil the Great, also known as Basil of Caesarea (c. 330–379), was one of the Cappadocian Fathers. He was instrumental in reconciling the Origenist tradition with conciliar orthodoxy.]

17. [John Chrysostom (c. 347–407), sometime bishop of Constantinople and one of the great preachers of the early-church period (his name *Chrysostom* means "golden-mouthed"). Cyril of Alexandria (d. 407), Patriarch of Alexandria and greatest representative of the Alexandrian tradition. Theophylact was an 11th-century Byzantine commentator and bishop.]

significance of it may, nevertheless, be viewed as vitally incorporated with the sacrament of the Supper as here brought to view. This would seem to be implied in the force of the words: "Except ye eat the flesh of the Son of man, and drink his blood, ye have *no life* in you."[18] Baptism is the sacrament in which Christian life is properly said to take its rise in the subject, and yet, in the order of nature and of time, it precedes that of the Supper. Perhaps this may be accounted for in part from the fact that, in the early ages of Christianity, the two sacraments were very closely connected in time, even in the case of children who were admitted to both.

Regarding, then, these sacraments as the things designated, next to the person of the Redeemer, we are called upon to examine their significance in the light of the explanation given by our Saviour, as this explanation stands connected with the previous representation of the whole chapter: "The words that I speak unto you, they are spirit, and they are life." Of course we are bound, in all fairness of reason, and urged by what we conceive to be the promptings of a true faith, to regard them as the bearers of the Divine-Human Life of the Redeemer in just as real a way as we have seen his life itself to be real, as connected with his person. We cannot, indeed, escape from this faith, if we regard the Church and Sacraments, on the one hand, as the only divinely constituted channels of his grace, and on the other, recognize the necessity of a real contact of that grace with our persons, for the general purpose which the gospel contemplates. It will not do, as we have already seen, that this Divine-Human Life, in which alone salvation is comprehended, should be real in the person of Christ as separated from all vital connection with our persons. This were indeed for hungry, starving men to *look* upon a rich and royal banquet, only that the sense of their starving condition might become deeper and more dreadful by the contrast. The spiritual demand of our nature is real—the remedy in the person of the adorable Redeemer is real, and the means connecting that remedy with our disease must be just as real. We can recognize no room for fancy or picture in a matter pregnant with the momentous importance peculiar to this subject. He must have a strangely contorted heart, and a deeply jaundiced eye, who can feel and see nothing more in this whole representation than a mere feasting upon the merits of Christ by means of what passes for pious feeling and devout! meditation. No view

18. [John 6:53.]

certainly can satisfy the explanation, unless we make the explanation to ignore virtually the positions assumed in the previous representation, but that which recognizes in the sacraments the real Divine-Human life of Christ, which in this real way we receive into us as the "Bread" or principle of our life.

To say that the mere water in the case of Baptism, and the mere bread and wine in the case of the Supper, involved, of themselves and by the force of their own nature, the real Life of Christ as now explained, would be to speak great folly. But when infinite wisdom selects these emblems, and when infinite power ordains and sets them apart, and through his servants specially consecrates them as the bearers of the Divine-Human Life of Christ to the persons of believers, who is he to set in judgment upon that wisdom, or for one moment to limit that power! Baptism and the Supper have been thus selected and ordained, and consecrated, and it is one of the boldest acts of unbelief and rabid infidelity to deny their grace. They are God's special creatures, and true faith is always prepared to see in them God's special grace.

The same unbelieving objection might have been urged by the man impotent from his mother's womb against the waters of Bethesda, which were reported to contain healing efficacy. What could these waters in themselves contain of curative power, beyond other ordinary waters? But God's angel, in certain seasons, entered and troubled these waters, and therefore they became powerful as a remedial agent. Can you see *how*, precisely, or explain the mystery? This same objection was indeed urged by the leprous Syrian, when directed by divine authority to "go and wash in Jordan, that his flesh might come again to him, and that he might be clean." In the wickedness of his unbelief he replies: "Are not Abana and Pharpar, rivers of Damascus, better than all the waters of Israel? May I not wash in them and be clean?"[19] And yet, as the sequel discloses, nothing but a full surrender to, and a living faith in God's plan as such, accomplished the end sought. This is just as absolutely and unbendingly true now as it was then. His Bethesda and Jordan now are the Sacraments, borne in the divine stream of the Church, starting simultaneously in his sacred person as the God-man, Immanuel.

But what do they involve respectively?

---

19. [2 Kgs 5:10, 12.]

[Baptism the Sacrament of Initiation]

1. Baptism is the primary sacrament. By it the person is *initiated* into the Church—planted into God's vineyard, and made thus a plant of God's own planting. By it, his relation to the corrupt, Adamic life is broken, and he becomes ingrafted into the Divine-Human Life of the second Adam, inducing thus the possibility of a positively holy character. The term *initiation* refers, not simply to the Church in its outward organization, but to the Church in its inward life and power, as the *real Body of Christ*. This is the real spiritual power to which Baptism gives its subjects a living connection. It makes them members organically—members of his Body. In its own nature it can mean nothing less, and thus much Scripture abundantly confirms. We are represented as *being buried with Christ* in Baptism; that is, not only deadened in a real way to sin, but removed out of its sphere, and placed beyond its reigning power and control. *We are raised with him* in the same way, to a new and more elevated sphere of existence. "Whosoever of you that are baptized have put on Christ."[20] "According to his mercy he *saved us* in the *washing* of *regeneration*."[21] And referring to the circumstance of Noah's temporal salvation by the flood, we hear the Scriptures say, "The like figure whereunto even baptism doth now save us (not the putting away of the filth of the flesh, but the answer of a good conscience towards God) by the resurrection of Jesus Christ."[22] But we cease our quotations; it is enough to say that such and similar passages are scattered all through the New Testament, in all which Baptism is represented clearly as implying the *substance* of the various types and shadows by which it was pre-figured in the Old Testament; the one is complementing to the other.

Now, whether we regard the Divine-Human Life of Christ as planted by holy baptism into the person of the subject, or the subject as planted into this Life, in either case, the contact of Christ's humanity, as well as divinity, with his person is most real and vital. He does participate really in his human nature, raised by the Spirit, beyond the carnal and gross conception of it, and does, in consequence, possess spiritual real life. As a plant, planted in God's own way, into a Divine-Human

---

20. [Gal 3:27.]
21. [Titus 3:5.]
22. [1 Pet 3:21.]

soil, he is in a condition to grow up into the image of Christ, if the necessary conditions are at hand. In this respect there is a perfect analogy between the child baptized and the young and tender plant. Although the plant may be properly planted, and into the very best soil, adapted perfectly in every respect to its nature, yet, if the conditions of light, warmth and moisture are not at hand, death will be the inevitable result. The conditions in the case of the baptized child, which God has supplied in his moral government, are just as indispensable, if life is to be maintained.

The family, in its nature and constitution, is designed as the first of these conditions. The very idea of baptism in the case of the child implies the existence of piety on the part of the parents. They are constituted, in a sense that goes far beyond the merely figurative, the priest and priestess at the altar of the little home over which they are placed. The child exists in them—forms part of their nature, and they can bear it to the altar in prayer and supplication, in just the same way in which they carry themselves thither. The family is divine in its constitution, and adapted to the spiritual as well as the natural wants of the child. It is a vital part of the Church, and implies not only the presence of obligations arising in the Church, but also the presence of special spiritual grace, whereby it is possible to discharge these obligations in a proper and becoming manner. As baptism, in its practical operations, is granted, to a very considerable extent, upon the ground of the obligations which parents or sponsors assume at the time the act is performed, it is not an unreasonable conclusion that the practical discharge of these obligations will be the measure of benefit experienced by the child. Did parents feel the deep inward significance of baptism on the one hand, and the importance of a faithful discharge of their obligations on the other, in order to give to it its inward meaning and due practical application in the case of the child, they could neither be as indifferent to the baptism of their children, nor as careless in regard to their vows as they are. But it is not my purpose now to refer in lengthy detail to the various duties which parents, by their vows, are under obligations to discharge to their children in the family. They are known already far better than discharged. I shall only endeavor to excite the faith of Christian parents, if possible, in the great spiritual benefit which the institution, as such, contains for their children, and the real way in which it is imparted, and leave the force of their solemn vows, and the love they bear to their children, urge them on actively in the way *that* faith may lead them.

The Sabbath school, too, is no ordinary help in giving the baptism of our children its proper practical significance. It is a legitimate expression of Church piety when, by the Church as such, its power for good is applied diligently to the unfolding of the life in the children, implanted by baptism. But how often, as in the case of indifferent families, is the whole spiritual interest of the child in this respect placed into the hands of hirelings, who have no natural sympathy either with the Church, school, or spiritual nature of the child, which it is the object to draw out and develop. This habit is as infidel in the Church as it is unnatural in the family; and never (we speak confidently) will the Church, through the Sabbath school, accomplish the end here proposed until this habit is broke. The royalty of Christianity consists in each one's attending to his own duties, and permits not one to wear the crown and fold his hands in royal ease, whilst the part involving duty is shifted off upon others. The Sabbath school, to carry in it the life and power of the Church, need not necessarily be held in the church building, but must have the active piety of its members, evinced by the practical discharge of *their* duties in way of teaching, &c.

The catechetical class is next in order both as to nature and time. Unless this be the result in the end, the design of the school is frustrated, and our labors are in vain. And what reason have we to expect this to be the issue, unless the school is so organized as to make the whole cause tend to this as the highest interest it comprehends? Unfortunately for the Sabbath school in this country, it has very little sense of any higher interest than that which is comprehended in the bare familiarizing of the child with the Scriptures in an outward and mechanical way; and after this is accomplished, it is dismissed to the world to become more the child of sin than it was originally. It has no pervading appreciation at all, as it would seem, of the baptismal *life* of the child, which looks to the Church, through confirmation, as the only element in which it can live and expand. This is the grand defect—a defect which spreads through the whole Sabbath school of America, blighting, like the deadly Simoon,[23] the lovliest flowers planted by baptism, by the river of God. Oh when will the interests of God's heritage, the affection we bear for the dear little ones whom God has given us, in connection with the

---

23. [A hot, dry Saharan wind.]

earnest and deep sense of baptismal vows, arouse us to the tremendous interest which is here at stake! When shall we regard the Church as containing the highest end to be reached in our militant Christianity? And when shall we be so drawn to it as to a common centre, that all our efforts shall be regarded as failures unless they result in fixing ourselves and children more deeply and permanently in the Divine-Human life of the Church—the "Body of Christ?"

This is the course of Christian training which the Bible plainly lays down: "Train up a child in the way he should go, and when he is old he will not depart from it."[24] Led upon this course, through the door of confirmation, into the Church—the communion of saints, the child is safe, perfectly safe, because it has complied fully with God's plan; and now, agreeably to his promise, he will guard it from every harm and lead it constantly beside the still waters and the rich pastures of his grace, making it grow and expand, and ever tend forward towards the fulness of a perfect Christian character in Christ Jesus.

[The Lord's Supper as Real Reception of Christ's Humanity]

2. But in what form will he now find the grace particularly which is here so fully promised? In the *Lord's Supper*. This is the sacrament which is more especially referred to in this chapter. It is an eating of the flesh and a drinking of the blood of Christ, under the form of spirit and life. That it involves the humanity of Christ under a real form, there cannot remain the least shadow of doubt. It is humanity, however, penetrated by divinity, by the power of the Holy Ghost, and is hence made an object, not of oral manducation, but of faith in Christ through the sacrament of his flesh and blood. This is spiritual real food, typified by the manna, and accomplishes the same purpose in regard to the Christian or baptismal life, as *that* did in the natural life of the body. How otherwise could it be *Spirit and life*?

This does not mean the literal or corporeal presence of Christ's humanity no more than the germ, comprehending the *power* of the actual, contains the actual. The *spiritual real* presence is not by any means the *real actual* presence. The difference, I apprehend, is the difference and distance, at the same time, between the Protestant and Roman Churches. The distance is great enough, God knows, to keep us

---

24. [Prov 22:6.]

travelling towards each other for centuries yet to come, without coming so near as to afford opportunity for a very loving embrace. There is no inward reason at all why the one should, at any point, become the other. Transubstantiation, as commonly held, is an absurdity, contradicting reason, and destructive to faith. The same may be said generally of consubstantiation, one of the pet theories of the great Reformer, Luther. This last does not absorb and annihilate the natural properties of the emblems, bread and wine, as the other does, but it does make the *actual* humanity of Christ so penetrate these, as to render faith, in their reception, entirely nugatory and unnecessary as a condition. The merits of Christ go with the emblems in all cases of their reception. This, too, is extreme ground, which the Reformed Church has never occupied. Her steady adherence has ever been to the doctrine of the spiritual real presence, as brought out specially by Calvin. It is the medium between the extreme of Zwingli on the one hand, who regarded the whole transaction in the light of a mere outward memento, and that of Luther, just mentioned, on the other. It ever contends for the spiritual real presence, that is, the presence of Christ under the form of a Divine-Human life—thus retaining in the Church in a real way Christ as a Saviour, to the end of time. This is the doctrine of our symbol so plainly drawn out, that he that runs may read.[25]

Notwithstanding the difference between this view and the common view of transubstantiation in the Roman Church is so necessary and great, yet, as a Church we have been charged over and over again with Romanizing tendencies just with reference to this very doctrine.[26] Often times have these charges emanated from individuals who ought to have known better. Nor can we excuse them upon the ground of ignorance; for this is not the ground in the most of instances. We have been denying, explaining and correcting even for years, and yet the

---

25. [An allusion to Hab 2:2.]

26. [Charges of Romanizing dogged the Mercersburg movement from its inception. In part this was due to simple ignorance of the historic Reformed tradition with its liturgical concerns, healthy regard for the historic ecclesial structures and tradition of the church, and conceptions of sacramental efficacy, all of which ran afoul of the emerging American populism and rationalism. But it was also due to the trajectory of the movement itself, which increasingly exalted the sacraments at the expense of the pulpit, and for which the problem of religious authority became increasingly pressing (as the Biblicism of much American Protestantism was seen as more and more problematic). A later volume in this series will deal with these debates.]

same charges fifty times demolished, are hatched up from their non-entity again, and again hurled with the same pious zeal as before, until we have actually become so used to this kind of treatment that we are beginning to think we were born for it. We cannot but regard them, for the most part, as slanderous; nor can we help but look upon those who lend themselves, tool-like, to the nefarious business of report making, as wholly destitute of that charity "which thinketh no evil, but rejoiceth in the truth."[27]

[INCARNATION AND CHURCH: THE GRAND DIVINE PLAN FOR SAVING THE WORLD]

These things, in their proper connection—starting with the person of Christ—continued really and truly in the Church—and opening themselves to real contact from generation to generation in the sacraments, in the way of real Human-Divine life, constitute the grand Divine Plan for saving the world. If this be so, then it follows that our confidence in the plan shall hold in precise proportion to our faith in the person of Christ itself. We cannot separate the two: the first is the means to the last; and the individual who imagines he has faith in Christ as separated from his plan of salvation, gives the lie to his fancy in that very fact. Every one who has a true, living faith in Christ will at the same time be willing to cast himself wholly upon Christ's plan; nor will he have any confidence in any other scheme that might be devised by human ingenuity. It must in the end come to this—either God's plan alone, or none at all: and this is just the same thing as the salvation of God, or no salvation at all.

A want of faith in God's plan of saving man has, heretofore, led to the adoption of other systems of human origin.[28] Happily a re-action has widely spread all over the land, and we are beginning to feel once more the warm encirclings of a proper Church-life closing in around us. It is to be hoped that we are all sufficiently tired supping at the empty cistern that can hold no water, and that we are willing, with thankful

---

27. [1 Cor 13:5, 6.]

28. [On this "adoption of other systems of human origin," see John W. Nevin's *The Anxious Bench* in the forthcoming volume 5 of the Mercersburg Theology Study Series.]

hearts, to return in the full confidence of our spirits, to the Church—the Body of Christ, the fountain of divine life for the world.

These—imperfectly portrayed, I know—yet these are some of the glorious peculiarities of the Bible, and of the Reformed Church, and this briefly is the determination to which we are coming more and more intelligently every day. If these singly, or combined, be heresy, our enemies being judges, then with Paul we are ready to confess, "that after the way which they call heresy, so worship we the God of our fathers."[29]

Much, indeed, has been written, and still more spoken, of a harshly denunciatory character against the German Reformed Church in consequence of her honest adherence to these and similar views. How all this can be reconciled with the doctrine of *private judgment,* which these speakers and writers hold as one of the most precious interests of their faith, we are at a sad loss to understand. To an ordinary mind it would certainly seem that the right, in the case of any one class of men, to enter the Bible and interpret its teachings according to the tastes and bias that may be peculiar to them, would imply a concession of the same privilege (if such it may be called) to all other classes. Why then should the Reformed Church, seeking earnestly to maintain the views in which she had her origin—whether on the ground of private judgment separately, or *private* judgment standing freely in the *universal* judgment of the Church, it does not matter here—be denounced in the rabid and unchristian style so common and even fashionable in many newspaper prints, reviews, &c. The jewel of consistency has certainly been very much marred. The fact is remarkable, which observant minds cannot but have noticed, that those very Bodies, in which the *most* account is made of private interpretation, are the strongest in their denunciation against those who, in differing from them, *seem* to stand upon the same right. But this, after all, is the legitimate and only illustration which the principle is capable of giving. Selfishness, arrogance and pride are its natural fruits. Each mind singly it makes the measure of the whole truth; how can it consistently admit the same measure in the case of other minds that may differ in the least degree from them? It leaves no room for unity, and still less, if possible, for a peaceful and harmonious diversity. Charity, which is the bond of perfectness, it can never understand.

---

29. [Acts 24:14.]

[The Church No Mere Outward Organization]

1.) This whole subject should lead to a correction of our grovelling views of the Church of Christ. It is not a mere outward organisation, but a divine-human life-power, originating in the Person of Christ, with an inward, historical connection with the world, containing the very help we need and must have as sinners.

That the presence of such grand spiritual realities in the Church require faith and a great deal of subordination on the part of the individual to the power of a deeper and more comprehensive life than his own, there can be no doubt; and there can be just as little doubt that, in this age of rationalism, empiricism and individual wilfulness under other forms, many will be found unable to cast themselves freely into the grand comprehending Christian mystery; and, becoming offended with what they conceive to be carnal, because they have no faith to apprehend it as raised into the sphere of the real and spiritual, they will pass off into the open arms of infidelity and the world. This was the result of Christ's teaching and explanation, in regard to this very subject, in this chapter. "From that time many of *his disciples went back, and walked no more with him.*"[30] The same result in the present age, for the same reason, is no less an evidence that the doctrine is God's, and therefore marvellous to the eyes of unbelief. "They go out from us, thereby to show that they are not of us."[31] Occasions of this kind, therefore, instead of causing our faith to waver in regard to these things, should only serve to establish and confirm that faith in their divine truthfulness.

[The Church As the Place of Spiritual Life and Growth]

2.) It should also lead us to see the utter absurdity of the opinion entertained by many even in this day of intelligence, that a real and acceptable Christian character can be secured beyond the pale of the Church, as well as in it. If so, the whole grand superstructure of the Church is only a grand imposition! The wisest and best men that ever lived were demented and the veriest fools! The Bible is a fable! and all real hope of heaven a dream.

As well might we expect our grain to germinate in our granaries, and our flowers, nursed tenderly perhaps in the hot-house, to grow out

---

30. [John 6:66.]
31. [1 John 2:19.]

of the rock! The earth is their womb; air, light, heat, moisture are their conditions.

Thus the Church. In her we are born spiritually in Baptism—and fed in the Supper—and clothed jointly in the garments of the Saviour's righteousness: and thus we are carried forward gradually, by the progressive and expanding power of Christ's life, until we shall reach finally the "stature of the fulness of the perfect man in him."[32]

As I speak on the ground of God's testimony, sealed by a Saviour's blood, I must be believed when I say, it is no vain thing to confess Christ before men, by connecting with his Church. It is his own institution, divinely appointed for divine ends. It is inseparably connected with the Church triumphant in heaven, and is the only door that opens to it. "He that climbeth up any other way, the same is a thief and a robber."[33]

All need and want salvation; and for it are all willing to strive. If the fact then be once incorporated into the faith of men that it is inseparably connected with Zion, then will they flock unto her as doves unto their windows; Zion will arise and shine; her daughters will fill her courts with music; her sons will clap their hands for joy, and her fathers, like good old Simeon, will say, "Now Lord let thy servants depart in peace, for our eyes have seen thy salvation."[34] Then will Zion be gladly hailed as the Lamb's Bride, clothed in her beautiful garments, hanging tenderly upon the arm of her Beloved, and with tearful anxiety awaiting the day when her anguish shall all be o'er and her bliss consummated in heaven. This is the revival that we need as an entire American Protestant Church. This only can save us from the abnormal and wild tendencies of the age, and uplift a standard that, amid the wide-spreading commotions of the times, both in the Church and State, shall serve as does the light-house to the tempest-tossed mariner upon the deep, to guide both to the calm and peaceful moorings of spiritual and eternal truth.

Hagerstown, Md.
D. G.

---

32. [A paraphrase of Eph 4:13.]
33. [John 10:1.]
34. [See Luke 2:29, 30.]

Bibliography

WORKS INCLUDED IN THIS VOLUME:

Gans, Daniel. "The Person of Christ." *Mercersburg Review* 6 (October 1854): 505–31.
Nevin, John Williamson. "Cur Deus Homo." *Mercersburg Review* 3 (May 1851): 220–39.
———. "Jesus and the Resurrection." *Mercersburg Review* 13 (April 1861): 169–91.
———. "Liebner's Christology." *Mercersburg Review* 3 (January 1851): 55–72.
———. "The New Creation in Christ." *Mercersburg Review* 2 (January 1850): 1–12.
———. "Sartorius on the Person and Work of Christ." *Mercersburg Review* 1 (March 1849): 146–64.
———. "Wilberforce on the Incarnation." *Mercersburg Review* 2 (March 1850): 164–96.
Schaff, Philip. "The Moral Character of Jesus Christ." *Mercersburg Review* 13 (July 1861): 321–73.

WORKS CONSULTED:

Ahlstrom, Sydney E. "The Scottish Philosophy and American Theology." *Church History* 24 (1955): 257–72.
Athanasius. "On the Incarnation." In *Christology of the Later Fathers*, edited by Edward R. Hardy. Philadelphia: Westminster, 1954.
Aubert, Annette G. *The German Roots of Nineteenth-Century American Theology.* New York: Oxford University Press, 2013.
Augustine, *Confessions*. Translated by Henry Chadwick. New York: Oxford University Press, 1991.
———. "On Rebuke and Grace" (*De Correptione et Gratia*). In *Nicene and Post-Nicene Fathers*, 1st series, V:471–491. Edited by Philip Schaff. Grand Rapids: Eerdmans, 1971 [reprint].
Barth, Karl. *Church Dogmatics.* 4 vols. Edited and translated by G. W. Bromiley and T. F. Torrance. Edinburgh: T. & T. Clark, 1936–69.
———. *Protestant Theology in the Nineteenth Century.* Valley Forge: Judson Press, 1973.
Bonaventure. *S. Bonaventurae Opera Omnia.* Paris, 1855.
Bozeman, Theodore Dwight. *Protestants in an Age of Science: The Baconian Ideal and Antebellum Religious Thought.* Chapel Hill: University of North Carolina Press, 1977.

Brown, Charles Rufus. "American Old Testament Scholars: Oakman Sprague Stearns." In *The Old and New Testament Student* 10 (1890): 7–13.

Bushnell, Horace. *God in Christ*. Hartford: Brown and Parsons, 1849.

———. *Nature and the Supernatural, as together constituting the one System of God*. New York: Charles Scribner, 1858.

Calvin, John. *Calvin's New Testament Commentaries*. 12 vols. Edited by David W. Torrance and Thomas F. Torrance. Edinburgh: Oliver and Boyd, 1959–72.

———. *Institutes of the Christian Religion*. 2 vols. Translated by Ford Lewis Battles, edited by John T. McNeill. Philadelphia: Westminster, 1960.

———. *Theological Treatises*. Edited and translated by J. K. S. Reid. Philadelphia: Westminster, 1954.

Canlis, Julie. *Calvin's Ladder: A Spiritual Theology of Ascent and Ascension*. Grand Rapids: Eerdmans, 2010.

Clemmer, Robert. "Historical Transcendentalism in Pennsylvania." *Journal of the History of Ideas* 30/4 (1969): 579–92.

Copleston, Frederick C. *Fichte to Nietzsche, A History of Philosophy*, vol. 6. London: Burns and Oates, 1965.

Crisp, Oliver. "Did Christ have a Fallen Human Nature?" *International Journal of Systematic Theology* 6/3 (2004): 270–88.

Cunningham, William. *The Reformers and the Theology of the Reformation*. Edinburgh: T. & T. Clark, 1866.

Cunnington, Ralph. "Calvin's Doctrine of the Lord's Supper: A Blot Upon His Labors as a Public Instructor?" *Westminster Theological Journal* 73 (2011): 215–36.

D'Aubigné, J. H. Merle. *History of the Reformation of the Sixteenth Century* 4 vols. Translated by H. White. Edinburgh: Oliver & Boyd, 1853.

DiPuccio, William. *The Interior Sense of Scripture: The Sacred Hermeneutics of John W. Nevin*. Macon, GA: Mercer University Press, 1998.

———. "Nevin's Idealistic Philosophy." In *Reformed Confessionalism in Nineteenth-Century America*, edited by Sam Hamstra, Jr. and Arie J. Griffioen, 43–67. Lanham, MD: Scarecrow, 1995.

Dorner, Isaak August. *History of the Development of the Doctrine of the Person of Christ*. Translated by William Lindsay Alexander. 5 vols. Edinburgh: T. & T. Clark, 1861–63.

———. *History of the Development of the Doctrine of the Person of Christ*. 5 vols. Edinburgh: T.& T. Clark, 1872–82.

Ebrard, Johann Heinrich August. *Das Dogma vom heiligen Abendmahl und seiner Geschichte*. 2 vols. Frankfurt: Heinrich Zimmer, 1845–46.

Erb, William H. ed. *Dr. Nevin's Theology*. Reading, PA.: I. M. Beaver, 1913.

Evans, William B. *Imputation and Impartation: Union with Christ in American Reformed Theology*. Milton Keynes, UK: Paternoster, 2008.

———. *Imputation and Impartation: Union with Christ in American Reformed Theology*. Eugene, OR: Wipf & Stock, 2009.

———. "Twin Sons of Different Mothers: The Remarkable Theological Convergence of John W. Nevin and Thomas F. Torrance." *Haddington House Journal* 11 (2009): 155–173.

Fackenheim, Emil L. "Immanuel Kant." In *Nineteenth Century Religious Thought in the West*, edited by Ninian Smart, et al, 3 vols., I:17–40. New York: Cambridge University Press, 1985.

Fairweather, Eugene R., ed. *The Oxford Movement*. New York: Oxford University Press, 1964.
Frei, Hans. "David Friedrich Strauss." In *Nineteenth Century Religious Thought in the West*, edited by Ninian Smart et al (3 vols), I:215-260. New York: Cambridge University Press, 1985.
———. "Niebuhr's Theological Background." In *Faith and Ethics: The Theology of H. Richard Niebuhr*, edited by Paul Ramsey, 9-64. New York: Harper & Brothers, 1957.
"Daniel Gans." In *Franklin and Marshall College Obituary Record* 8, Vol. 2/4 (1904): 108-10.
Garcia, Mark. *Life in Christ: Union with Christ and Twofold Grace in Calvin's Theology*. Milton Keynes, UK: Paternoster, 2008.
Göschel, Karl Friedrich. *Beiträge zur speculativen Philosophie von Gott und dem Meschen und dem Gottmenschen*. Berlin, 1838.
Grave, S. A. *The Scottish Philosophy of Common Sense*. Oxford: Clarendon Press, 1960.
Gunton, Colin E. *Yesterday and Today: A Study of Continuities in Christology*. Grand Rapids: Eerdmans, 1983.
Hamilton, Neill Q. *The Holy Spirit and Eschatology in Paul*. Edinburgh: Oliver and Boyd, 1957.
Harris, Murray J. *Raised Immortal*. London: Marshall, Morgan and Scott, 1983.
Hart, D. G. *John Williamson Nevin: High Church Calvinist*. Phillipsburg, NJ: P&R Publishing, 2005.
Hatch, Nathan O. *The Democratization of American Christianity*. New Haven: Yale University Press, 1989.
Hegel, G. W. F. *Lectures on the Philosophy of Religion: One-Volume Edition, The Lectures of 1827*. Edited by Peter C. Hodgson. Berkeley: University of California Press, 1988.
Hodge, Charles. "Beman on the Atonement." *Biblical Repertory and Princeton Review* 17 (1845): 115.
Hodgson, Peter C. "Georg Wilhelm Friedrich Hegel." In *Nineteenth Century Religious Thought in the West*. 3 vols., ed. Ninian Smart et al, 81-121. New York: Cambridge University Press, 1985.
Holifield, E. Brooks. *The Gentlemen Theologians: American Theology in Southern Culture, 1795-1860*. Durham, N.C.: Duke University Press, 1978.
Holte, Ragnar. *Die Vermittlungstheologie. Ihre theologischen Grundbriffe, kritisch untersucht*. Uppsala: Almquist & Wiksell, 1965.
Hunsinger, George. "The Dimension of Depth: Thomas F. Torrance on the Sacraments of Baptism and the Lord's Supper." *Scottish Journal of Theology* (54/2 (2001): 155-76.
Irenaeus. *Against Heresies*. In *The Ante-Nicene Fathers*. Edited by Alexander Roberts and James Donaldson. Grand Rapids: Eerdmans, 1981 [reprint.], I:315-567.
Irving, Edward. *The Orthodox and Catholic Doctrine of our Lord's Human Nature*. London: Baldwin and Cradock, 1830.
Kant, Immanuel. *Critique of Practical Reason*. Translated by Lewis White Beck. Indianapolis: Bobbs-Merrill, 1956.
———. *Critique of Pure Reason*. Translated by Norman Kemp Smith. New York: St. Martin's Press, 1965.

Kennedy, Earl Wm. "Reformed Orthodoxy Redivivus: Heinrich Heppe's 'Reformed Dogmatics' in Historical Perspective." *The Reformed Review* 33 (1980): 150–157.

Kuklick, Bruce. *Churchmen and Philosophers: From Jonathan Edwards to John Dewey*. New Haven: Yale University Press, 1985.

Lange, Johann Peter. *The Life of the Lord Jesus Christ: A Complete Critical Examination of the Origin, Contents, and Connection of the Gospels*. Edited by Marcus Dods. 6 vols. Edinburgh: T. & T. Clark, 1864.

Littlejohn, W. Bradford. *The Mercersburg Theology and the Quest for Reformed Catholicity*. Eugene, OR: Pickwick, 2009.

Loetscher, Lefferts A. *Facing the Enlightenment and Pietism: Archibald Alexander and the Founding of Princeton Seminary*. Westport, Conn. Greenwood Press, 1983.

Luther, Martin. *Against the Heavenly Prophets in the Matter of Images and Sacraments*. Translated by Bernhard Erling and Conrad Bergendoff. In *Luther's Works*, edited by Helmut T. Lehmann, 40:79–223. Philadelphia: Muhlenberg Press, 1958.

Mackintosh, H. R. *The Doctrine of the Person of Jesus Christ*. New York: Scribner's, 1912.

May, Henry. *The Enlightenment in America*. New York: Oxford University Press, 1976.

McCormack, Bruce L. "The Person of Christ." In *Mapping Modern Theology: A Thematic and Historical Introduction*, edited by Kelly M. Kapic and Bruce L. McCormack, 149–173. Grand Rapids: Baker, 2012.

Muller, Richard A. *Christ and the Decree: Christology and Predestination in Reformed Theology from Calvin to Perkins*. Grand Rapids: Baker, 1986.

———. "Emanuel V. Gerhart on the 'Christ Idea' as Fundamental Principle." *Westminster Theological Journal* 48 (1986): 97–117.

Müller, Julius. *The Christian Doctrine of Sin*. Translated by William Pulsford. 2 vols. Edinburgh: T. & T. Clark, 1852.

———. *The Christian Doctrine of Sin*. Translated by William Urwick. 2 vols. Edinburgh: T. & T. Clark, 1868.

Neelands, David. "The Use and Abuse of John Calvin in Richard Hooker's Defense of the English Church." *Perichoresis* 10 (2012): 3–22.

Nevin, John Williamson. *The Anxious Bench*. 2nd ed. Chambersburg, PA: Publication Office of the German Reformed Church, 1844.

———. "The Apostles' Creed." *Mercersburg Review* 1 (1849): 105–127, 201–221, 313–347.

———. "Catholic Unity." In *The Mercersburg Theology*. Edited by James Hastings Nichols, 33–55. New York: Oxford, 1966.

———. "The Church." In *The Mercersburg Theology*, edited by James Hastings Nichols, 56–76. New York: Oxford, 1966. Originally published in pamphlet form as *The Church: A Sermon Preached at the Opening of the Synod of the German Reformed Church at Carlisle, October 1846*. Chambersburg: German Reformed Church Publishing House, 1847.

———. "Hodge on the Ephesians." *Mercersburg Review* 9 (1857): 46–83, 192–245.

———. *The Mystical Presence: A Vindication of the Reformed or Calvinistic Doctrine of the Holy Eucharist*. Philadelphia: J. B. Lippincott, 1846.

———. *The Mystical Presence And the Doctrine of the Reformed Church on the Lord's Supper*. Edited by Linden J. DeBie. The Mercersburg Theology Study Series, vol. 1. Eugene, OR: Wipf & Stock, 2012.

———. "Natural and Supernatural." *Mercersburg Review* (1860): 176–211.

———. "Noel on Baptism." *Mercersburg Review* 2 (May 1850): 231–265.

———. "Trench's Lectures." *Mercersburg Review* 2 (1850): 604–619.
Nevin, John Williamson and Charles Hodge. *Coena Mystica: Debating Reformed Eucharistic Theology*. Edited by Linden J. DeBie. The Mercersburg Theology Study Series, vol. 2. Eugene, OR: Wipf & Stock, 2013.
Newell, Roger. "Participation and Atonement." In *Christ in Our Place: The Humanity of God in Christ for the Reconciliation of the World*, edited by Trevor A. Hart and Daniel P. Thimell, 92–101. Exeter: Paternoster, 1989.
Nichols, James Hastings, ed. *The Mercersburg Theology*. New York: Oxford University Press, 1966.
———. *Romanticism in American Theology: Nevin and Schaff at Mercersburg*. Chicago: University of Chicago Press, 1961.
Niebuhr, Richard R. *Schleiermacher on Christ and Religion*. New York: Charles Scribner's Sons, 1964.
Noll, Mark A. *America's God: From Jonathan Edwards to Abraham Lincoln*. New York: Oxford, 2002.
———. "Common Sense Traditions and American Evangelical Thought." *American Quarterly* 37 (1985): 216–238.
Pfleiderer, Otto. *The Development of Theology in Germany Since Kant: and Its Progress in Great Britain Since 1825*. Translated by J. Frederick Smith. New York: Macmillan, 1893.
Plato, *The Republic*. In *The Collected Dialogues of Plato*. Princeton: Princeton University Press, 1961.
Riley, Woodbridge. *American Thought: From Puritanism to Pragmatism and Beyond*. New York: Henry Holt, 1915.
Rousseau, Jean-Jacques. *Emile, or On Education*. Translated by Allan Bloom. New York: Basic Books, 1979.
Schaff, Philip. *The Creeds of Christendom*. 3 vols., 6th ed. New York: Harper and Brothers, 1931.
———. "General Introduction to Church History." *Bibliotheca Sacra* 6:23 (August 1849), 409–41.
———. *Germany; Its Universities, Theology, and Religion*. Philadelphia: Lindsay and Blakiston, 1857.
———. *History of the Apostolic Church; with a General Introduction to Church History*. Translated by Edward D. Yeomans. New York: Charles Scribner, 1853.
———. *The Person of Christ: The Perfection of His Humanity Viewed as a Proof of His Divinity*. London: James Nisbet, 1880.
———. The *Principle of Protestantism*. Chambersburg, PA: German Reformed Church, 1845.
Schleiermacher, Friedrich. *The Christian Faith*. Edited by H. R. Mackintosh and J. S. Stewart. Edinburgh: T. & T. Clark, 1928.
Strauss, David Friedrich. *The Life of Jesus Critically Examined*. Edited by Peter C. Hodgson, translated by George Eliot. Philadelphia: Fortress Press, 1972.
Sweeney, Douglas A. *Nathaniel Taylor, New Haven Theology, and the Legacy of Jonathan Edwards*. New York: Oxford University Press, 2003.
Sykes, Norman. *Old Priest and New Presbyter*. Cambridge: The University Press, 1956.
Taylor, Hannis. *Cicero: A Sketch of His Life and Works*. 2nd ed. Chicago: McClurg, 1918.
TeSelle, Eugene. *Christ in Context: Divine Purpose and Human Possibility*. Philadelphia: Fortress Press, 1975.

Thompson, Curtis L. *Between Hegel and Kierkegaard: Hans L. Martensen's Philosophy of Religion*. New York: Oxford University Press, 1997.
Torrance, Thomas F. *Incarnation: The Person and Life of Christ*. Edited by Robert T. Walker. Downers Grove: IVP, 2008.
———. "Karl Barth and the Latin Heresy." *Scottish Journal of Theology* 39/4 (1986): 461–482.
Ullmann, Karl (or Carl) Christian. "Ueber den unterschiedenen Charakter des Christenthums, mit Beziehung auf neuere Auffassungsweisen." *Theologische Studien und Kritiken* 18/1 (1845): 7–61. [This article was translated and published as a "Preliminary Essay" in John W. Nevin's *The Mystical Presence*.]
Vos, Geerhardus. "The Eschatological Aspect of the Pauline Conception of the Spirit." In *Redemptive History and Biblical Interpretation: The Shorter Writings of Geerhardus Vos*. Edited by Richard B. Gaffin, Jr., 91–25. Phillipsburg, NJ: Presbyterian and Reformed, 1980.
———. *The Pauline Eschatology*. Princeton: Princeton University Press, 1930.
Wallace, Ronald S. *Calvin's Doctrine of Word and Sacrament*. Grand Rapids: Eerdmans, 1957.
Welch, Claude, ed. *God and Incarnation in Mid-Nineteenth Century German Theology*. New York: Oxford University Press, 1965.
Welch, Claude. *Protestant Thought in the Nineteenth Century, Vol. 1, 1799-1870*. New Haven: Yale University Press, 1972.
Wolff, B. C. "German Reformed Dogmatics." *Mercersburg Review* (April 1857): 249–272.
Xenophon. *Xenophon IV: Memorabilia and Oeconomicus* Translated by E. C. Marchant, Loeb Classical Library. Cambridge, Mass.: Harvard University Press, 1968.
Yerkes, James. *The Christology of Hegel*. Missoula: Scholars Press, 1978.

WORKS CITED IN THE ORIGINAL:

Alexander, James W. "The Character of Jesus, an Argument for the Divine Origin of Christianity." In *Lectures on the Evidences of Christianity delivered at the University of Virginia*, 193–211. New York: Robert Carter, 1852.
Bushnell, Horace. *Nature and the Supernatural, as together constituting the one System of God*. New York: Charles Scribner, 1858.
Channing, William Ellery. "Character of Christ." In *The Works of William Ellery Channing*, 6 vols., IV:7–29. Boston: American Unitarian Assoc., 1903.
Cicero. *On the Nature of the Gods. Academics*. Translated by H. Rackham. Loeb Classical Library, 268. Cambridge: Harvard University Press, 1933. [Cited by Schaff as Cicero, *De Natura Deorum*.]
E. Dandiran, E. *Essai sur la divinite du caractere moral de Jesus-Christ*. Genève: Jullien, 1850.
De Pressensé, Edmond. *Le Redempteur*, Paris: Ch. Meyrueis, 1854.
Diodorus Siculus. *The Historical Library of Diodorus the Sicilian, in Fifteen Books. To which Are Added the Fragments of Diodorus*. 2 vols. Translated by G. Booth. London: J. Davis, 1814.
Dorner, Isaak August. *Entwicklungsgeschichte der Lehre von der Person Christi*. 2nd ed., 2 vols. Berlin: Gustav Schlawitz, 1853.

Bibliography   245

Ebrard, Johannes Heinrich August. *Christliche Dogmatik*. 2 vols. Königsburg: A. W. Unzer, 1851-52.

Gervinus, G. G. *Shakespeare*. 4 vols. Leipzig: Engelmann, 1849-50.

Gess, Wolfgang Friedrich. *Die Lehre von der Person Christi entwickelt aus dem Selbstbewusstsein Christi und aus dem Zeugnisse der Apostel*. Basel: Bahnmeiers Buchhandlung, 1856.

Hase, Karl. *Das Leben Jesu*, 4th ed. Leipzig: Breitkopf und Härtel, 1854.

Hase, Carl. *Life of Jesus, A Manual for Academic Study*. Translated by James Freeman Clarke. Boston: Walker, Wise, and Co., 1860.

Hippolytus, *Philosophumena, or the Refutation of all Heresies*. Translated by F. Legge. London: SPCK, 1921.

Hofmann, Rudolph. *Leben Jesu nach den Apokryphen im Zusammenhang aus den Quellen erzaehlt und wissenschaftlich untersucht*. Leipzig: Friedrich Voigt, 1851.

Hooker, Richard. *Of the Laws of Ecclesiastical Polity*. Edited by R. W. Church. Oxford: Clarendon Press, 1868.

Irenaeus, *Libros Quinque Adversus Haereses*. Edited by W. Wigan Harvey. Cambridge: Typis Academicis, 1857.

Lange, Johann Peter. *Leben Jesu nach den Evangelien*. 3 vols. Heidelberg, Karl Winter, 1844-47.

Liebner, Karl Theodor Albert. *Christologie oder die christologische Einheit des dogmatischen Systems*. Göttingen: Vandenhoek and Ruprecht, 1849.

M'Clintock, J. "Short Reviews and Notices of Books." *Methodist Quarterly Review* (January 1849): 154.

Müller, Julius. "Untersuchung der Frage: Ob der Sohn Gottes Mensch geworden sein würde, wenn das menschliche Geschlecht ohne Sünde geblieben ware." *Deutsche Zeitschrift für christliche Wissenschaft und christliches Leben* (1850): 314-320, 333-341.

Nevin, John W. *The Mystical Presence: A Vindication of the Reformed or Calvinistic Doctrine of the Holy Eucharist*. Philadelphia: J. B. Lippincott, 1846.

Paulus, H. E. G. *Das Leben Jesu als Grundlage einer reinen Geschichte des Urchristentums*. Heidelberg: C. F. Winter, 1828.

Sartorius, Ernst. *Die Lehre von Christi Person und Werk in populairen Vorlesungen*. 5th ed. Hamburg: Friedrich Perthes, 1845.

———. *The Person and Work of Christ*. Translated by Oakman S. Stearns. Boston: Gould, Kendall & Lincoln, 1848.

Schaff, Philip. "General Introduction To Church History." *Bibliotheca Sacra* 6:23 (August 1849), 409-441.

———. *Geschichte der Christlichen Kirche von ihrer Gründung bis auf Gegenwart: Die Allgemeine Einleitung, und die erste Periode, vom Pfingstfeste bis zum Tode des heil. Johannes, (A. 30—100)*. Mercersburg, 1851.

———. *History of the Apostolic Church; with a General Introduction to Church History*. Translated by Edward D. Yeomans. New York: Charles Scribner, 1853.

———. *History of the Christian Church: From the Birth of Christ to the Reign of Constantine*. New York: Charles Scribner, 1859.

Schleiermacher, Friedrich. *Der Christliche Glaube*. Berlin, 1836. [Schaff cites the edition printed in *Friedrich Schleiermachers Sämmtliche Werke*. Berlin, 1834-64.]

Sextus Empiricus. *Against Professors*. Translated by R. G. Bury. Loeb Classical Library, 382. Cambridge: Harvard University Press, 1949. [cited by Schaff as Sextus Empiricus, *Adversus Mathematicos*.]

Strauss, David Friedrich. *Die christliche Glaubenslehre in ihrer geschichtliche Entwicklung und im Kampf mit der modernen Wissenschaft*. 2 vols. Tübingen: Osiander, 1840–41.

———. *Das Leben Jesu, kirtisch bearbeitet*. Tübingen: Osiander, 1835–36.

Trench, Richard Chevinix. *Christ the Desire of All Nations, or the Unconscious Prophecies of Heathendom*. Cambridge: MacMillan, Barclay, and MacMillan, 1846.

Ullmann, Carl. *Die Sündlosigkeit Jesu. Eine apologetische Betrachtung*. 6th ed. Hamburg: Friedrich Perthes, 1853.

———. *The Sinlessness of Jesus: an Evidence of Christianity*. Translated by Lundin Brown. Edinburgh, T. & T. Clark, 1858.

Wilberforce, Robert Isaac. *The Doctrine of the Incarnation of our Lord Jesus Christ in its relation to Mankind and to the Church*. Philadelphia: H. Hooker, 1849.

Wilson, Daniel. *The Evidences of Christianity*. 2 vols. Boston, 1830.

Wigram, George V. *The Englishman's Greek Concordance of the New Testament*. New York: Harpers, 1855 [Cited by Schaff as "Bagster's"].

Young, John. *The Christ of History: An Argument Grounded in the Facts of His Life on Earth*. New York: Robert Carter, 1857.

Subject and Author Index

A

Adam (*see also* Second Adam), xxvii–xxviii, xxx–xxxi, 47, 64–66, 72, 115, 120, 131–32, 160, 177, 194, 207, 224
Ahlstrom, Sydney, xvii
America, xvii, xxxvi, 34, 49–50, 159, 231, 233
angels, 90, 129–30, 134
apostles, 7, 9, 82, 122, 155, 163, 166, 178, 184–85, 190, 198, 201, 205
appropriationist soteriologies, xvi, xxiii–xxiv
Aquinas, Thomas, 89, 115, 184
Arianism, 74, 197
Athanasius, 71, 184
atonement (*see also* Mediator, Christ as), viii, xxiii–xxiv, xxviii, xxxiii–xxxiv, 2, 43, 57–58, 60, 64, 90, 125–26, 137, 141, 146, 211
Augsburg Confession, 4, 14, 27
Augustine, 164, 177

B

baptism, 2, 20–22, 27, 42, 57–58, 68, 79, 157, 211, 225, 227–31, 237
  infant, 27, 230–31
Baptists, 19, 21–22, 24–26
Barth, Karl, xxix
the Bible, 32–34, 38–39, 44–45, 59–60, 121–22, 235–36
blood of Christ *see* Christ, blood of
body (in relation to soul), xvii, xxvi, xxx, 76, 155, 211, 222–23
body, Church as Christ's, xxvi–xxvii, 16, 36–37, 66, 77, 83, 85, 92, 126, 156, 211, 225, 229, 232, 235
bread, 21–22, 157, 228, 233
bread of life, 68, 207, 210, 213–14, 216–17
Bushnell, Horace, 54, 163, 167, 170, 179

C

Calvin, John, xxii–xxiii, xxvii, 25, 30, 35, 38, 68–69, 89, 110, 116–17, 184, 212, 224, 233
Channing, William Ellery, 186, 198–200, 202
Christ
  blood of, 21, 43, 68, 140, 146, 194, 210, 212, 214, 219, 223–24, 227, 232
  body of, 73–74 *see also* body, Church as Christ's
  character of, 181–93
  death of, xxiv, xxviii, 37, 90, 113, 121–22, 125, 136, 140–41, 144, 146–47, 153–54, 188–90, 226
  divine-human life of, 2, 21, 124, 211, 222, 227–29, 232–33
  divine nature of, xxiv, 16–17, 69, 74, 79, 217–18
  divinity of, 6, 8, 13–17, 67, 71–72, 74, 88, 98, 160–61, 165–67, 174, 195–99, 211, 214–16, 219
  flesh of, 21, 67–69, 77, 220
  historical, 207–8
  human life of, 167–79

Subject and Author Index

human nature of, 16–17, 66, 69, 72–73, 78–79, 83, 128, 148, 161, 211, 214–15, 217–21, 224
humanity of, xvi, xxi–xxiii, xxx, xxxii, 19, 47, 66, 68, 74, 164–66, 193–95, 210–11, 214–17, 219–20, 232
life of, xxx–xxxi, 2, 19, 25, 30, 33, 36–38, 47, 65, 69, 123, 226, 237
mediation of *see* Mediator, Christ as
person of, xvi, xxxiii, 2, 19, 25, 54, 57–58, 70–71, 122–23, 137, 141–42, 217–18, 221–25, 234
personality of, 17, 57, 217
resurrection of, xvi, xxviii–xxix, xxxii–xxxiii, 38, 42, 58, 136–38, 145–48, 150, 152–56, 158, 211, 219
sinful humanity of, xxix, 46–47, 109
sinlessness of, xx, xxix, 111, 160–61, 177, 179–80
Christology, xv, xix, xxi–xxii, xxvi–xxvii, xxxi, 2–3, 18–20, 25, 48, 88, 97–99, 114, 128, 160
christology from below, xvi, xxi
Church (*see also* body, Church as Christ's), xxv–xxvi, 21, 25–27, 36–38, 48, 50, 58–59, 66, 75–78, 81–86, 92, 124, 156–58, 210–12, 225–37
early, 59–60, 83, 85, 226
Common Sense Realism, xvii–xviii, 29, 33, 47, 163
communion with God, 78, 80, 88, 108, 125, 133
creation, xv, xxxiv, 66, 89, 99–101, 104, 107–10, 117, 119–20, 127, 131–33, 222
Creed, 57–60, 66, 68, 75, 79, 82–86
Cunningham, William, 68

D
D'Aubigné, Merle, 23
death, xxviii–xxix, 43, 58, 60, 69, 137, 143–48, 150, 153–54, 162, 207
death of Christ *see* Christ, death of
deity of Christ *see* Christ, divinity of
divine nature, 6, 8, 13, 130, 154

docetism, xxvi, 41, 88
Dorner, Isaak, xxi, 52, 96, 114, 159, 166–67
dualism, xvii, 88, 100, 102 *see also* body (in relation to soul)
Duns Scotus *see* Scotus, John Duns

E
Ebionitism, xxvi, 41, 61, 88, 154
Ebrard, Johann H. A., 166–67, 186
ecclesiology, xv, xxv–xxvii, 48, 138, 210
Edwards, Jonathan, vii, xxiv
England, Church of, 67, 81
Episcopacy, 46, 48, 81–84
Episcopal Church, 53
Eucharist *see* Lord's Supper

F
Father, the, 6–9, 73–74, 104, 132, 134, 153, 169–70, 182–83, 189, 191, 194–97, 199
federal theology, xxiii–xxiv, 224
Fichte, Immanuel Hermann, 110
first Adam *see* Adam
flesh of Christ *see* Christ, flesh of
freedom, human, 88–89, 101, 108–9, 111, 126
freedom of God, xxxv, 90, 118–19, 121

G
Gans, Daniel, xix, 210–13, 224
Gnosticism, 19, 39, 41, 61, 164, 222
God, personal, 90, 118, 121
Godhead, 6, 8, 15, 66, 70–71, 104, 165, 196
Göschel, Karl Friedrich, 96, 102

H
Hart, D. G., xxxv
head, Christ as, 8, 13, 36, 38, 47, 64, 74, 78, 90, 92, 109, 124–26, 132, 156, 194
Hegel, Georg W. F., viii, xviii–xix, xxi, 15, 52, 71, 88–89, 92–94, 96, 105, 110, 119
history, xix, 39–41, 44, 65–66, 108–9, 162

Subject and Author Index

Hodge, Charles, vii–ix, xxiii–xxiv, xxvi, 68, 211, 224
Holy Spirit, xxii, xxiv, xxxi–xxxiv, 47, 69, 72–73, 90, 133, 147–49, 155, 163, 196, 211, 220, 224
Hooker, Richard, 67–68
human life, 47, 60, 65–66
human nature, 15, 44, 47, 61–62, 64, 66, 68–69, 116, 120, 124, 130–31, 133, 180, 194, 218–19
  fallen, xxix, xxxv
  general, 65
human nature of Christ *see* Christ, human nature of
human race, xxvii, 15–16, 30, 42, 45, 56, 63–67, 69, 71, 74, 78, 90, 124–26, 130–31, 193
humanity, xxvii–xxx, 30–33, 39–41, 44, 47, 61–62, 64–67, 90, 98–99, 101–2, 108–9, 111–12, 126–28, 132–33, 207
  fallen, xxviii, xxxiii, 40, 58, 146
humanity of Christ *see* Christ, humanity of
Hume, David, xvii
Hunsinger, George, xxxi
hypostatic union *see* union, hypostatic

I

idealism, viii, xvii–xix, xxi, xxxi, 32–33, 110
image of God, 21, 130, 132, 144
imputation, xxiv, xxviii, 68, 211, 224
Incarnation, necessity of, xxxv, 88–90, 100, 107–8, 111, 115, 117–18, 120–25, 129–31
Irenaeus, xxvii–xxviii, 64, 89, 115, 160, 168
Irving, Edward, xxix

J

Jews, 147, 150, 185
justification, xxii–xxiv, 2, 23–24, 102, 117, 164

K

Kant, Immanuel, xviii–xx, 71, 92, 208
kenoticism, 52, 103, 107, 193

kingdom of Christ, 150, 156
kingdom of God, 123, 129, 137, 143, 150–52, 156
Kurtz, Benjamin, 2, 27, 103

L

Lange, Johann Peter, 96, 167, 169, 180, 186
Liebner, Karl, xxxiv–xxxv, 87–89, 91–93, 95–96, 100, 106–8, 110–11, 114–15, 124, 126–28, 134
Logos, xxviii, xxxiii, xxxv, 52, 90, 103–4, 107, 119–20, 122, 124, 129–33, 137, 193
Lord's Supper, xxii, xxvi, 20–22, 25, 27, 68, 73, 79, 157, 212, 224–28, 232, 237
Luther, Martin, 3, 24–25, 27, 30, 38, 116–17, 172, 184, 233
Lutherans, xxii, 3–4, 11, 18–20, 26, 79, 88, 102–3

M

manhood, 65–66, 74, 77 *see also* human nature
manhood of Christ *see* Christ, human nature of
mankind *see* human race
Mediating theologians, viii, xvi, xxi, xxvii, xxxi, xxxiv–xxxv, 30
Mediator, Christ as, 7–9, 15, 18, 46, 55–58, 61, 67, 69–70, 72–80, 133, 136, 141, 196
metaphysics, xix, xxxv, 47, 90, 127–28
miracles, 165, 171, 189, 193, 196, 203, 206
Moses, xxv, 55, 57, 61, 139, 162, 184, 196
Müller, Julius, xxxiv–xxxv, 87, 89–90, 114–16, 118–21, 128, 131
mystical body, 13, 36, 48, 75–76
mysticism, xxx, 14, 183, 185
myth, 15, 161, 204

N

nature, 63, 142–43, 145, 151
Neander, August, xxi, xxxi, 159, 167
Nestorianism, 19, 69

250 Subject and Author Index

new creation, xxv, xxvii, xxx, xxxii, xxxiv, 30, 33–34, 36–37, 40–41, 43–44, 66, 120, 123, 162–63
New England theology, xxii–xxv, 54
Newman, John Henry, 51, 81
Nichols, James Hastings, xxv, xxvii–xxviii, xxxv
nominalism, 47, 62

O
offices of Christ, 18, 20, 58, 123
Olshausen, Hermann, 35, 167, 169, 180
ordo salutis, xxiii–xxiv
Origen, 95, 225–26
Oxford Movement, 51, 81

P
pantheism, xviii, xxxv, 51, 88, 98–99, 102, 107, 112, 118, 120, 130–32
participation, real, xxii, 210, 217, 223, 225
Paulus, H. E. G., 161, 203
Pelagianism, 61, 72, 89, 116
person of Christ *see* Christ, person of
personality, xxxi, 65, 70, 90, 129–30, 132–33
personality of Christ *see* Christ, personality of
philosophy, 15, 88, 94, 97–98, 207
posse peccare, 160, 177
predestination, 115–17
Princeton, vii–viii, xxii, xxv, 211, 224
Protestantism, 50–51, 165
Puritans, 2–3, 26

R
rationalism, 39, 44–45, 51, 54, 60, 77, 80, 95, 105, 203, 216, 222, 236
realism, 62–63
reconciliation, 8, 13, 16–17, 43, 55, 58, 60, 125
Reformation, 3, 24, 50, 68, 89, 101, 164
Reformed, xxii–xxiii, 3, 25, 79, 88, 102–3, 117, 211, 233, 235
regeneration, xxx, 21, 28, 72, 229
Reid, Thomas, vii, xvii–xviii
resurrection, 35, 58, 123, 149, 152

of believers, 35, 38, 58, 130, 137, 149, 152, 154–56
of Christ *see* Christ, resurrection of
Roman Church, 22, 50, 83, 233
Rothe, Richard, xxi, 52, 110–11

S
Sabellianism, xxxiv, 74, 80, 197
sacramental grace, 20, 22, 26–27, 48, 76, 78–79
sacraments, xxv–xxvi, xxxvi–3, 18, 20, 22, 24–27, 48, 68, 76, 78–80, 85, 157, 210–11, 225–28, 232–34
sacrifice, 55, 73–74, 140
Sartorius, Ernst W. C., 1–23, 25–27
Schaff, Philip, xv, 29, 32, 34–35, 52, 95–96, 159–61, 199
Schelling, Friedrich W. J., viii, xviii–xix, xxxi, 92–94, 175
Schleiermacher, Friedrich D. E., xvi, xx–xxi, 30, 88–89, 92, 95, 105, 110–11, 120, 160, 179–80
Schöberlein, Ludwig Friedrich, 102, 114
Scottish Common Sense Realism *see* Common Sense Realism
Scotus, John Duns, 89, 116, 184
Second Adam, xxvii–xxviii, xxx, 47, 56, 61, 66, 78, 115, 120, 132, 168, 177, 194, 223–24, 229
sects, 24, 27, 59
Shakespeare, William, 173, 184
sinlessness of Christ *see* Christ, sinlessness of
Socinianism, 89, 117, 161, 199
Socrates, 181, 184, 192
soteriology, xv, xxiii–xxiv, xxvii, xxxi, 210
soul (in relation to body), xxvi, xxx, 16, 76, 154–55, 211, 222–23
Spirit *see* Holy Spirit
Stahl, Friedrich Julius, 63
Stearns, Oakman S., 1–2, 4–5, 10–13, 17–20, 22, 25–26
Strauss, David Friedrich, xix, 15, 71, 96, 161, 179–80, 204–7
supernatural, the, xvii, xix, 163
supralapsarianism, 116–17

T

Tholuck, Friedrich A.G., 35, 159, 167
Thomasius, Gottfried, 88, 106–7, 111–12, 114, 120
Torrance, Thomas F., xxix, xxxi
transcendentalism, xx, 29, 32–34, 37
transubstantiation, 212, 233
Trench, Richard Chevinix, 87, 113
Trinity, xxi, 38, 100–101, 104, 106, 109, 114, 119

U

Ullmann, Karl C., xxxi, 166–67, 179
union
  hypostatic, xxvi, 2, 19, 54, 58, 70, 217
  legal, xxiii–xxiv
  moral, xxiv–xxv, 36
  mystical, xxvi, 35, 38, 47, 69, 71
Unitarianism, 44, 55, 161, 186, 198–200
universalism, xxxv, 90, 223–24

V

Virgin Mary, 19, 165, 180

W

Wilberforce, Robert I., 46, 48–49, 51–53, 57, 62, 67, 69, 71, 81, 84–85
Witherspoon, John, vii, xvii
The Word (*see also* Logos), xxxii, 34, 41, 58, 60–61, 66–68, 70, 84, 122, 141, 153
worship, 48, 76, 78

Z

Zinzendorf, Nikolaus Ludwig, 103
Zwinglian memorialism, viii, 212, 233

www.ingramcontent.com/pod-product-compliance
Lightning Source LLC
Chambersburg PA
CBHW071933240426
43668CB00038B/1547